Jörn W. Scheer, Kenneth W. Sewell (Eds.)
Creative Construing

The Psychology of Personal Constructs, as devised by the American psychologist George Kelly, stresses the importance of the meanings that individuals attach to persons and events in the world surrounding them. Originating in clinical psychology, it has increasingly attracted the interest of scholars and practitioners working in education, in organisations, and in other disciplines working with people. As there are hardly more "personal" processes than creative ones, it seems appropriate to look at the arts from a personal construct psychology perspective. This book presents for the first time analyses of creative processes, but it features also personal accounts by creative people – who write, sing, dance, act, and make music.

Jörn W. Scheer
Kenneth W. Sewell
(Eds.)

Creative Construing

Personal Constructions
in the Arts

Psychosozial-Verlag

Editors:
Prof. Dr.phil. Dipl.-Psych. Jörn W. Scheer
Abteilung für Medizinische Psychologie
Zentrum für Psychosomatische Medizin
Justus-Liebig-Universität Giessen
Friedrichstr. 36
35392 Giessen
Germany
Prof. Kenneth W. Sewell, Ph.D.
Department of Psychology
Box 311280
University of North Texas
Denton, Texas 76203-1280
USA

Bibliographic information of Die Deutsche Bibliothek (The German Library)
Die Deutsche Bibliothek lists this publication in the Deutsche Nationalbibliografie
(German National Bibliography). Detailed bibliographical data can be accessed
via internet (http://dnb.ddb.de).

Original edition
© 2006 Psychosozial-Verlag
E-mail: info@psychosozial-verlag.de
www.psychosozial-verlag.de
All rights reserved. No portion of this publication may be reproduced
in any manner without the written permission of the publisher.
Cover: Grafik von Michael Catina
Draft design cover: Atelier Warminski, Büdingen
Printed in Germany
ISBN 978-3-89806-438-5

Contents

Contributors	7
Preface	8

READING AND WRITING

A PCT view of novel writing and reading *Don Bannister*	12
People, poetry and politics – the novels of Don Bannister *Max Farrar*	17
George Kelly and literature *Fay Fransella*	30
What-if versions of ourselves: Creative writers speak *Chris Stevens*	51
Two roads converge: Poetry as Personal Construct Theory *Richard Bell*	63
Haiku poetry: Escape from constriction *Sean Brophy*	74

EXPERIENCING MUSIC

Music and the person *Eric Button*	88
Construing sounds, constructing music and non-music *Devorah Kalekin-Fishman*	99
Living with jazz: Construing cultural identity *Jörn Scheer*	110

SINGING

Becoming a singer: PCT and voice *Vivien Burr*	120
Stand at the back and pretend - the experience of learning to sing *Mary Frances*	128

DANCING

Construing through body: The dancing experience 144
    Sabrina Cipolletta
Music and mirrors: Dance as a construction of self 157
    Sara K. Bridges

ACTING

Construing characters and casts: Personal constructs on the stage and in the dressing room 166
    Kenneth W. Sewell
Sociality and the sitcom 176
    Jonathan D. Raskin

COMING TO TERMS

Art proustifies Kelly's PCP: Personal searchings and revisitings 196
    C. T. Patrick Diamond

APPENDICES

A short introduction to Personal Construct Psychology 210
    Jörn W. Scheer
Constructive criticism 216
    Editors

Contributors

Don Bannister, Deceased.

Richard C. Bell, PhD, Prof., School of Behavioural Science, University of Melbourne, Victoria, Australia. rcb@unimelb.edu.au

Sara K. Bridges, PhD, Assist. Prof., Dept. of Psychology, University of Memphis, Memphis,TN, USA. sbridges@memphis.edu

Sean Brophy, PhD, Dublin, Ireland. seanbrophy@eircom.net

Vivien Burr, PhD, Division of Psychology, University of Huddersfield, UK. v.burr@hud.ac.uk.

Eric Button, PhD, Brandon Mental Health Unit, Leicester General Hospital, Leicester, UK. Eric.Button@leicspart.nhs.uk

Sabrina Cipolletta, PhD, Dept. of Psychology, University of Padova, Italy. sabcip@unipd.it

C. T. Patrick Diamond, PhD, Prof. em., Ontario Institute for Studies in Education, University of Toronto, Canada. ctpdiamond@oise.utoronto.ca

Max Farrar, PhD, School of Social Science, Leeds Metropolitan University, Leeds, UK. max.farrar@ntlworld.com

Mary Frances, Leamington Spa, UK. mary.frances@virgin.net

Fay Fransella. PhD, Prof. em, University of London, UK. Ffransella@lambslane.eclipse.co.uk

Devorah Kalekin-Fishman, PhD, Faculty of Education, University of Haifa, Israel. dkalekin@construct.haifa.ac.il

Jonathan D. Raskin., PhD, Prof., Dept. of Psychology, State University of New York, New Paltz, N.Y., USA. raskinj@newpaltz.edu

Jörn W. Scheer, Dr. phil., Prof. em., Dept. of Medical Psychology, University of Giessen, Germany. joern.scheer@joern-scheer.de

Kenneth W. Sewell, PhD, Prof., Dept. of Psychology, University of North Texas, Denton, Texas, USA. sewellk@unt.edu

Chris Stevens, Ph.D., Communicorp Pty Ltd, Coogee, NSW, Australia. cdstevens@optusnet.com.au

Preface

Personal Construct Psychology (PCP), developed by the North American psychologist *George Alexander Kelly*, holds that – irrespective of the existence of a 'real' world – every individual develops a personal view of the world. This is not just a personal way of 'looking at' things (and people) but implies a more general way of interpreting the world from the point of view of the individual. 'To construe' has two meanings: to build and to interpret. Thus, this verb lends itself nicely to describe the process of actively developing a personal world – by using *personal constructs*: the tools used to attach meaning to things, people and events, and, moreover, to develop individual ways of dealing with them. In the Theory of Personal Constructs Kelly provided a systematic elaboration of how this works, and how people 'in trouble' may be helped in coping with their troubles – after all, Kelly was a psychotherapist. Construing, however, occurs whenever we deal with the world...not just when we are in trouble. It implies trying out possibilities, comparing different options, choosing alternatives, revising choices. This is a process of loops or cycles, moves from 'loose' construing to 'tight' construing and back and forth until a person feels something has been 'created' that can be tested out. Creativity thus is at the core of human activity – of living.

Creativity is also considered as being at the core of artistic activity. By creating a work of art, artists *construe* – but so do the people who enjoy a piece of art, such as a painting or a performance. We all know that 'beauty lies in the eye of the beholder' (Margaret Wolfe Hungerford, *Molly Bawn*, 1887, but in similar words dating back to Shakespeare's times) – it is the beholder who 'attaches meaning' to the object of admiration. It is somehow surprising that Personal Construct Theory has not been used extensively to analyse and interpret artistic endeavours. Fay Fransella, in the comprehensive *International Handbook of Personal Construct Psychology* which appeared in 2003, mentions 'the world of music' and 'literary criticism' in the concluding section on 'new avenues to explore' – it seems there is work to be done! In fact, there are some foundations to build on. Kelly himself wrote about Hamlet in his *Magnum Opus* (Kelly, 1955); at an international conference on PCP held in 1985 several papers were presented on literature and music (Fransella & Thomas, 1988); and in 1991 a short-lived journal titled 'Constructive Criticism' presented analyses of novels and plays from a PCP perspective (Whitehead, 1991; see Appendix B). But since then not much has been published.

The idea for this book was born when a number of people involved in Personal Construct Psychology discovered more or less accidentally that they shared an interest in the arts. Some were avid readers or listeners, and some considered themselves, cautiously, as artists: writing poems, painting, acting, making music. All of them found it worthwhile to see what a PCP perspective might have to offer when dealing with the arts. So we invited a number of colleagues to contribute to this volume.

In view of the gigantic body of literature on the arts, we refrained from engaging in a definition of 'the arts'. Instead we worked with a liberal, enumerative notion of the arts that includes visual arts, literature, music, and performing arts, (such as dancing and acting). Some of the chapters present analyses (e.g., of poems or of music), or report on the use of arts in psychotherapy or research in a more traditional way. Others are written by non-professional practitioners. This raises the interesting question of who is (or can be considered to be) an artist. Is an artist only someone who makes a living out of it, or who publishes his/her works? Certainly not; some great writers of world fame never published a single line while alive. On the other hand: hundreds of thousands of people write poems, with or without attending 'Creative Writing' workshops, that are never published (except these days maybe on the Internet), others paint 'for fun' or sing in a church choir – are they artists? They are 'amateurs' or 'dilettanti' – which in the original sense means not 'incompetent' but 'lovers'. We think they are creative in the realm of arts and therefore *are* 'artists' – and not only because we count ourselves among them.

Certainly, in editing this book, we do not intend to re-invent the wheel. But we think that as a discipline concerned with *persons* and *meanings*, PCP is particularly well prepared to deal with the *persons* who create art and enjoy art, and with what art *means* to them. This refers to the analytical tools that the theory provides, but also to the willingness and capability of its practitioners to open up – to give accounts of their personal experience in producing and enjoying art.

In keeping with the spirit of constructive alternativism, we kept editing to a minimum and especially accepted the spelling (e.g., British or American) the authors preferred. We attempted to strike a balance between the coherence of the volume as a whole and the freedoms afforded to the individual contributors.

Obviously, some areas within the arts are not covered in this book. For example, we know that there are people who paint or compose music in the PCP community, and we are sure that there are a large number of colleagues who could contribute to the development of what might tentatively be named 'a Personal Construct Theory of art'. Since a network of people interested in 'PCP and the arts' has recently been formed (http://www.arts-con.net), there is hope that this might happen one day. We would be pleased if this book would have a part in it.

References

Fransella, F., Thomas, L. (eds.) (1988). *Experimenting with personal construct psychology*. London: Routledge & Kegan Paul.

Hungerford, M. W. (1878*). Molly Bawn*.

Kelly, G. A. (1955/1991). *The psychology of personal constructs. Vols. 1 & 2.* New York: Norton (London: Routledge).

Whitehead, C. (ed.) (1991). *Constructive Criticism. A Journal of Construct Psychology and the Arts.* Vol.1.

Jörn W. Scheer, Kenneth W. Sewell
January, 2006

READING AND WRITING

A PCT view of novel writing and reading[1]

Don Bannister

Novel reading is an exercise in continuous anticipation. As you turn the pages, on the basis of your elaborating understanding, you anticipate what will happen next. 'Happen next' refers not only to events and narrative turns of plot but also to the unfolding over time of what the people in the story are saying and experiencing, the way in which the nature of the context reveals itself, the way in which the harmonics of the novel's world are developing. You may be only intermittently and partially aware that you are predicting, and (as in daily life) it is often misprediction that brings the process into conscious focus.

If the act of novel reading is truly an act of constructive anticipation, then the reader is constantly subject to validation or invalidation or to experiencing the unfolding events as being outside the range of convenience of his or her construing. In swift sequence, a novel packages for us those confrontations which Kelly thought basic to life, in which we find our forecasts right or wrong or totally irrelevant.

Perhaps most markedly, in our novel reading, we crave validation. We have the experience of having our anticipations confirmed, of seeing the significance of what is presently portrayed, verified by outcome. Children grasp at narrative validation in a very direct way when they demand to have the same story read to them over and over again. Familiarity deepens their understanding and endows them with a sense of anticipative control. Adults often achieve the same guarantee of validation not by re-reading the same story but by reading endlessly the same kind of story. Thus much popular fiction caters to our craving for validation by working out, in varying detail, unvarying sequences, such as that of the heroic hero triumphing over the villainous villain. Detail may vary, but the essential landmarks are where we expect them to be, signposts are clear and the landscape is broadly familiar. So the most successful popular fiction is that which offers us comforting superordinate validation while, in its colourful detail, it invites us to widen (not too uncomfortably) the range of convenience of our construing. Thus the historical romance depicts for us a world in which the physical paraphernalia and customs are curious and unfamiliar, while the central psychology and metaphysic is conventional and of our time.

Nevertheless, novel reading is not a risk-free occupation. The story may, in some essential way, run contrary to our expectations and we may be in-

---

[1] originally published in F. Fransella & L. Thomas (1988). *Experimenting with Personal Construct Psychology*. London: Routledge & Kegan Paul (509-514). Reprinted by permission of the Don Bannister estate.

validated. When this happens we may see the story as untrue, badly written and misleading. Alternatively, we may come to see it as true and revise our initial construing. This is the most powerful effect that a novel can have, in that it provides us with the kind of puzzlement and dismay which becomes insight and enables us to elaborate our understanding.

Equally, a novel can take us to the frontiers of our range of convenience, not comfortably (as on a tourist excursion to well-ordered foreign parts) but so that we find ourselves in a threatening and confusing landscape. At such times we may simply abandon the novel as a literal nonsense. Alternatively, we may find enough points of contact between worlds we have lived in and the world we are exploring in the novel, contact by analogy, metaphor, through a scatter of small but significant clues, to encourage us to complete the journey and learn.

Novel writing

Novel writing is an exercise in the controlled elaboration of an author's construct system.

Whatever the formal working system of the author, a novel stems from some personal intersect of elements and constructs which has vast implicative mass. As, for example, from childhood memory of seeing miners drinking at night time in a town square, I found myself drawn outwards into unfolding reflections and themes to do with the colliery on which my village centred, the texture of the village and its manner of life, the *mores* of childhood, unchosen life paths, and so forth (Bannister, 1979).

True, the starting point can be pre-empted into the form of a plan, and the novel be constructed to fulfil that plan rather than having its form evolve from the detail of exploration. These two processes represent varying forms of the creativity cycle, described by Kelly (1955) as a cycle which starts with loosened construction and terminates with tightened and readily validatable construction. Many novels (such as the classic 'whodunnit' mystery, which is not at all mysterious) seem written by rapidly tightening their vague and speculative origins into specific superordinate constructions from which a mass of subordinate detail can be mechanically read off. Then the cycle is worked through (in major form) once only, from loose to tight. Contrastingly, a novel can involve a perpetual cycling from loose to tight to loose construing. Thus its total shape and meaning is generated in play with its detail, rather than acting as dictator of specific content.

If a novel is thus unfolded by (for and from) the author, then just as readers may have their anticipations of what is forthcoming denied, so the author may experience invalidation. Authors may recognise that what they have written is, in an essential sense, false. That is to say, that it is untrue in the light of the construct system of the author, it is false to that total way of understanding of the world from which the particular narrative is derived. The author realises that the people on the pages could not have done or said or experienced at this point and in this context what he or she has set them down as doing, saying, experiencing. Then comes a moral choice: whether or not to consign eminently plausible pages of narrative to the wastepaper basket.

Kelly depicts the act of construing as partaking of both invention and discovery. We invent the terms in which we will view the word and thereby discover what is to be seen by taking such a view. This inextricable mixing of what we create with what we are confronted by, is most manifest in novel writing. I have grown used to working on a novel spurred on by the thought that now I shall find out what happens next. Perhaps the very length of novels emphasises this quality of 'finding through making' in our construing. We *construe* through *constructs*. Novels remind us that elaborative construing takes time, that it is a long search for what is hidden, not a simple detailing of what is manifest.

Central to elaborative construing is the movement between subordinate and superordinate construing (and back and forth again) already referred to in relation to the creativity cycle. At the heart of novel writing is exactly this deriving, working out, of the subordinate (the detail and content of the novel) from the superordinate (the theme of the novel). Equally, new aspects of the superordinate theme are generated by subordinate exploration. I had written a substantial part of the novel already referred to (Bannister, 1979) convinced that its sole theme concerned the nature of the pit village community before I realised that the specific events adumbrated an alternative autobiography — a super-ordinate which then I consciously articulated into yet further narrative. But in novels, as in life, we sometimes fail to listen to the new melodic lines implicit in the notes we are playing. Thus it is that the novel *Walden II* did little for Skinner's abstractions except to illustrate them.

Writers and readers

The relationship of novel writer to novel reader is precious but mysterious. It is intimate without being conversational. Letters are written to someone, but novels are written to whom it may concern. Kelly's Sociality Corollary asserts that it is by construing the construction processes of others that we enter into a social role with them. We might conclude that novelists are essentially construing not the construction processes of their readers but the construction processes of the characters in the novel. In the final analysis, perhaps our genius for standing in angled relationships to aspects of ourselves and others is such that the novelist is construing his or her own construction processes and representing this construction through the figures in the novel. The reader, it is, who provides sociality by construing the construction processes of the author. True, many novelists annotate their narrative, they tell the reader what to think, but in so doing they are essentially writing for a 'typical' reader. Thereby, they restrict themselves to some easily accessible and mundane part of their own construing, which is taken to represent the 'typical' reader.

This is not any kind of injunction to novelists to disregard their readers. It is the reading of a novel that ultimately gives it life. Rather, it is argued that novelists must respect readers and acknowledge both their right and their ability independently, to read significance *into* the novel. In chess there is the notion of playing the board rather than playing the man. It is argued that the best kind of chess is played when you do not try to capitalise on what you imagine to be the particular weaknesses or foibles of your opponent but play each move as if your opponent were a perfect chess player who will make the perfect reply. Thus it is that novels might be written. Novelists should struggle to represent their experience as truthfully and as vividly as they can, resting secure in the belief that, through our common humanity, the novel will have its significance affirmed and properly transmuted by the construct system into which it passes.

The novel, in PCT terms, is not unique. It is a special case of the anecdote, the poem, the play, the daydream. Indeed, Kelly argues it is close kin to that other great public enterprise in make-believe, Science. He set out the relationship thus:

But there are two differences between him [the novelist] and the scientist; he is more willing to confide his make-believe — even publish it — and he is willing to postpone the accumulation of factual evidence to support the generality of characters and themes he has narrated.

But neither of these differences between the novelist and the scientist is very fundamental. Both men employ nonetheless typically human tactics. The fact that the scientist is ashamed to admit his fantasy probably accomplishes little more than to make it appear that he fits a popular notion of the way scientists think. And the fact that a novelist does not continue his project to the point of collecting data in support of his portrayals and generalizations suggests only that he hopes that the experiences of man will, in the end, prove him right without anyone's resorting to formal proof.

But the brilliant scientist and the brilliant writer are pretty likely to end up saying the same thing — given, of course, a lot of time to converge upon each other. The poor scientist and the poor writer, moreover, fail in much the same way — neither of them is able to transcend the obvious. Both fail in their make-believe. (Kelly, 1979, p. 150)

References

Bannister, D. (1979). *Sam Chard*. Routledge & Kegan Paul. London.

Kelly, G. A. (1955). *The psychology of personal constructs*, Vols. I and II. Norton: New York.

Kelly, G. A. (1979). *Clinical psychology and personality: The selected essays of George Kelly*. Ed. B. A. Maher. Krieger: New York.

People, poetry and politics – the novels of Don Bannister

Max Farrar

This chapter addresses three central themes in the novels of Don Bannister, who is perhaps better known as a follower of George Kelly, and a leading British exponent of Personal Construct Theory. I selected these themes – the vividly constructed people in Don Bannister's imaginary world; the poetry of everyday speech; and the remarkably sexual and class-laden anarchist politics spread throughout his novels – and delivered a conference paper[2] before I read Bannister's own Kelly-inflected writing on the novel (Bannister, 1988). I have modified the paper in light of Bannister's observations, but these issues remain pertinent to an understanding of Bannister the man, Bannister the psychologist, and Bannister the novelist.

The novels – briefly

In an extraordinary outburst of creative energy, Don Bannister had five novels published between 1979 and 1987 by prestigious, mainstream British companies. Routledge and Kegan Paul published the first three, *Sam Chard* (1979), *Long Day at Shiloh* (1981) and *Burning Leaves* (1982), while Heinemann took *The Summer Boy* (1984) and Secker and Warburg published *Hard Walls of Ego*, posthumously, in 1987. To get these companies interested in your work is a significant achievement, but to get favourable reviews in important journals is even more impressive. On the dust jacket of *Burning Leaves*, Angela Carter, herself a writer of the first rank, is recorded of praising *Sam Chard* as a "quite exceptional first novel", while the *New Yorker* wrote: "A brilliant piece of story-telling, alternating between dialogue rendered in dark and bitter dialect and cool, measured narrative, that is as vivid as Zola's *Germinal*, but without Zola's hyperbole". On *Long Day at Shiloh*, *The* [London] *Times* wrote: "His command of historical detail and uncanny ability to get inside his characters make this an unforgettable if sometimes harrowing book"; the *Times Literary Supplement* praised its "intellectual

---

[2] The XV International Congress on Personal Construct Psychology, University of Huddersfield, 14 -18 July 2003. I am grateful to Trevor Butt for asking me to submit a paper on Don Bannister's novels, for the positive feedback on the paper at the XV Congress, and to the editors of this volume for including this re-working of the original paper.

vigour", while Max Hastings, war historian and quality newspaper editor wrote: "Bannister's earthy dialogue is superb, his feel for the confusion, dirt, exhaustion and fear of war cannot be faulted". On the cover of *The Summer Boy* you find *The Times* saying of *Burning Leaves*: "We still understand precious little about where and why madness strikes . . . there is plenty to relish in this funny and beautifully written exploration of life beyond the end of the tether." *The Times Literary Supplement* was equally impressed.

Of the five novels, *Long Day at Shiloh* is the only one which departs from what I take to be Bannister's central concern: what happens to a working class northern English man when his fierce, critical and political intellect pushes against the limits imposed by his situation[3]. *Long Day at Shiloh* is, as its title suggests, an hour by hour description of one of the decisive battles of the American Civil War. But even here, Bannister's focus is mainly on the ordinary working men, normally farmers, as they battle against circumstances that they are making, but which are not of their making. While the book is meticulous in detailing the military maneuvers of that day, Bannister presents us with the fears, the longings, the anecdotes (usually sexual) and the memories of the everyday lives of these men before they became soldiers. And *Shiloh* is not so out of phase with the other books as it first appears, since Bannister is clearly as interested in history as he is in psychology. *Sam Chard* can be enjoyed simply as a piece of social history, with its beautiful evocation of life in a small mining village somewhere around Barnsley or Doncaster in Yorkshire, in the north of England, in the late 1930s. Paul Killick, the protagonist in *Burning Leaves*, is a university history lecturer, and he loses no opportunities, before, during and after his psychotic journey, to lecture anyone who will listen about historical episodes and the meaning of history. Joe Telford, the elderly man at the centre of *Hard Walls of Ego*, spends much of his time instructing his young girl-friend Janis about the history of anarcho-syndicalism. The latter is the only book in which Bannister places in the foreground another of his over-riding, but usually masked, concerns: what are the possibilities for working people to decisively alter the oppressive and exploitative circumstances in which they are placed?

---

[3] I use this word in the sense that Jean-Paul Sartre used it: 'The For-itself's engagement with the world. It is the product of both facticity and the For-itself's way of accepting and acting upon its facticity' (Sartre, 1958, p. 634). I don't know if Bannister was interested in Sartre, but it seems to me that Bannister's novels are a rather English form of the existentialist novel.

How to read a novel: Personal Construct Theory meets materialist literary theory

Bannister (1988, p. 510) argued that "Novel writing is an exercise in the controlled elaboration of an author's construct system". Readers, he argued "read significance *into* the novel" which is a close as he gets to emphasizing the point that literary theorists in the Marxist tradition have made: that readers read from a position which is highly influenced by structural factors such as their class, gender, sexual orientation and ethnicity. In PCT terms, these are the factors which influence the type and range of constructs through which the reader makes sense of what he or she reads. Migrating across theories in this way brings to mind a sharp rebuke Bannister and Fransella offered to those who misuse the term 'theory':

The term 'theory' should be reserved for extensive and elaborated systems of ideas cast in terms of an integrated language. Users should not have to borrow, in every intellectual emergency, from elsewhere and conclude by assembling a ragbag of concepts which cannot be cross-related. (Bannister and Fransella, 1986, p. 2)

If we take seriously the injunction from PCT that the social world is best understood as a process of negotiating personal constructs, it is as useful in the academic world as it is in everyday life to understand the types of constructs an author uses. To some extent, this chapter tries to unpick some of Bannister's own fundamental constructs. At this stage, I am setting out the theories which underlie my constructs. To meet the 'rag-bag' complaint I should start by pointing out that my main reference points are drawn from sociology, but I adhere to a form of sociology which seeks to integrate the personal, the psychological, and the intimate fields of life with the social, material and public spheres. Applying this to reading novels, I take from Marxism a focus on ideology and the social context in which the novels are set, and I take from phenomenology a concern with the text in itself, taken as a specific mode of representing experience. Feminist and queer theory leads me to an interest in the particular modes in which gender and sexuality are manifested in these texts. I aim to move (sometimes rather uncomfortably) between theories of structure and of agency, between the personal and the political. If this looks like a rag-bag, academic apartheid is to blame.

My theoretical perspective accepts that novels are read from a variety of subject positions, and thus that what is offered here is a partial, value-laden, subjectivist interpretation of these novels for which I will offer justifications but which makes no claim to 'truth'. (This is not an 'anything goes' relativism, however. My reading can and should be tested for adequacy against other readings.) My underlying literary theory is a version of reception theory inflected by Marxism and feminism, which sees the act of reading as the construction of meaning in an interaction between the text and a reader, who is himself or herself embedded in a particular cultural niche, which includes a conglomerate of other readers (Eagleton, 1996). Don Bannister pin-pointed the human's "genius for standing in angled relationships to aspects of ourselves and others" (1988, p. 512). I think he is capturing here a version of literary reception theory, for he is emphasising the 'angles' in ourselves and between us and others which we notice when we see the act of reading as a deeply social act, where a seemingly isolated reader is actually sitting all the time in a set of (usually ignored) relationships with other readers, and other authors, all of whom are situated in a material context. He continues: "the novelist is construing his or her own construction process and representing this construction through the figures in the novel" (p. 512). A few lines further on he states that "through our common humanity, the novel will have its significance affirmed and properly transmuted by the construct system into which it passes" (p. 513). My sociological theory would sharpen this formulation. It would not be quite so quick to point to what humans have in common (though, in resisting the anti-humanist excesses of post-structuralist theory, it would welcome Bannister's invocation of the human). It would put greater emphasis on the 'transmutation'. Thus, the position from which I read is not simply a product of abstract theory; it is a product of my embodiment as a heterosexual male of advancing years, of my life-world within, historically, the white, English middle class in a northern city, not far from the places Bannister evokes in his English novels. I therefore have significant identity-positions in common with Bannister, namely gender, sexuality, age, 'race' and class. We share a commitment to radical, left-wing politics. But even within these locations, I have significant differences from Bannister: he acquired his class position through his education and his occupation, mine was donated by birth. His aggressive heterosexuality is not mine. Perhaps more significantly, as a long-term inhabitant of a multi-cultural working class neighbourhood, my white Englishness has been reconstructed. So Bannister's presentation of the novelist's constructs, exemplified in all their variety by the character he or she imagines, being simply passed into – and perhaps modified – by the reader places too little emphasis on these structural differences and too much on what readers have in common. Thus I would emphasise the variety of readings to which his novels can be subjected, particularly by readers whose identifications are significantly different from Bannister's, or mine.

I see these novels as ideological constructions, which I read through my own ideological leanings. It is this combination of theoretical and political interests that leads me to pull out the three themes I'm addressing in these novels: people, poetry and politics. In the conference paper on which this chapter is based, I stressed that my analysis specifically rejected any inference from, or imputation about, Don Bannister the man. I aimed to treat the novels as texts independent of the author's biography. This was partly out of respect to the sensitivities of his friends and family attending the conference, but it was mainly because I align myself with those who argue that the author's motives and intentions are far less important than the work itself; the work is so important that it should be treated in its own right. Nevertheless, just as the reader is positioned by his or her situation, so is the text itself, and thus I made evaluative and critical remarks through the process of placing the novels in the social and political settings of the 1930s, the 1970s and the 1980s – the times evoked in the novels. At the conference, both one of Don Bannister's children, and several people who knew him personally, made affirmative remarks about the content of the paper, including its critical notes, and so in this chapter I shall hazard some guesses about 'Don the man' as I re-construct the author from the novels.

The people Don Bannister constructs

Sam Chard is the novel which is most precise about its historical setting, the 1930s. It makes explicit reference to the war in Abyssinia (1979, pp. 157-161) and the reader is continually drawn back to the mine at which Sam works until he is made redundant. It is also the most tightly focused on a discrete sector of the British population: the white, English, northern, Yorkshire, working class. It sets out an abiding theme of Bannister's: that these people are intelligent, argumentative, hard-working, funny, sexually energetic, skillful and utterly capable in everything that they do. But if that is his over-arching construct of the working class, it is portrayed as highly differentiated in terms of personality and politics. Thus some people are more dedicated than others, some are more left-wing than others, some more snobbish than others. The latter is a feature to which Bannister always returns: when working class boy meets girl – who may be an inch up the class ladder from him (as in *Sam Chard* and *The Summer Boy*) or a mile higher (as in *Hard Walls of Ego*) – how heavily does this class differentiation bear down on the man. And when this working class man acquires middle class status, as in *Burning Leaves*, it could be that the contradiction which he perceives in his situation drives him crazy.

It is important to note that while Bannister's main focus is on men, his novels are significantly populated by women. It is too crude to divide these women into saints and sinners, Madonnas and whores – but there is this sentimental, polarising tendency in Bannister – because even the female saints are as sexually active as Sam Chard, Paul Killick (*Burning Leaves*), Martin Morley (*The Summer Boy*) and Joe Telford (*Hard Walls of Ego*). All the women in Bannister's novels are exuberantly interested in sex, several of them reveal the same levels of intellectual ability as the leading men, and the saints are able to dissect the men's many failings with forensic accuracy. Read from a feminist position, this could be taken as one reason why most of the men walk away from these erotic, intelligent, but highly critical women. Whether Bannister realised that 'his' men were not ready for these types of women, or whether he was himself unable to cope with them in real life, is an open question which only those who knew him can answer. Bannister does not let us in on this question because we learn much about their intellect and very little about the emotions of the people in these novels. Perhaps this is because, in his psychological theory, Bannister adopts Kelly's rejection of the assumed dichotomy between the emotional and the intellectual (Bannister and Fransella, 1986, p. 4). If so, why do the novels give us so much material about how people are thinking, rather than how they are thinking/feeling? One emotional moment is described at the end of *Burning Leaves*, when Paul walks away from the home in which his mental well-being has been restored feeling "sickened by a sense of wrongdoing". But this is immediately dismissed in words which he speaks aloud: "No, I'm not responsible. That's as daft as not caring at all" (1982, p. 273). This passage seems to me to suggest that another person's emotional state is his or her own responsibility, not that of the person with whom they are emotionally engaged. You may care about the other's position, but this does not imply responsibility. This would fit with a primitive version of existentialist psychology – primitive, because it is an act of bad faith to persuade yourself that you are a monad, who can shrug off responsibility for the other. This, I fear, is what is happening in these novels: because these men rationally understand themselves to be free, they can quite easily bracket off their emotions and negate the demands of the other.

The poetry of everyday speech

Bannister never describes how people look – their features, their hair, their build, their style of dress all seem to be quite irrelevant in these novels. They are, nevertheless, entirely vital. Bannister brings them to life through his extraordinary facility with the spoken word. These novels, even *Shiloh*, read like very long conversations and monologues. Gifted dialogue is the hallmark of all good writing and to that extent Bannister is simply following a literary convention, but he is offering us two other possibilities in taking this approach. Firstly, he is working as an oral historian – he is capturing the poetry of the Yorkshire vernacular. Most of this dialogue is in single sentences and its effect is built by the too-ing and fro-ing of the conversation. But here is a rare long speech:

> *'I came off night shift late this one time, after seven, and I'm walkin'*
> *past that cottage that stands by itself just before you come to the Ter-*

race. There's little lad standin' by the gate in his night things, roarin' his eyes out. When I asked him what was up he kept sayin' his mam and dad wouldn't wake up. So I went into t' cottage and there's the pair of 'em lying in bed, dead wi' t' flu. There's no wonder the poor little bugger couldn't wek 'em up. Willis they were called.'

(*Sam Chard*, 1979, p. 152)

Here is the plain, direct but expressive language of a Yorkshire miner. No flourish, no sentimentality, giving us the simple facts of everyday life in the 1930s: flu kills poor people, children are orphaned and they grieve. The dignity of the language fits the solemnity of the occasion. Here's the angry dialogue when Sam Chard hears that he is being made redundant.

'Why am I sacked.'
'Tha knows full well we've been layin' two and three men a week off for months. Company policy. We've more men than work.'
'Don't talk fuckin' daft. Tha knows the rule is last in first out. I've bin at this pit seventeen year. Sin' I left school. You'd 'ave to sack 'alf the pit afore you come to me.'
The head clerk fidgeted with the pay-book.
'It's Patricks in't it. Patricks said I was to be sacked.'
'It's a company decision.'
'Company be buggered Fattie Scott. It's Patricks as wants me nobbled.'
'I'm not at liberty to disclose who says what. 'Appen it was felt the pit would be better off without you.'
'Y' mealy-mouthed fucker. You'd lick Patricks' arsehole if he told you too.'

(*Sam Chard*, 1979, p. 115)

The blunt, scatological language of the angry worker is nicely offset here by the hint of class pretension in the book-keeper's "I'm not at liberty to disclose . . ." This fragment is consistent with Bannister's approach throughout his work – when people speak in their own terms the language is often poetic and its meaning is transparent. Bannister can mercilessly parody the mealy-mouthed language of the middle class academics in *Burning Leaves* (1982), but his real interest is the expressive and intelligent language of those who have not had the dubious advantages of higher education. They deploy the poetry of the vernacular spoken word.

Politics

This section presents an analysis of the politics of 'race', gender and class in Bannister's novels, followed by some brief remarks about anarcho-syndicalism, one of the themes of *Hard Walls of Ego*.

Firstly, 'race' is an absent presence in Bannister's work. It is never addressed in any detail, but it inserts itself insidiously into most of his novels. Because his technique is observational, and meaning is conveyed through dialogue, the reader is always left to make up his or her mind about which side to take in the arguments that Bannister's characters have over issues where 'race' is at stake. I put 'race' in inverted commas because this is, according to the sociological theory I subscribe to, a bogus concept (Miles 1989). Such is its resonance in everyday life, however, that the conversation recorded in *Sam Chard* about the Jews has to be taken as a racialised conversation. During a Workers' Education Association evening class on economics, specifically on the way that market forces make some rich and others poor, Bannister provides us with this bit of dialogue:

> '*You can bet it'll be the Jews at the back of it*' and several voices chimed in.
> '*You old blather, you all'us blame the Jews.*'
> '*Well they're running things.*'
> '*Go on Old gaffer Owen runs the Donny collieries an' he's been on thy back all thi life an' he comes from Sheffield.*'
> '*An' what's at the back of him.*'
> '*Wust capitalist I ever knew were a Lancashire chap.*
> '*And if the Labour lot ever got to be the top dog they'll show you what bossin's about.*'
>
> (*Sam Chard*, 1979, p. 23)

Reading this in the long shadow of the Holocaust, is a complex matter. We might want to place our stress on the last two contributions, which seem to close down the anti-Semitic claim. We might simply want to note that this conversation reminds us that the working class is no less prone to racism than any other class. But if we refer also to the racialised dialogue in the other novels we might be more disturbed by the racial politics of these books. In *Long Day at Shiloh* we hear that the rebels (the South) are incapable of fighting because they've had sex with "nigger women" (1981, p. 10) and that the Northern government is bickering over whether or not they should enlist "nigger soldiers" (1981, p.74) – comments which are simply recorded, naturalistically, leaving interpretation to the reader. Similarly, a visit to "the Chinky" for a takeaway meal in *The Summer Boy* is presented as just another example of vernacular speech. A debate is staged in a pub about whether or not jokes which lampoon the Irish are prejudiced (1984, p. 20), and there's a desultory discussion about "Pakis and the others comin' here that's makin' us short of jobs" in *Burning Leaves* (1982, p. 260). In these fleeting moments in which 'race' is foregrounded in these novels, the left-wing view seems to be given equal weight with the right-wing view. Never is the whiteness, the racialised construction of Yorkshire-ness, brought into focus in these books.

Secondly, if the reticence on 'race' is a notable gap in the politics of these novels, the focus on gender and sexuality is a theme shouted from the rooftops. These novels open themselves to feminist and queer theory readings which place them as extremely masculinist and heterosexist. I suspect that would be to over-read the relevant sections of these novels – to allow theory to over-determine our reading – but it is hard to resist such a reading in books which compete with each other to see how quickly they can introduce the word 'cunt' into the narrative. *Sam Chard* sets a lively pace with "Let's talk about cunt" appearing on page 9, while Paul waits till page 10 in *Burning Leaves* before he can stare at Wendy's cunt. Martin ties with Paul when he feels Helen's cunt moisten on page 10 of *The Summer Boy*. Writing in light of the feminist critique of the use of this word, it is hard not to assume that Bannister is offering a specific provocation. It may or may not be significant that feminist arguments about language are defied in the title of Bannister and Fransella's important text on personal construct psychology: *Inquiring Man* (1986).

The lack of same-sex activity in these novels, like 'race', is an absence which makes itself present in throw-away lines such as the re-writing of popular songs in *Hard Walls of Ego* – where, apparently, you can create a 'fine homosexual anthem' by substituting 'arse' for 'heart' in the song 'You Are My Heart's Delight'. Further fun can be had from the 'gay bloke's chant of terror', "You're Breaking my Arse with Your Heaving'" (1987, p. 67). When Martin ruminates on his coruscating critique of council policy in *The Summer Boy* he describes it as "an arsehole tearing analysis" (1984, p. 226). You begin to wonder whether to read this, and the frequent references to buggery in other novels, in Freudian terms as unconscious desire, or to take it at face-value: this is how straight men talk.

I try to suppress my discomfort at these passages in the novels by searching for another reading, which I have just hinted at. Perhaps Bannister is setting out for us a particular construct of masculinity, one which is predicated on the man thrusting his penis into the vagina as often and as vigorously as possible. In this reading, all Bannister is doing is describing a version of heterosexuality, and it is significant that the context in which this sexual activity is placed is one where informed consent and mutual pleasure are always affirmed. None of the male protagonists is presented to the reader as a hero. Each of them wants the woman on his terms, and his terms alone, and each of them is capable of alarming self-deception, remorselessly revealed by the women. Bannister might redeem himself of the charge of anti-feminism in his representation of the leading women in these novels as independent, intelligent, assertive and critical beings, and in *Sam Chard* and *Burning Leaves* the woman are presented as capable of rejecting the charms of the men who penetrate them. In the most unusual relationship (in terms of the normalised narrative of sexual love), the one between the elderly Joe and the young Janis (*Hard Walls of Ego*), Janis is portrayed as completely besotted with Joe, and he seems highly committed to her, but he deserts her without explanation at the end of the novel, just as Paul vanishes from Wendy's devoted love in *Burning Leaves*. Can we impute anything to Bannister himself here? Perhaps he merely presents us with relationships which all readers know are, in everyday life, routinely incomprehensible to outsiders, and often to the couples themselves. This version of masculinity is one which many readers will find troubling, but it is the proper function of the novel to expose the contradictions in our intimate lives, just as much as in the public arena.

Thirdly, I want to examine Bannister's approach to the issue of class. It should be clear by now that the overt message of these novels is that the northern English working class is to be valued, understood, admired – but not uncritically – and placed at the centre of representation. For most radicals, including myself, this makes for pleasurable reading, despite the caveats I have lodged about the politics of 'race', gender and sexuality. But it has to be noted that this is a message which is very much of its time and place. Bannister was writing at a specific period in British history when the industrial working class was in its death-throes, and he was writing about a generation of working class people, mainly men, unlike any other: the first one that had some access to free state education of a high standard, the grammar school and university. The problems posed when people newly acquire cultural capital, with no significant economic capital in their family history, have by no means gone away. There are plenty of people working in the British universities which were until 1997 polytechnics, and entering them today as students, who will viscerally recognise the discomfort experienced by Paul Killick (*Burning Leaves*), Martin Morley (*The Summer Boy*) and Joe Telford (*Hard Walls of Ego*) when they find themselves face-to-face with representatives of the class that has an excess of both cultural and economic capital. If for no other reason than recording the subtleties of the class-conflicts of everyday life in the late Twentieth Century, these novels have great value. Their defect, sociologically, is that they pay no attention to the changing configurations of class in this period. This may be because Bannister was either uninterested in the rampant individualism and consumerism of Britain from the 1980s onwards, or because he rejected the 'myth of classlessness' that was promulgated throughout that period.

Finally, a note on the anarcho-syndicalist politics that a close reader will have detected in *Sam Chard*, and which are placed in clear focus in *Hard*

Walls of Ego. George Woodcock explains that anarcho-syndicalism shares with anarchism the commitment to federalism and workers' associations, and with anarcho-communism the attack on the wage-system as a whole. Woodcock points out that the anarcho-syndicalists added the distinctive idea that the revolutionary trade union was to be both an organ of political struggle and the foundation of the new society (Woodcock, 1963, pp.17-18). Joe Telford puts it this way, in one of his many lectures to his lover Janis, who is writing her thesis on anarcho-syndicalism:

An' the significance of a real industrial democracy is that it's the only way to get a real political democracy. Syndicalism's not just a pretty idea about a few co-operative factories, liberal crap about co-ownership, it's the only answer to class rule.
(*Hard Walls*, p. 101)

But neither *Sam Chard* nor *Hard Walls* offer any hope that this vision might be achieved. The union deserts Sam, and Joe, author of the pamphlets which inspired Janis to track him down, has long since given up his activism. Martin Morley's assault on council corruption forcefully reminds us of the limits of local democracy and the over-weaning power of big capital. The viciousness of the state apparatus and its ability to crush even minor efforts to reveal the extent of Special Branch phone-tapping is the other plot-line of *Hard Walls*. The political message is one of complete pessimism. Given the strength of this message, it would be easy to conclude that Bannister had himself retreated from anarcho-syndicalism. Bannister lived through the 1983-4 strike by the National Union of Mineworkers, taken by many as the definitive battle between socialism and Thatcherite conservatism. He witnessed the defeat of the British trade union movement by a government and its police force. Only his friends and family can tell us if this actually resulted in a jettisoning of his anarchism, or whether he was merely pessimistic about the possibility of revolution when faced with such a powerful class enemy. My guess is that he would not have provided Joe Telford with such a compelling account of this ideology if he actually thought it was to be consigned to the dustbin of history. Perhaps more significantly, he would not have provided Joe with such an attractive lover if he had thought that these ideas would never again inspire a younger generation. Bannister would no doubt have been reinvigorated when, from the mid-1990s, anarchism became the most important political theory inside the movements against global capital.

Conclusion

Don Bannister wrote:

> *If the act of novel reading is truly an act of constructive anticipation, then the reader is constantly subject to validation or invalidation or to experiencing the unfolding events as being outside the range of convenience of his or her construing. In swift sequence, a novel packages for us those confrontations which Kelly thought basic to life, in which we find our forecasts right or wrong or totally irrelevant.* (Bannister, 1988, p. 509)

One of the great achievements of Bannister's novels is that he forces readers to engage in a battle between our own constructs and those of the characters set before us. Even when the result, sometimes, is discomfort – as, for me, when I wonder if I am construing racism or homophobia – this can still provide a pleasurable reading experience. If we were to examine reading positions in terms of personal constructs, I suggest we need to include ideological constructs such as left or right wing, anti-racist or racist, pro-feminist or anti, and personality constructs such as optimistic or pessimistic, forward-looking or nostalgic. On such dimensions as this, I place myself in the cautiously optimistic, radical and future-directed camp. Thus I read Bannister's work as a fascinating and immensely worthwhile effort to imaginatively re-construct recent British history in both its personal and its political dimensions. Being incurably optimistic, the deeply pessimistic tenor of some of these texts does not daunt my enthusiasm for them. The pessimism arises from Bannister's commitment to a specific type of trade union politics which, like Leninism, has been swept away in the UK by the pitiless march of capitalist restructuring. But the underlying message – that working people have the intelligence and the capability to democratically run their own affairs, given the right conditions – remains as true today as it ever did. And the example that Don Bannister has set here for academics in successfully finding an accessible and lyrical language for communicating profound and radical ideas should inspire us for years to come. In imagining the recent past in this way, he provides us with a marvellous tool-box for thinking about our own lives, and for inspiring the dreams we should be hatching for our personal futures, and those of our fellows.

References

Bannister, D., & Fransella, F. (1986). *Inquiring Man: the Psychology of Personal Constructs (Third Edition)*. London: Routledge

Bannister, D. (1979). *Sam Chard*. London: Routledge and Kegan Paul

Bannister, D. (1981). *Long Day at Shiloh*. London: Routledge and Kegan Paul

Bannister, D. (1982). *Burning Leaves*. London: Routledge and Kegan Paul
Bannister, D. (1984). *The Summer Boy*. London: Heinemann
Bannister, D. (1987). *Hard Walls of Ego*. London: Secker and Warburg
Bannister, D. (1988). A PCP view of novel writing and reading. In Fransella F, and Thomas, L (Eds.). *Experimenting with personal construct psychology.* (pp. 509-514). London: Routledge & Kegan Paul. *(reprinted in this volume).*
Eagleton, T. (1996). *Literary theory – an introduction (Second Edition).* Oxford: Blackwell
Miles, R. (1989). *Racism.* London: Routledge
Sartre, J.-P. (1958). *Being and nothingness.* London: Methuen and Co.
Woodcock, G. (1963). *Anarchism.* Harmondsworth: Penguin

George Kelly and literature

Fay Fransella

What is literature?

When Jörn Scheer asked if I would contribute a chapter on George Kelly and literature to this book I returned the compliment by asking him a question. "What do you mean by 'literature'?" But I realised that was an unfair question when I looked the word up in dictionaries. They all basically say that literature is written by scholars or 'men of letters'. Not too helpful. Perhaps I have the wrong dictionaries. But I went then to a book of quotations and came up with what I think are some intriguing examples.

> There is first the literature of knowledge, and secondly, the literature of power. (Thomas de Quincey, 1848).

That is certainly something to dwell on. How about this?

> Our American professors like their literature clear and cold and pure and very dead. (Sinclair Lewis, 1969).

That can be said of Kelly's two volumes, but certainly not about his essays.

> Great literature is simply language charged with meaning to the utmost possible degree. (Ezra Pound, 1931).

Yes, I would say some of Kelly's essays are charged with meaning to the utmost possible degree.

> The virtue of much literature is that it is dangerous and may do you extreme harm. (John Mortimer, 1969).

That can indeed be said of some of Kelly's writings.

So, if we substitute 'influence' for 'power' I think nearly all those definitions can be related to many of George Kelly's essays. Many of these have been published by Brendan Maher (1969) and others have popped up in other edited books.

But there is another aspect of literature that I particularly want to focus on and that is the poetry that George Kelly wrote, none of which did he publish. In these verses we find him talking about how he, personally, sees things in a way not found in his other work. It is possible that he used this form of loose construing – the very opposite to the tight, sometimes overly tight, way in which he wrote his two volumes – to come to grips with some of the deep-seated personal conflicts he could have been experiencing. Thus, I see two contributions George Kelly made to literature, his essays and his poems.

George Kelly story teller and story inventor

George Kelly was an inveterate teller of stories as Miller Mair has graphically described (1989, 1990). His love of stories may have come in part from his maternal grandfather, a sea Captain. He says, for example, in 'Confusion and the Clock', written in 1960, that one of the things he thought about as he lay suffering a heart attack was of "*our first grandchild, expected in a few weeks, whom I might never see, and to whom I might never tell the wonderful stories that all grandchildren should hear*" (Kelly, 1978, p. 226).

When I visited George and Gladys Kelly in Brandeis in 1966 he described, in an interview he kindly allowed me to record, the book he was in the process of writing, which would be called *The Human Feeling*. He was tired of people saying he had not dealt with feeling and emotion in his two volumes and so this book was being written never mentioning psychology. He said "and Fay has snitched copies of the chapters I have written so far" (Fransella, 1966).

Identifying exactly which chapters I "snitched" was not easy. Some people have commented on the short quotations by Kelly at the beginning of each chapter in the *International Handbook of Personal Construct Psychology* (Fransella, 2003) saying it was nice to be reminded of 'that unique style'. But what is that style? I am no expert on literary style but there is certainly much humour in Kelly's writings, often with a serious meaning enmeshed within it. For instance, "my nightmare is that one day I will wake up and find that my best friend is a psychologist". Others have said he writes in a 'folksy' way. For me one other very important quality is the way in which he makes one want to read a piece of writing right to the end. His meaning is often obscure. He uses metaphor and draws verbal pictures leaving the reader uncertain whether or not one has a complete understanding. That often leads me, and no doubt others, to read his writings more than once.

If I were to pick one central theme in many of his essays I would say it is about searching, always asking "what is around the corner", "what might have been" and in absolute terms, struggling with the nature of truth. He presses himself and the reader to "transcend the obvious". He often takes us unawares as we read. He seems to want to unsettle us. He makes sitting back in the armchair uncomfortable. We should not be surprised at this because he actually spells his view out in the Preface of Volume 1.

To whom are we speaking? In general, we think the reader who takes us seriously will be an adventuresome soul who is not one bit afraid of thinking unorthodox thoughts about people, who dares peer out at the world through the eyes of strangers, who has not invested beyond his means in either ideas or vocabulary, and who is looking for an ad interim, rather than an ultimate, set of psychological insights.
(1955/1991, p. xi, Vol 1, p. x).

Of some significance for the story unfolding in this chapter is that the reader should be someone "who is looking for an ad interim, rather than an ultimate, set of psychological insights".

George Kelly and his writings

The focus of much of his essay writing is on prediction, anticipation, truth, and what might have been. These are, of course, linked but I am giving examples of Kelly's writings about them separately for the sake of clarity.

Prediction and anticipation

One chapter that was definitely intended for the book on the *Human Feeling* is that on 'Hostility'. He takes the story of Procrustes to explain his understanding of the nature of hostility. I give this at some length because it is, in my view, a wonderful bit of writing.

> *There was a young man by the name of Theseus who had been reared under the domination of his mother. One day, out in the garage or some place, he ran onto an old sword and a pair of shoes that had belonged to his father. Right then and there he decided to make a break for it and go look up his father, who, it appears, had gone away to a national convention a number of years before and somehow had managed to stay away on urgent business ever since.....*
>
> *Now this young victim of "momism", as it existed in the classic Greek era, became quite a hero by the time he caught up with his old man ...along the road Theseus ran into a character by the name of Procrustes...people thereabouts all called him by his nickname, "Stretch", which is what the word "procrustes" means in English.*
>
> *Stretch....was hostile. That, of course, is the whole point of telling this story. I don't think he ever meant to be hostile. His feelings would probably have been hurt if anyone had even suggested the idea. As a matter of fact, it is quite possible that no one ever did mention it to him. In those times not many people went in for psychoanalysis and you could easily go for weeks without so much as once having someone interpret your unconscious motivation to you....*

Because he happened to be hostile, Stretch was one of those unlucky souls in this world whose fate it is to be grossly misunderstood. Why? In the first place he was genuinely interested in people. I mean genuinely! *He had bought this little chicken ranch, or whatever it was, with the express purpose of setting up a kind of wayside motel where travellers who found themselves in this lonely spot at nightfall could be assured of some old-fashioned hospitality......Stretch, like most hostile people, had a pretty clear idea of how guests should be treated. He really fancied himself as a host and along about sundown he used to stand out by the front gate, lean against the mailbox, and wait to see if he could persuade some traveller to stop in for supper. At the table he always proved to be an excellent conversationalist and, before his guest realized how late it had gotten to be, it would be time to go to bed.....He would fluff up the pillows, press down on the mattress to show how soft it was, and keep murmuring something about how much he hoped that the bed would be neither too long nor too short....Showing all this solicitude was what really got him into trouble.* (Kelly, 1969a, pp. 268-9)

Kelly goes on to paraphrase the story and couch it in personal construct terms.

There is something humanly plausible about Procrustes. He did what people do. He could not bear the thought of being wrong in his estimate of the stature of his guests. Rather than change his estimate he corrected his guests. And so this part of the Thesean story has lived and the poetic imagery of the procrustean bed has survived to this day.

It is at the point of Procrustes' failure to anticipate correctly the stature of his guests that the legend places the fulcrum of his hostility ...... in my paraphrasing I have underscored one original feature of the tale by describing Procrustes as an ardent host who was genuinely interested in people. It was only because so much of his world was centered in his claim to knowing the true dimensions of man that the invalidating evidence assumed such overwhelming proportions. When he peeked through the bedroom door that world of his threatened to collapse.

How to save it! If his bed – his only bed – did not fit his guest, his guest must be made to fit the bed. Regardless of the cost, the validity of his bed and the integrity of his world – which were one and the same thing – must be sustained. That piece of psychological furniture was for him, not just a bed, but a vital institution – more important by far than the physical well-being of just one guest. It was a key to his way of life. Under the circumstances he did the only thing as far as he could see, that made sense. (Kelly, 1969a, p. 274)

He later makes a very firm statement about the importance of prediction:

It is in terms of his predictions, then, that the mind of man comes at last into firm contact with reality. I would go even further and say that it is only in terms of his predictions that man ever touches the real world about him. (Kelly, 1969a, p. 275).

The first part of this excerpt shows Kelly the storyteller and the whole essay is, to me at least, a great read. There can be no doubt that he thoroughly enjoyed this type of writing. The second part shows how he was able to put the story into psychological terms without having to change his literary style too much. In the third excerpt he succinctly makes his crunch-point. It is only when we put our predictions to the test by behaving that we are in touch with reality.

There are many other essays to choose from but I have decided on 'Confusion and the Clock' (Kelly, 1978) because it is about what prediction means in daily life. How would it be possible to predict what tomorrow will bring? Would we really want to know? How would we be able to test out how correct we had been in our predictions? As one might expect, he links prediction with what might have been.

Now that I come to think of it, I have never staked my existence wholly on the practical 'facts of life', though I have repeatedly told myself that I should. But how can one spend his whole life, the one and only life that is given us, taking notes on things as they are, without once using his pencil to make a little sketch in the margin depicting things as they might be. Must we always pretend that truth is only what is: Even on the one day, the one that is different from the thousands before, must we still pretend that? (Kelly, 1978, pp. 224-225)

What might have been

Kelly's fascination with alternatives can be clearly seen in his essay 'Psychotherapy and the nature of man' written in 1963. Again, in my view a great piece of writing. As in several of his essays, he uses the Biblical story of Adam and Eve. In talking about Adam he says:

....Man, the poor fellow, chose the toil and confusion of knowledge instead of the pleasant and obvious rewards of unquestioning obedience.

> *It should be said, I suppose, that Man probably would not have had the initiative to take this fateful step if he hadn't had some encouragement from his girlfriend. Without her he would probably have been content to do what he was told, as men are inclined to be when they are part of an all-male society..... But when women are around, or you can't get your mind off them material security and inner contentment don't always add up to the same thing. No matter how much happiness is available at hand, you are likely to become restless and itchy to test the limits of your instructions. **We wonder just what would happen if....? All the luminous possibilities of the future become so fascinating that we are blinded to the obvious rewards of the present.*** (Kelly, 1996b, pp. 207-8, bolding added)

This topic comes up again in 'Ontological acceleration':

> But human anticipation – the stuff that life is made of – unfolds its full meaning only when one is keenly appreciative of what might actually happen instead, and when he comes to forecast the events of his future in the rich context of all else that may be possible. (Kelly, 1969c, p. 8)

The nature of truth

In 'The language of hypothesis' (Kelly, 1969d) Kelly focuses more directly on another central theme running through these essays – the nature of truth. He looks at the results of using the *invitational mood* of speech instead of the *indicative mood* as we normally do. Kelly cites Vaihinger's 'as if' philosophy (1924) in which he suggests that both God and reality might be regarded as paradigms rather than 'truths'.

> *This was not to say that either God or reality was any less certain than anything else in the realm of man's awareness, but only that all matters confronting man might best be regarded in hypothetical ways* (Kelly, 1969d, p. 149).

George Kelly continues this theme of make-believe and the use of the invitational mood in seeing it an essential feature of science and also as a way of coping with threat. He explains it in this way:

> *Instead of insisting that old truths are about to give way to new, that we are shifting from one indicative to another, we can take the view that it is not the truth that is changing, but rather that we are tentatively exploring the possibilities of a new approach to the truth.* "Sup-

pose we regard the floor as if it were hard." **We approach the truth through the door of make-believe.** (Kelly, 1969d, p. 152, bolding added)

In his essay 'Confusion and the clock' he talks at some length about what truth means to him. The first paragraph sets the scene:

> *What is not so easy to help is the failure of those "truths" that have served to make so many thousands of days turn out as expected. We believe them because how else is one to know what is really so, or how else to bridge the chasm between past and future over which we always find ourselves suspended, how else to find continuity and thus to live. These "truths" – they can be a little tick-tock-tick-tock truths that keep repeating themselves in the corner – and always so impersonal about what is going on that you don't mind having them around – or they can be big round shining truths – brittle as all perfect things must be – that roll along majestically until they crash against the day that was not meant for them, and leave you with nothing but their fragments, a litter of words – leave you shattered too.*
>
> *I suppose one solution is to forge bigger, rounder, fuller truths – really perfect truths this time, or, if not perfect, so hard they will not be shattered by the crash of single events. Then, when that one day comes along, we can simply regard it as an exception to the rule, a statistical improbability , or, if it is something nice, as a miracle. The trouble with this is that once you come face to face with this pesky statistical improbability you have to be an awfully fast talker to keep yourself convinced that it is not genuine. But then, some of us are awfully fast talkers, and quite ready to believe something does not exist if we keep telling ourselves it is not there.* (Kelly, 1978, p. 227)

There is no end of the different ways in which George Kelly is saying the same thing. "Let us use our imagination a bit more". "Let us glimpse what might be around that corner". With this seemingly almost desperate need to strive to see over the horizon it is not surprising that Kelly put 'anticipation' into his Fundamental Postulate.

Did George Kelly see himself practicing what he preached?

In these essays as well as in his theory, George Kelly talks about not trapping oneself in the known world, of looking at what might be, thinking what might be round the corner, not getting hooked on thinking you have the truth. But did he see himself putting these ideas into practice? Kelly does not often talk about himself in his essays – except for 'Confusion and the Clock', but he does occasionally as in 'Ontological acceleration'. He says:

> *But what eludes me still is an understanding of human behaviour, and particularly that of my students. I have only the faintest idea of what they might have achieved if they had made the most of their opportunities, or what failures otherwise awaited them in that depression-ridden, drought-stricken dustbowl of the 1930's.* **Only in the context of what was possible can I make a proper assessment of their behaviour, or of mine.** (Kelly, 1969c, pp. 17-18)

George Kelly's poems give us a clearer idea of how he saw himself as matching up to his ideas of how we all might be.

George Kelly's contribution to literature through his writings

Comparing his writings with the definitions of literature cited at the beginning of this chapter I think they pass the test. Thomas de Quincey (1848) says:

> *There is first the literature of knowledge, and secondly, the literature of power.*

There will be few who will argue that he does not exhibit knowledge but power is a more difficult criterion. If that means in one sense 'influence' then I would say his writings meet that criterion too.

With Kelly's two volumes in mind, the point made by Sinclair Lewis does not need labouring:

> *American professors like their literature clear and cold and pure and very dead.*

However, taking just those few excerpts from his essays cited in this chapter, it is clear to me that they can be said to be 'great literature' in Ezra Pound's definition as they are:

> *simply language charged with meaning to the utmost possible degree.*

Lastly there is John Mortimer's definition that:

> *The virtue of much literature is that it is dangerous and may do you extreme harm.*

Perhaps support for this definition in Kelly's writings is summarised by Bill Perry's comment (personal communication) after reading 'Ontological Acceleration' (Kelly, 1969c):

> *The vision he put forward impressed me so deeply, was so far-reaching, so futuristic, that I had a sense of dealing with a new scripture.*

So much for his writings, now to a few of his poems.

George Kelly and his poetry

He wrote several poems. Some are obscure, especially the last one I mention, ONTA. What I am now sure of is that George Kelly used verse to express, even explore, some ideas and issues that he felt strongly about. In particular, he may have used verse to 'talk' about how he feels he matches up to the ideals he talks about in his essays. He talks personally in his poems in a way that is rare in his other writings. I wonder if that is why none of the following poems was published in his life-time. He is known to have been 'a very private man'. Also, his construing is very loose as befits poetry but it is also a favourite way of construing for him although he was a very tight construer in his dealings with most people most of the time (Fransella, 1995).

The switching from tight to loose construing is one of the personal characteristics that students found most difficult about Kelly as a teacher. His poem about being a teacher has been published in Fransella (1995) and shows some of the conflicts he experienced. In this poem we have 'truth' being what he and others teach and to contradict that is 'sinful'.

'Nursery rhymes for older tots: to all you kettles, from all us pots'

> Teacher, teacher – strict upbrought,
> Truth is that which you've been taught.
> All that contradicts is sin;
> Therefore man needs discipline.
>
> Never question any saint;
> Question only those who ain't.
> Never seek an answer new;
> Only answers old are true.

It is necessary to instil a single faith because people need guidance and discipline.

> Install a monolithic faith
> To guide each step a man may take.
> Thus, tuned to your authority,
> His life shall run perpetually.

But then he asks that vainly sought teacher, Kelly himself, "where do you stand on this issue?"

> Teacher, Teacher, vainly sought,
> Noble skeptic, bold in thought,
> Keen assayer of all man's gains,
> Where stand you amidst these claims?

Sean Brophy (personal communication) offers these interpretations of the following and the last verse:

> Still, you are part of us, the part
> Denied when safer lusts our heart
> Desired, and in us gaped instead
> A dark, where truth is raped by dread.

Still, *you* are part of us –	*You* – the questioning you, the personal scientist within you.
The part denied when safer lusts –	the part that put questions for which no answer currently exists, the part that wishes to experiment and take risks in pursuit of truth – the part which is denied in favour of the safer harbour of the heart where the emotions remain serene on the calm waters of unknowing.
And in us gaped instead A dark, where truth is raped by dread	The dark revealed as the badly lit passage out of a secure well-lit well-watered and well provisioned cave, where the search for truth is assaulted as an idea which threatens us with the dreaded possibility that our secure cave could be a prison!

Kelly seems to be saying that he has been teaching what he is 'supposed' to teach rather than what he believes he 'should' be teaching. He has not been practising what he has been preaching. Perhaps we are not all as free as we would like to think. All is tied up in his last verse:

> Teacher, teacher, if our will
> To comprehend shall dare not fill
> This void in our society,
> Then in what sense *can* we be free?
> Critics, teachers, kettles, pots,
> Boobies, bullies, and bigots,
> Whilst flushing freedoms down the drain,
> Cry, '*Education* is to blame!'

He spells out his view of how students at university level should be taught in the following unpublished talk:

> *We have to teach our students how to replace certainty with uncertainty. There's a line in the musical play "The King and I" where it says that people fight most violently for the things they are not quite sure are so, but which they don't want to admit they are questioning. The things that you really feel comfortable about you don't usually get quite so violent over. But things which you feel you must believe even though you doubt, those are the things we become unreasonable about. And so I think we have to teach students how to live with uncertainty.* (Kelly, 1958, p. 3)

I think these thoughts may well have a bearing on my interpretations of his poem ONTA later in this chapter in which he says: "To save their dreams all men must fight". Do we glimpse here what Kelly was referring to when he told Al Landfield that "I live my life under constant threat" (Fransella, 1995, p. 12). Was he saying: "I am aware that I am living a lie"?

Some of his verses were light-hearted and very tongue-in-cheek. One such verse comes at the start of his chapter on 'Aldous the personable computer' (1963). It is very much Kelly – humorous, succinct, but making a point. It is unusual in its clarity and shows his love of playing with words and ideas.

> There once was a passionate dame
> Who wanted some things made plain,
> So she punched up the cards,
> Filled tape by the yards,
> But - somehow - *it just wasn't the same*!
> (Kelly, 1963, p. 229)

I have the feeling he allowed his love of loose construing to take over at times because it expressed his meaning better than prose. But we move on to a poem that is very complex. I wonder if that is deliberate in order to hide its 'true' personal meaning. Or was it written, indeed, as part of his personal struggle to get his thoughts straightened out. Readers must be the judge of that.

ONTA

To me, this is the most profound of Kelly's writings and, perhaps, the most autobiographical. Apparently written in 1963 he seems to be setting out his quandary about being true to oneself. His poem about teachers indicates he is aware of this issue. Also, when acknowledging those whose ideas can be found in his theory he says: "and, of course, that distinguished and insightful colleague of all personal-construct theorists, Mr William Shakespeare" (Kelly, 1955/1991, p. xii/Vol 1, p.xiii). Perhaps he warmed to Shakespeare's Hamlet:

> This above all:
> To thine own self be true,
> for it must follow as dost the night the day,
> thou canst not then be false to any man.

Did George Kelly see something of himself in Hamlet? Was Kelly questioning the extent to which he had been true to himself? One of the few occasions on which Kelly becomes a literary critic is when he uses the soliloquy 'To be or not to be' to explain the CPC (decision-making) and the Creativity Cycles. This last poem, ONTA, takes us into the realm of the nature of 'being'. My interpretations are based mainly on what I have discovered on that wonderful source of knowledge – the Internet.

The title of the poem, ONTA, is the Greek for 'Being'. In his chapter 'The Question of Being' in his *Basic Writings* (1927), Martin Heidegger says that "Aristotle's broadest and deepest question, which demanded an account (logos), was the 'Being of beings' (onta)" and out of that arose 'ontology'. Kelly wrote a whole essay on 'ontolotical acceleration' as already mentioned. It was a subject clearly of great importance to him.

So this poem, ONTA, is about 'being', which in turn relates to both the nature of reality and to the nature of truth. But perhaps also in this poem we begin to glimpse some of the things that troubled George Kelly, the person. Whether you will agree with me or not remains to be seen. Kelly writes each of the four verses 'as if' written by someone else and then gives his personal comment on the verse in the last three lines.

Verse 1: Parmenides

Parmenides of Elea is a Greek philosopher who was born around 510 BC and is said to be one of the most significant of the pre-Socratic philosophers. He was the first to ponder the question 'What is Being?' His work 'On Nature' exists in fragments and is made up of two parts. One part, the 'Way of Truth', discusses what is real. The reality of the world is 'One Being', it is an unchanging, indestructible whole. The second part, the 'Way of Seeming', discusses the contrary, more conventional view of the world, which is illusory. Movement and change are simply illusions of a static, eternal reality. No doubt Kelly liked the bi-polarity here. The title of each verse summarises its content.

Is so!

The men who grasp and clutch at objects say,
"Now look; this is reality.
It's firm. It's bold and clear.
So straight would be tomorrow's flimsy way
If you would only deign to see
Just that that's here, that's here."

Kelly's reply:

To this what shall I say?
One cannot but agree.
I too am surely here.

No doubts here.

Verse 2: Alexander

Kelly accepts the point Parmenides made about reality but questions it in the second verse through the mouth of Alexander. My first question was "Who is this Alexander?" I found there were at least three philosophers to choose from. To my surprise I found that Alexander the Great was also known for his philosophical ideas as, in fact, he had been educated by Aristotle. Indeed, Aristotle shared with Alexander not only his doctrines of *Morals* and of *Politics*, but also some of the more abstruse and profound theories the philosophers reserved for oral communication only among themselves, the initiated.

As evidence of this I came across a letter Alexander wrote to Aristotle on hearing that he had published some of these treatises meant for oral communication to the initiated only, he was not well pleased. He wrote:

> Alexander to Aristotle, greeting. You have not done well to publish your books of oral doctrine; for what is there now that we excel others in, if those things which we have been particularly instructed in be laid open to all? For my part, I assure you, I had rather excel others in the knowledge of what is excellent, than in the extent of my power and dominion. Farewell.

Through the mouth of Alexander – both The Great and the philosopher - George Kelly asks:

But why for man?

The men who talk and talk in order to be wise
Yap loud and long at shadows in our night
And snarl at strangers constantly.
Alone, they strive their dreams to guard with peering eyes
Till dawn, or death – or both – shall prove them right
And what is not at last shall be.

And what is Kelly's reply to all this? Back to truth.

But who utters truth until he tries?
To save their dreams all men must fight.
My world shall take its shape from me!

These philosophers talk and talk, keep all strangers away and guard their dreams from peering eyes. That is not right. You have to test your predictions by behaving. Philosophy is no good if it cannot be used. If you have a dream you must fight for it. I am grateful to Al Landfield for suggesting that Kelly was referring here to threat. He knew his theory would be threatening to others and that he would have to fight for it. Landfield says: "New ideas threaten holders of old ideas. New ideas may invalidate people. Invalidated people will fight back and try to invalidate the holders of new ideas" (2005). Kelly then reminds himself and others that "*My world shall take its shape from me!*". *And I will fight to shape it – particularly if I am not absolutely sure I am right.* As already cited, Kelly said that:

43

> .. *people fight most violently for the things they are not quite sure are so, but which they don't want to admit they are questioning.* (Kelly, 1958, p. 3)

Is there additional threat here? Does he want to be a power in the world and shape the worlds of others? Is he not so sure that his theory is such a good idea after all?

Next he speaks through the mouth of Paul and asks what comes after we die?

Verse 3: Paul

I am assuming this must be the Paul who changed from being Saul, the slayer of every Christian that could be found, to become one of the greatest Christians. The voice of Jesus Christ on the road to Damascus and Saul's resulting blindness brought about this change. Kelly mentions this conversion in the context of the psychological importance of name change. Through the mouth of Paul Kelly says:

> Man lives. Man dies. What then?
>
> The men who climb the distant heights to gain some crystal tower,
> From whence to visualize the space beyond their time.
> Chart past and future as one coursing stream,
> And find themselves, borne in its flow, transcending troubled hours.
> So thus, in lives with greater destinies aligned,
> Self's immortality is seen.

Once you get into your crystal tower you can free yourself from the present and "bridge the chasm between past and future over which we always find ourselves suspended" (quoted above from 'Confusion and the clock'). Paul was borne along by the Will of the Lord and was able to rise above all adversity. If we align ourselves with such visionaries, or with God, we can, perhaps, see our own immortality.

What seems possibly to be at the kernel of these first three verses was suggested to me by Ian Stubbs, a Church of England clergyman. He pointed out that, to him, Parmenides, Alexander and Paul were all 'Shapers'. They all changed the world by thinking and by action. Kelly has just said that his world will be shaped by him – and not others. Could he be really concerned about being a 'shaper' himself? In the quotation from 'Psychotherapy and the nature of man' Kelly says he is against 'unquestioning obedience' (Kelly 1969, p. 207).

But in Kelly's reply to Paul we perhaps come to a statement of what may have been a vital personal conflict for Kelly.

> And I? Why dare not I attune to greater power?
> Indeed, all's lost, astray from its majestic line
> I'll dangle neither truth nor gods upon a string!

"Why shouldn't I be a shaper?" "What if my personal construct psychology were to become a model for people to live by – such as happens with prominent philosophers and psychologists?" "Why don't I dare to be such a powerful person?" Perhaps because you can lose everything if you stray from that 'majestic line'. I puzzled long over everything being lost if one strays from 'its majestic line' but found a connection in Confusion and the Clock. There are those 'big round shining truths' which are 'brittle' and 'roll along majestically until they crash against the day that was not meant for them and leave you with nothing but their fragments, a litter of words – leave you shattered too'. Threatening indeed.

Is he saying that those who allow themselves to be influenced by these great thinkers and theorists are lost or even shattered if they do not follow the rules they ascribe to? This links to Kelly saying in 'Psychotherapy and the nature of man':

> *No matter how much happiness is available at hand, you are likely to become restless and itchy to test the limits of your instructions.* (Kelly, 1969b, p. 208)

Whatever the rights and wrongs of that, I interpret Kelly clearly deciding that being seen as powerful was 'definitely not for me'. "I will *not* be someone who pretends to have 'the truth' and treat others as if they were puppets having no will of their own'." Was he perhaps aware of imminent comprehensive change in his core construing if he came to believe that he had followers? He did joke about writing another theory if he started to have followers. Yet I have personal evidence that he did not see me or Don Bannister or Franz Epting or Rue Cromwell or Jack Adams-Webber and many others as followers. Why not, I wonder? Perhaps it was because he thought these people were using his theory to develop their own understanding of themselves and others. How did he construe 'followers'? I, for one, do not know.

Another possible threat is his ambivalence about the publication of his theory. On the one hand we have him saying in a talk with me that only one of the five books he had written to be published, and *that might have been a mistake* (Kelly, 1966). On the other hand, Al Landfield says that, after reading a missing letter Kelly wrote to Neil Warren in 1964 "I knew beyond a shadow of a doubt that Kelly's hopes for the theory went way beyond ordinary ambition. His hopes went beyond himself, I believe". ONTA suggests here was a conflict indeed. Now to the last verse spoken not through the mouth of a person but focusing around a concept.

Verse 4: xenos

> Once this I knew and had forgot
>
> The men who lived to live, whose names are lost among discarded years,
> No pedant questions posed. Their words stood not for things apart,
> But only served to draw them close to what was theirs.
> Self was for them a woman's voice, a tiny hand, a storm, a tear,
> A sorrow etched in love. They left no legacy of art,
> Yet overhead we hear their children climbing up the stairs.
>
> To whom but them has what is real approached so near?
> This is no alien world; its keys are in my heart.
> I touch, I try, I scan, I feel, and stumble up my stairs!

My internet searches told me that *xenos* is the Greek word for 'stranger' or 'one with whom one is not acquainted'. Hence the word xenophobia. I came across a piece entitled *What does it mean that, 'Some have entertained angels unawares?'* by Tony Warren. He says that we need to understand two things about the source of this title, which comes from Hebrews 13: 1-2:

> *Let brotherly love continue.*
> *Be not forgetful to entertain strangers: for thereby*
> *Some have entertained angels unawares.*

First, the word angel is the Greek word *aggelos* meaning messenger. That is, it is talking about people and not angelic beings. The second is that 'entertain strangers' comes from the Greek word *philoxenos* meaning being friendly to those we don't know. Warren interprets this as saying we must be friendly to those we do not know because sometimes we may entertain messengers – all believers are God's messengers – *aggelos*. Christians show hospitality to all and by so doing show their Love of God. So, where does that get us with Kelly's last verse?

> The men who lived to live, whose names are lost among discarded years,
> No pedant questions posed.

There are, first of all, all those strangers, some of whom may be God's messengers, who lived simply to live. We must remember that Kelly was a devout Christian although by no means seemingly an orthodox one. These people were not philosophers and shapers with great ideas. They did not ask purely academic questions but spoke in order to bring themselves closer to those they know.

> Self was for them a woman's voice, a tiny hand, a storm, a tear,
> A sorrow etched in love. They left no legacy of art,

These strangers left no legacy like those shapers and visionaries. They did not write a psychology that has made some impact on the world. They did not shape the world in any tangible way. BUT overhead we hear their children climbing up the stairs.

Now we come to Kelly's comments to the xenos verse. He brings us back to the central issues of the poem, reality and being and truth.

> To whom but them has what is real approached so near?
> This is no alien world; its keys are in my heart.
> I touch, I try, I scan, I feel, and stumble up my stairs!

It is these people who get close to reality. Their legacy is their children. These unknown people did not ask academic questions, instead they were busy testing out their predictions by behaving and so getting in touch with the 'real' world. That world is not an alien world, because 'its keys are in my heart', that is, the Kingdom of God is within us all. Could this be what he is referring to in the title 'Once this I knew and had forgot'? In his essay 'A psychology of the unknown' (Kelly, 1977) he mirrors that last line in this way:

> *If a man, say a psychologist, remains aloof from the human enterprise he sees only what is visible from the outside. But if he engages himself he will be caught up in the realities of human existence in ways that would never have occurred to him. He will breast the onrush of events, **He will see, he will feel, he will be frightened, he will be exhilarated, and he will find himself feared, hated, and loved.** Every resource at his disposal, not merely his cognitive and professional talents, will be challenged. So involved will he be that, in order to survive, he will have to cope with his circumstances inarticulately as well as verbally, primitively as well as intelligently, and he will have to pull himself together physically, socially, biologically, and spiritually.* (Kelly, 1977, p. 11, bolding added).

Did he use this poem and perhaps other writings or poems to 'pull himself together'? One other interpretation occurs to me that relates to what he said in 'Confusion and the Clock'. He talks there about his thoughts while experiencing his heart attack and of his pregnant daughter with a husband overseas, already under stress and of the grandchild to whom he would never be able to tell stories. He then talks about his son 'and realised how like him it would be to try to sacrifice his own opportunities to make life easier for his widowed mother. '*He would undertake the sacrifices I had failed to make.*' He wrote again later in that essay of the importance of his family to him:

> *I looked at my family that morning and it occurred to me that if I had wished for the most wonderful thing in the world to happen it would turn out to be just such a family. And I realised that while life had given me only a small proportion of all the miscellany I had, at one time or another, grasped for, it had generally ended up supplying me with the very best that could be managed under the circumstances, better than anything I could claim to have deserved.* (Kelly, 1978, p. 228).

As in ONTA – which is about 'being' – George Kelly perhaps realised as he lay having a heart attack that the most important thing in his life was the creation of this family. It was more important than whether he wanted to be a 'shaper', someone who had the power to influence people.

What to say at the end of this over-long search for George Kelly the person through his writings. I end up with the feeling of having been in touch with someone of enormous intellectual power who perhaps was unable or unwilling to accept that power and, because of that, often felt he was living a lie. It is as if he had a construct something to do with 'being a shaper' as opposed to 'being a family man' who has the keys to the Kingdom of God in his heart. And, like all people, he makes contact with reality by touching, trying, scanning, feeling and stumbling up his stairs. ONTA suggests that he opted for 'being a family man' – 'Once this I knew and had forgot'.

Is it possible that the real threat to George Kelly was that his conflict over practising what he was preaching and of wanting and yet not wanting his theory to be taken up by 'followers' had lead him to question his religious faith? Had he been faced with the threat of religious doubt? Would that perhaps not have been guilt also – he would be dislodged from his core role of being a devout Christian? It was Kelly himself who said that 'the wages of guilt is death'.

ONTA as a self characterisation

The poem can be seen as a self characterisation written in both the first and third person. If we take the personal lines first and look at the first sentence as a statement of the present, he agrees about reality:

Is so. I too am surely here

And the last line as an indication of where a person might be going:

Once this I knew and had forgot. This is no alien world; its keys are in my heart.
I touch, I try, I scan, I feel, and stumble up my stairs!

In between we have conflicts examined. One should not keep one's ideas locked away from all but the favoured few. One has to publish them and then fight to save them. 'The world shall take its shape from me'. That means if you are not careful that you 'gain some crystal tower', away from the present rush of events and so glimpse your own immortality. But he then decides that that is wrong. One's ideas may be proved invalid and then one is shattered. But perhaps most important, perhaps it is wrong to dangle truth on a string before the unsuspecting.

I am left wondering whether, having written ONTA George Kelly was at peace with himself. It is good to think that possible.

References

de Quincey, Thomas (1848). Review of the *works of Pope*, *North British Review*, *9*, 301.
Fransella, F. (1966). Unpublished interview with George Kelly.
Fransella, F. (1995). *George Kelly* London: Sage Publications
Fransella, F. (2003). *International handbook of personal construct psychology*. Chichester, UK: John Wiley & Sons.
Heidegger, M. (1927). The question of being. *Basic Writings*
Kelly, G. A. (1955, 1991). *The psychology of personal constructs*. Vols I & II. First published by Norton, 1955, then by Routledge in collaboration with the Centre for Personal Construct Psychology, UK
Kelly, G. A. (1958). Teacher-student relations at the university level. Unpublished manuscript, Fransella PCP Collection, University of Hertfordshire, UK.
Kelly, G. A. (1963). Aldous the personable computer. In Tomkins, S. S. and Messick, S., (Eds) *Computer Simulation of Personality* New York: John Wiley & Sons
Kelly, G. A. (1969a). Hostility. In B. Maher (Ed) *Clinical psychology and personality: The selected papers of George Kelly* New York: John Wiley & Sons

Kelly, G. A. (1969b). Psychotherapy and the nature of man. In B. Maher (Ed). *Clinical psychology and personality: The selected papers of George Kelly.* New York: John Wiley & Sons.

Kelly, G. A. (1969c). Ontological acceleration. In B. Maher (Ed) *Clinical Psychology and Personality: the Selected Papers of George Kelly* New York: John Wiley & Sons

Kelly, G. A. (1969d). The language of hypothesis: man's psychological instrument. In B. Maher, (Ed) *Clinical Psychology and Personality: The Selected Papers of George Kelly* New York: John Wiley & Sons

Kelly, G. A. (1977). The psychology of the unknown. In D. Bannister (Ed) *New Perspectives in Personal Construct Theory* London: Academic Press

Kelly, G. A. (1978). Confusion and the clock. In F. Fransella (ed.) *Personal construct psychology 1977.* London : Academic Press.

Landfield, A. W. (2005). Personal communication.

Lewis, S. (1969). The American fear of literature. In H. Frenz *Literature 1901-1967.*

Maher, B. (Ed) (1969). *Clinical psychology and personality: The selected papers of George Kelly* New York: John Wiley & Sons

Mair, M. (1989). Kelly, Bannister and a storytelling psychology. *International Journal of Personal Construct Psychology, 2,* 1-14

Mair, M. (1990). Telling psychological tales. *International Journal of Personal Construct Psychology, 3,* 121-135

Mortimer, J. (1969). Foreword to C. H. Rolph, *Books in the dock.* L'Andre Deutsch

Pound, E. (1931). *How to read,* Harmsworth

Vaihinger, H. (1924). *The philosophy of 'as if': A system of the theoretical, practical and religious fictions of mankind* (C. K. Ogden, Trans.). London: Routledge & Kegan Paul

Warren, T. (1999). *The mountain retreat.* www.mountainretreat.org.

What-if versions of ourselves: Creative writers speak

Chris Stevens

In interviewing leading Australian fiction writers about their creative processes and experiences (Stevens, 1999) a cluster of themes, concerning validation, participatory knowing, being oneself, the community of self and self-transformation became broadly evident. What emerged as each writer spoke was a profound sense of open-ended inquiry, emotional engagement to the point of identity with their characters and frequently the dissolution of a discrete or unitary experience of self. Significantly, this dissolution of self was simultaneously experienced as personal enhancement as their writing seemed to take on a life of its own and connected the writers in profound ways to the world 'beyond' him or herself. These themes are broadly related to Personal Construct Theory and to a pragmatist view of personal growth.

Non-validation that validates

The creative writer's lot can be a lonely, arduous one. The genesis of a major work can take years, with little or no guarantee of success. Writers may struggle with creative insecurities, despite records of public acclaim. Nonetheless, they report various experiences in writing that validate them deeply and that compensate for this suffering and effort and that keep them inspired to write.

Surprisingly all seven writers interviewed spoke about how they typically do not know in advance where their works were heading. They don't have formal plans and often only the most general themes or metaphors to guide them. They may have written many thousands of words or a number of 'drafts' but are still searching for what their book is about, what will happen and what it will mean. In Personal Construct Psychology (PCP) terms they spend a great deal of time in a state of loose construing and non-validation, perhaps with a dilated perceptual field in which to organise the system of construal at a more comprehensive level (Kelly, 1955, pp. 476-477).

It can be very challenging or distressing psychologically to be in this state of non-validation (where one is confronted by the lack of both validation and invalidation of one's construing). Such a state can lead one to be further and further removed from reality and can make the person extremely vulnerable (see Walker, Oades, Caputi, Stevens & Crittenden, 2000, for a more complete discussion). This is particularly so if, for example, children are left in this type of developmental 'vacuum' for an extended period of time leaving them bereft of ways to anticipate and test their world.

The writers interviewed appear, however, to have developed a positive and constructive use of non-validation; a contemplative holding off from completing the Experience Cycle (Kelly, 1963, 1966a). Their creativity is certainly related to this deliberate use of non-validation. As Walker et al. (2000) put it:

> *It seems to be important at times to utilize non-validation in order to preserve the integrity and coherence of one's overall system of understanding. Given such a superordinate construal of the validity of one's construing processes, however, loosening one's construing may provide periods of non-validation in which new elements, and new combinations of elements may enable us to see things in new ways.*

The writers spoke about this need to keep their sense of self coherent and integrated amidst this highly uncertain circumstance – a process that goes against the grain of our normal constructive tendency to resolve uncertainties. Writer 5 (W5[4]) spoke of the various 'ruses' he used to 'convince' himself that everything was going according to plan – even down to making a story line that he didn't follow. Another writer (W7) revealed that she distanced herself from the potential insecurity and anxiety of not knowing where she was going by writing many drafts. Of her early drafts she could truthfully tell herself: 'no-one will ever read this'. In general, the writers had various strategies they would use to avoid feelings of personal fragmentation and a sense of disorientation.

This suspension of the tightening phase of the Creativity Cycle (Kelly 1955) is related to what Heidegger (1959) called *meditative thinking*. In contrast to *calculative thinking* it is a type of active anticipation in which the person 'waits-upon' what the world will provide rather then 'looking for' or predicting something in particular. This may be considered to be the opposite of hostility (Kelly, 1955) in that it embodies an openness or "objective attitude" (Warren, 1998) that allows events to be other than we may predict or desire them to be. It is not avoidance in some defensive fashion, but a radical openness and determination to keep the constructive doors open for as long as possible.

In fact Writer 2 also suggested (before our formal interview) that the above strategy is like walking down a corridor with many doors. One looks through the doors to see what is there, but takes pains to not close them, to

---

[4] References to the 7 writers interviewed will be abbreviated to W1, W2 etc. The number references are to the transcript paragraphs in Stevens (1999), Vol. 2

leave them all open as long as possible. These writers are giving expression to Kelly's (1955) concern that people should not try to prematurely grasp for insight. It seems to me that the crucial stage in the creativity cycle is what Kelly (1955) called 'provisional tightening', where one is able to look through newly opened doors, but one does not enter that new room fully, closing the door behind oneself, and therefore closing oneself to other possibilities. Writer 7 suggested that such premature tightening slows down one's creative progress overall:

> (W7) *The danger, though... is that I will try to arrive at that structure too quickly... And of course the lack of time is another thing that distorts the process because the quicker you can get it structured... that's a real problem because it, it just takes twice as long, basically... if you truncate those, that exploratory part of the process.* (986)

This exploratory style of construction adds a new dimension to our PCP understanding of the active elaboration of one's perceptual field or 'aggression' (Kelly, 1955). As Walker et al. (2000) suggested:

> *... at a superordinate level there is an active elaboration of one's perceptual field, but the means for this is a more subordinate or 'local' cultivation of non-validation. It is a way of keeping construing loose enough to prevent premature completion of the validational cycle.*

Creative writers suffer. They experience in particular the anxiety of not-knowing and long-term uncertainty. The meditative creative strategy described above enables a periodic release from the anxiety of self-concern and self-consciousness and enables them to transcend invalidations thereby to experience a looser, freer, non-censored sense of self and being. The fact of not-knowing is backgrounded. All the writers talked emphatically about this not-knowing as being at the heart of their creative processes. The related ability to hold contradictories in mind with equanimity has been called 'omnivalence' (Briggs, 1990) and recalls the (Romantic poet) John Keats' 'negative capability':

> *... that is, when a man [sic] is capable of being in uncertainties, mysteries, doubts, without any irritable reaching after fact and reason.* [letter to G. and T. Keats, 21 Dec. 1817]. (Page, 1965, p. 53)

Participatory knowing

This equanimous state of awareness often leads to an experience of intimate relationship with the known or what I've called *participatory knowing* (Stevens, 1999). A pivotal concept in Merleau-Ponty's (1964) philosophy was the centrality of the *body subject* in anticipating or negotiating life. The body subject is the 'phenomenal body' as experienced by the person (as distinct from the 'objective body' considered as physiology from an 'external' perspective). Essentially, it is the person's experience that is present before reflexive consciousness is operative and which is the vehicle for all our object-directed experiences. In Radley's (1977) terms it is the 'from which' that characterises anticipation and which tacitly forms the basis for later, more predictive modes of understanding our world. *Anticipation*, in these terms, is one's bodily stance towards one's world: "one's attitude to it which embodies silent questions and the sort of answers one is open to" (Butt, 1998a, p. 108). This notion is essentially a relational one in which one is a body-subject enmeshed in activity and context, not a separate subject who happens to be in a body. It contrasts to a more predictive, external perspective and leads to an understanding of knowledge as participatory.

Participatory knowing is not knowing in some sort of detached, disembodied way, but is more about developing a way of being, of experiencing. The writers expressed just such a way of being:

(W6) *What you are trying to do is to get that other human soul, your reader and the rest of it, to find him, herself in all these other forms, all the time, experiencing reality in it, you know. It's a protean thing. Get them into this new, new form, new way of being in the world, new way of living.* (925)

Participatory knowing isn't 'knowing-about' but 'knowing–with'. It has an event-like character. It is represented in the oft-quoted experience of creative absorption. This experience sometimes develops into a felt sense of identity with one's creative product, where the creator has the experience of merging almost physically with his or her creation:

(W7) *... instead of saying, instead of identifying myself as a woman who is writing a book about an incestuous father, and that had become a role I could no longer do, instead of that I was now just a part of this world, and it was all open to me.* (1049)

We feel others' feelings because we live in a field that includes their expression. Their expression becomes a part of our experienced world. As Butt (1998a) put it: "I am a participant in it; it involves me" (p. 111). Butt (1998a) further considered that two people together are not 'interacting' but act as an 'indivisible system' where "the relationship between them in some sense precedes their individual psychologies" (p. 115). This sense of participatory knowing is what Shotter (1995) called 'joint action'. Notice how similar this is to Writer 2's experience:

> (W2) *So once they [the characters] get going on their own, they can do what they like. So it doesn't, it's not like writing from life... yes... You become them rather than they are you.* (435)

In the case of writers, then, 'joint action' involves created 'others' who develop a type of autonomous existence, an 'indivisible system' with the writers and, hopefully, with their readers.

Being oneself

Changing our awareness processes themselves is arguably more important in Kellian theory (particularly the later Kelly) than changing the particular contents of construing (see Kelly's paper on 'Ontological Acceleration', 1966b). In these terms practising creative writing could be understood partly as personal development. Being able to alter one's construing process is liberating and validating. It provides new worlds to inhabit, new possibilities of being, feeling and doing. The writers, in effect, create worlds in which they can 'be themselves' in new ways. Thereby they can come to transcend any particular way of identifying self. Such a conclusion is consistent with the findings of Butt, Burr and Bell (1997) who described this easy sense of acceptance:

> *There was a consensus that being oneself referred to the absence of self-consciousness and the relaxing of self-monitoring. Being oneself meant allowing oneself to be carried along in a social flow unreflectively and without exercising effort.* (p. 25)

These ideas also exactly fit the reported experiences of creative writers. The reverie, loosening and meditative style of thought bring about a freedom to be whoever, and to think whatever, comes along. Critical self-judgement is relaxed utilising the conceit of the characters. A feature of meditative thought is that one does not will or extort creativity. One must value all one's experiences, outlooks and intuitions, but in a non-grasping way. What is required is an affectionate, patient curiosity about what is going on. John Anderson, in discussing Heidegger's *meditative thinking*, expressed the same idea:

> *There is a sense in which we wait without knowing for what we wait. We may wait, in this sense, without waiting for anything; for*

anything, that is, which could be grasped and expressed in subjective human terms. In this sense we simply wait, and waiting may come to have a reference beyond ourselves. (in Heidegger, 1959, p. 57)

This 'reference beyond ourselves' has been called the *interbeing* by Thich Nhat Hanh (cited in Mair, 1995, p. 19) wherein distinctions between self and other begin to blur, especially within creative processes.

Community of self

Another way of thinking about these new ways of 'being myself' is to consider that we are not a unitary self (Colapietro, 1990; Mair, 1977) but rather contain multiple selves. This idea is directly expressed by novelist Kate Grenville who, in writing about one of her novels, *Lilian's Story*, described this direct experience of multiple selves:

> *There was an element of magic about writing the book. There were times when I felt in direct relation to that voice, that the book was, as they say, 'writing itself' through me. But I don't think it is magic. I think it's that my image of that person released something latent in me, released one of the voices in me. Lillian's voice felt very natural to me, although it's still not a voice I ever use in my own life. In taking on that persona – that voice, actually – I discovered an astonishing freedom. Perhaps that's the compulsion of writing: the freedom to be, not somebody else, but another of your selves.* (Grenville & Woolfe, 1991, p. 106)

The 'astonishing freedom' suggests that there has been constriction or suppression of aspects of self and that the writing allows these multiple selves to live together in a workable community. This multiple sense of self is commonplace among creative writers. Helen Garner in relation to *Cosmo Cosmolino* expressed a similar sentiment:

> *That character came down from heaven and landed on my page. I found such ease in him. I don't know why... A Jungian psychologist might say that Alby was a version of my animus; he seemed so intensely familiar to me. It was as if I were he.* (Grenville & Woolfe, 1991, p. 68)

I made reference earlier to research by Butt, Burr and Bell (1997) where participants were asked to complete 'social self grids'. This freedom to be multiple selves:

... was not identified with occupying particular construct poles, but with allowing themselves to be drawn pre-reflectively into social contexts. (p. 12)

As the authors noted, these findings do not mark the death of the 'self' nor diminish its importance. There is still a "personal constructor" (p. 12), as they put it, even though the self is dispersed and fragmentary. What was crucial for participants in this research was not that a particular self, or *content* was validated, but that one felt free to 'be myself' — in *whatever* spontaneous or pre-reflective form that took. What needed to be validated was the person as *process*, not so much any particular results of that process. In this way, 'self' is a process with a pre-reflective 'I' as the author and the 'me' as its context-specific production. It is important that we go on producing selves, as the world changes, as we face different circumstances.

Writer 4 expressed this adaptive function of multiple selves this way:

(W4) *You can't afford, in my line of work... to have a single notion of consciousness or of absolute privacy. You have to have a notion that one's psyche is made up of parallel and conflicting elements. That's not madness. It's a healthy way of being.* (680)

There is something definitively 'constructivist' about these accounts in that self is conceived as an ongoing constructive process, rather than as a fixed entity. One of the writers (W7) considered that at base most novel writing is autobiographical, but this is in a creative, generative sense, not as a description of a fixed entity. It would not be right to say that all fiction writing is strictly autobiographical. This is the case for at least two reasons. The first is that fiction writing is in part a means for ontological change and personal development for the writer rather than a description of an extant reality, that is, the writer's self.

The second is that there is this experience of the dissolution of self-other boundaries, so it becomes as much social observation as self-description. Perhaps it is better to understand creative writing as an experiential playground in which broader, more anthropological observations about the nature of human beings are explored. As Writer 4 expressed this somewhat paradoxical state of affairs: "Of course it's a distillation, of course it's been censored. These are what-if versions of ourselves" (613). These characters are therefore simultaneously symbols that are intensely personal yet also take on an archetypal reference for humankind.

Transcending self

This personal development theme is related to the permission that writers grant themselves to not self-censor; a relative liberation they seek from the constraints of 'social acceptability'. I believe it is a special case of the positive validation and emotion associated with being 'allowed to be ourselves' (Burr, Butt & Bell, 1997). Self-consciousness is relinquished and the person is free to be spontaneous. This concern with avoiding social inhibition is related to the fact that creative fiction involves explorations of core aspects of self:

> (W7) *It's more like you are allowing a self to speak that is normally censored... Which is why the more conscious you are of the audience, of course the more disastrous it is.* (1014)

These self-references are 'concealed' within characters as Writer 7 put it, and the writers appeared to find something inherently liberating about it, some sense of freedom and experimentation to 'be themselves' in new ways in their works without self-consciousness and inhibition. This experience is complex:

> (W2) *It's humbling and... what's the word, validating, yes. It's both. But they are not necessarily um... in opposition are they? Because humbling doesn't mean that you don't take pride in your work. You claim it as your own. You can't just say 'Oh shucks, I don't know how this happened!' [laughs]. Because I made it happen.* (433)

Inherent in this statement is an important distinction about self-validation: about what or who is being validated. There is one sense in which it is not one's self at all that is responsible, yet paradoxically it *is* the writer who is responsible:

> (W2) *Oh it's great. It's neat. Yes! That's great! It's a wonderful feeling to see it working there. And quite humbling in a way because it's as if you didn't do it [chuckles]. It's been given to you. And yet I know that it is my intelligence presiding over the whole thing... I'm not just a blank medium.* (421)

This paradox can be understood in terms of the distinction we have stressed between self as content or beliefs about self ('me'), and self as process ('I'). What is being primarily validated is the person as process, the person as non-self-conscious creator freed to be non-reflexively and spontaneously responsive to circumstances as they arise (Butt et al., 1997). There is a growth in self as old aspects of the 'me' can be relinquished and replaced by a broader sense of the 'I' as one who can be a type of conduit, a way of being that allows the world to speak. This may represent a higher form of the 'objective outlook' that I suggest is conducive of creativity. This represents one's capacity to be-with the world exactly as it is.

What emerges is a sense of fluidity and excitement as a narrow sense of self is transcended and the writer senses the arrival of a new integration both 'within' and 'without'. This is in keeping with Writer 2's expectation that the other writers would have mentioned 'resisting the excitement' of this looser stage:

> W2: *Resistance to the excitement... a pulling back. Have you heard, has anyone spoken to you about pulling back from the excitement?* (336)

There appears to be a paradoxical state here where the writers both want and fear to be in this non-directable, unpredictable state of being. Perhaps, as in a swimmer procrastinating before diving into water, once one has plunged into the 'water' it is fine, and one does not want to get out again.

In relation to this resistance, another useful concept Merleau-Ponty (1962) proposed was that of *sedimentation*. This refers to the strong tendency to maintain one's self-definition and tacit assumptive structures rather than change them. Just as sediments laid down in a river become hardened (may even turn into rock), one's assumptions and core constructs resist contradiction. This is because things become murky and upsetting when sediments are disturbed. We may lose our bearings and no longer know who we are.

Merleau-Ponty (1962) argued that the capacity to become aware of our tacit, superordinating system is the means to overcome sedimentation. He believed that the best way to do this is to create new projects.

Butt (1998b), in summarising this view, put it this way: "we 'find' that we have changed in the living of a new project" (p. 278). We change superordinating structures primarily by doing, not by intellectualising, even in 'intellectual' pursuits! Frequently, the existential project precedes the conscious one. The work of creative fiction, for example, appears in some way to 'write itself' using the creator as a medium or conduit. There is the suggestion, however, in the question concerning resistance to "excitement" raised by Writer 2 above, that writers sense these large-scale construct implications and experience some measure of 'threat' as Kelly (1955) defined it and therefore may hesitate on the threshold of substantial construct change.

The writers suggested another way they transcend self and overcome sedimentation. They tended not to show or share their work in-progress socially, even to respected peers and friends. This is for two reasons. Firstly such fear and anxiety about other's opinions and ideas about their work reveals a type of 'inverse' social influence. They were certainly not indifferent to social influences. Just as the writer is trying to escape the tighter, habitual and more predictable structures of his or her own thought, he or she needs to create a social 'vacuum' to prevent being drawn into conventional discursive channels which may inhibit their creativity.

The second reason is that writing creative fiction is a very private task. As Writer 7 said, perhaps writers have to assiduously disguise or 'conceal' their autobiographical or personal relation to the text, thus holding off till they feel relatively secure about this. It is significant, however, that at some (usually quite late) point, all writers have special people whose opinion about their work is highly valued.

Conclusion

We have seen that the creative writers interviewed have articulated a number of related themes concerning the creative use of non-validation; a qualitatively different mode of awareness I've called participatory knowing; the subsequent experience of a freedom to 'be myself'; which is then expressed in terms of the authentic experience of a person's 'multiple selves'. This leads to a different understanding of personal growth – one distinct from the enhancement of a unitary self, and more related to non-self-conscious engagement with the world. This pragmatist reading of personal development is centred in the paradoxical experience that the writers described of their works 'writing them' as much as being written by them.

When a person values his or her ongoing experience for its own sake and relinquishes somewhat the driving subjectivity that attempts to control and predict events, genuine creativity and personal change become more likely. What emerges is a patient 'waiting-upon', a receptive, looser style of anticipation that modulates between the provisional tightening of construing and looser, playful explorations. As the person becomes immersed in this style of thought and experience, there can be a progressive development of awareness such that one may become aware of one's interpretations or constructions *as* interpretations or *as* constructions. By suspending our immediate desire to know, the horizons of our understanding may themselves come into view. The assumptions we take for granted may be revealed to us as such, and the haste to jump to a ready interpretation may be inhibited. This can then lead to creative flow as the person enters into a psychological state characterised by non-validation.

In similar fashion, one may also become aware of the non-unitary nature of 'self' in favour of a more spontaneous presence to oneself as construer, as an 'I' at the centre of the production of many me's – what I've called the community of self. This relative freedom from the personal and social constraints on self-construal leads to a profound awareness of being spontaneously 'myself'. Such awareness may enable the person to suspend the 'normal' pragmatic engagement with the world, to suspend the habits of thought, to hold off knowing for long enough for new possibilities to emerge. This was frequently experienced by the writers as a spontaneity and lack of self-concern, as an experience of freedom accompanied by a strong sense of connectedness and meaningfulness. The writers demonstrated a deliberate use of non-validation to emotionally endure and maintain this exploratory stance.

The subsequent joy of creative insight can be considered to be a type of reunion with one's anticipatory 'fit' or 'coupling' with one's world after such open-ended explorations. Within this meditative awareness, it is 'self-as process' that predominates and allows one to relinquish one's habitual 'looking-for' an answer, and to instead be satisfied to 'wait-upon' creative insight. At the tightening phase of the creative process, the arrival of insight makes the writer feel whole once again, but now whole in a significantly new way. The burden of not-knowing and uncertainty is lifted. To express this adequately it is only right to leave the last words to a professional writer:

(W7) *Because it was like a physical, um, 'lightness' is the only word. I felt as if I were in danger of floating off the car seat. ... It was as if I had been dissociated and just, suddenly things were integrated.* (1045 –1047)

References

Butt, T. (1998a). Sociality, role and embodiment. *Journal of Constructivist Psychology, 11*, 105-116.
Butt, T. (1998b). Sedimentation and elaborative choice. *Journal of Constructivist Psychology, 11*, 265-282.
Butt, T., Burr, V. & Bell, R. (1997). Fragmentation and the sense of self. *Constructivism in the Human Sciences, 2*, 12-29.
Colapietro, V. M. (1990). The vanishing subject of contemporary discourse: a pragmatic response. *The Journal of Philosophy, 88*, 644-655.
Grenville K. & Woolfe, S (1991) *Making stories: how ten Australian novels were written.* Sydney: Allen & Unwin.
Heidegger, M. (1959/1966). *Discourse on thinking.* J. M Anderson & E. H. Freund (Eds.), New York: Harper and Row.
Kelly, G. A. (1955). *The Psychology of Personal Constructs.* New York: Norton.
Kelly, G. A. (1966b/1969). Ontological acceleration. I n B. Maher (Ed.), *Clinical psychology and personality: The selected papers of George Kelly* (pp. 7-45). New York: Krieger.
Kelly, G.A. (1963/1977). The psychology of the unknown. In D. Bannister (Ed.) *New perspectives in personal construct theory,* London: Academic, pp. 1-19.
Kelly, G.A. (1966a/1970). A brief introduction to Personal Construct Theory. In D. Bannister (Ed.) *Perspectives in personal construct theory,* London: Academic, pp. 1-29.

Mair, M. (1977). The community of self. In D. Bannister (Ed.). *New perspectives in personal construct theory* (pp. 125-149). London: Academic Press.

Mair, M. (1995). *A long term quest for understanding.* Paper presented at the XI International Congress on Personal Construct Psychology, Barcelona, Spain, 3-7 July, 1995.

Merleau-Ponty, M. (1962). *The phenomenology of perception.* London: Routledge.

Merleau-Ponty, M. (1964). *The primacy of perception: and other essays on phenomenological psychology, the philosophy of art, history and politics.* Northwestern University: Northwestern University Press.

Page, F. (1965). *Letters of John Keats.* London: Oxford University Press.

Radley, A. (1977). Living on the horizon. In D. Bannister (Ed.), *New perspectives in personal construct theory* (pp. 221-249). London: Academic Press.

Shotter, J. (1995). In conversation: joint action, shared intentionality and ethics. *Theory and Psychology, 5*, 49-73.

Stevens, C. D. (1999). *Crooked paths to insight: the pragmatics of loose and tight construing.* Unpublished Ph.D Thesis. Department of Psychology, University of Wollongong. Vols 1 & 2.

Walker, B.M., Oades, L.G., Caputi, P., Stevens, C.D. & Crittenden, N. (2000). Going beyond the scientist metaphor: from validation to experience cycles. In J.W. Scheer (Ed.). *The Person in society: Challenges to a constructivist theory.* Giessen: Psychosozial-Verlag.

Warren, W. (1998). *Philosophical dimensions of personal construct psychology.* London: Routledge, 1998.

Two roads converge: Poetry as Personal Construct Theory

Richard Bell

The link between Poetry and Personal Construct Psychology [PCP] writing began with Bannister and Fransella (1971) when they identified some bipolar constructs in a Bolingbroke speech in Shakespeare's Richard II.

Bipolar construing is fairly common in poetry as it follows from contrast, which is a common device in poetry. Choice too, follows from the dichotomy corollary as might be seen in the famous poem by Robert Frost that begins *Two roads diverged in a yellow wood....*

There is dichotomy and choice in this poem, but its Kellyian qualities are of course deceptive. The two roads represent the choice and in one sense are elements as they are variously construed as bent, fair, worthy of claim, grassy, wanting of wear, and leaf strewn.

If we set this up as a grid however, we can see the poet has not chosen according to Kelly (1955). Except for *Bent-Straight* both elements (roads) are located at the same pole of each construct.

Emergent pole ✔	The road taken	The road not taken	Implicit pole ✘
Bent	✔	?	*straight*
Fair	✔	✔	*Not fair*
Better claim	✔	✔	*Poorer claim*
Grassy	✔	✔	Bare
Wanted wear	✔	✔	Worn
Leaf strewn	✔	✔	Leaf free

Bannister (1977) also distinguished between personal construct theory and poetry when he quoted (albeit disparagingly) Pope, Keats, and Shakespeare in 'The logic of passion', criticizing them for contrasting cognition and affect. Closer perhaps to the process of poetry writing, he also spoke about the processes involved in novel writing (Bannister, 1988).

> *We invent the terms in which we will view the word* [world?] *and thereby discover what is to be seen by taking such a view. This inextricable mixing of what we create with what we are confronted by, is most manifest in novel writing.* (Bannister, 1988, p. 511)

Bannister was writing from the perspective of a novelist and we might expect such a mixture to also underlie the process of poetry writing. In fact Bannister noted

> *The novel, in PCT terms, is not unique. It is a special case of the anecdote, the poem, the play, the daydream.* (Bannister, 1988, p. 513)

Perhaps not unsurprisingly Bannister also referred to Kelly's creativity cycle in this context, moving from loose construing to 'tightened and readily validatable construction' and also a cycling between superordinate (the theme of the novel) and subordinate (the detail) construing. In poetry it might be argued that form [since poetry also involves aural and visual effects] also plays a role in such cycling.

PCP and poetry also have links in educational contexts. In the PCP world, David Miall (1985, 1988) has looked at the reading of poetry and presented some data on using repertory grids to assess students' reactions to a poem while Boscolo and Bernardi (1992) used repertory grid techniques to look at how students construe the process of writing in various contexts (although they did not explicitly consider poetry). However, the link between PCP and writing has also been dealt with more explicitly outside the traditional PCP arena. In the late 1960's and in the 70's there was a move in English teaching, primarily in Britain but also in Australia, to improve the literacy of school children by encouraging them to write, write from personal experience. One of the proponents of this movement was James Britton, who was in part influenced by the writings of George Kelly. Britton (1970, p. 18) wrote:

> *We have spoken so far as though the 'successive reconstruing', the modification of our representations, took place only as our expectations were put to the test in our moment-to-moment encounters with the actual. But we habitually use talk to go back over our events and interpret them, make sense of them in a way that we were unable to while they were taking place. This is to work upon our representation of the particular experience and our world representation in order to incorporate the one into the other more fully. We may of course achieve a similar end without talking: we may simply meditate in silence on past events. In doing so we should, in my view, be using processes which we had acquired as a direct result of our past use of language.*

Such reflecting on experience is also to be found directly in poetry as in:

> I gazed--and gazed--but little thought

>What wealth the show to me had brought:
>For oft, when on my couch I lie
>In vacant or in pensive mood,
>They flash upon that inward eye
>Which is the bliss of solitude;[5]

Or less familiarly

>These beauteous forms,
>Through a long absence, have not been to me
>As is a landscape to a blind man's eye:
>But oft, in lonely rooms, and 'mid the din
>Of towns and cities, I have owed to them,
>In hours of weariness, sensations sweet,
>Felt in the blood, and felt along the heart;
>And passing even into my purer mind
>With tranquil restoration:--feelings too
>Of unremembered pleasure: such, perhaps,
>As have no slight or trivial influence
>On that best portion of a good man's life,[6]

Both of these sets of lines come from Wordsworth, who is, in a couple of senses, the key to a link between poetry and PCP.

One of these senses follows directly from Wordsworth[7] himself. In the *Preface to the Lyrical Ballads*, he wrote: *...our continued influxes of feelings are modified and directed by our thoughts, which are indeed the representatives of all our past feelings...* and he went on to say

> *The principal object, then, proposed in these Poems, was to choose incidents and situations from common life, and to relate or describe them, throughout, as far as was possible in a selection of language really used by men, and, at the same time, to throw over them **a certain colouring of the imagination**,[8] whereby ordinary things should be presented to the mind in an unusual aspect; and, further, and above all, to make these incidents and situations interesting by tracing in them, truly though not ostentatiously, the primary laws of our nature...*

---

[5] William Wordsworth. *I wandered lonely as a cloud*
[6] William Wordsworth. *Lines composed a few miles above Tintern Abbey, on revisiting the banks of the Wye during a tour. July 13, 1798.*
[7] This and other quotes and poems by Wordsworth are taken from Hutchinson (1906)
[8] **Bolding** added.

The way Wordsworth throws over events a *"certain colouring of the imagination"* has echoes of Kelly's *"Man looks at his world through transparent patterns or templets which he creates and attempts to fit over the realities of which the world is composed"* (Kelly, 1955, pp. 8-9) and the '*tracing*' of '*the primary laws of our nature*' in these '*ordinary things*' is aligned with Kelly's notion of superordinate core constructs. Interestingly, Wordsworth sees this kind of relationship as making things '*interesting*' for the audience, which has implications in terms of sociality and commonality corollaries.

The other sense in which Wordsworth plays a role in the linking between PCP and poetry, is as a motivation for the work of Samuel Levin (1976, 1977, 1988) on metaphor in poetry, which we will consider in more detail in a moment.

Metaphor has been considered in personal construct perspective, principally by Mair (1977) who briefly considered poetry in a paper entitled 'Metaphors for living'. In that paper he referred to three poems as follows:

> *In poetry, of course, metaphor is vital and omnipresent. T. S. Eliot (1936) speaks, for example, of the "the yellow fog that rubs its back upon the window panes", as if the fog were some kind of animal. Norman McCraig (1972) speaks of male pigeons on the roof as "wobbling gyroscopes of lust." Kathleen Raine (1970) likens "time" to a storm at sea when she writes, "Time blows a tempest – how the days run high, deep graves are open between hour and hour."*

Many years later Freeman (Freeman, 1999) has written about the 'poetic construction of selfhood' from a clinical perspective, and in doing so has drawn upon poetry (with reference to a Seamus Heagney essay) and metaphor (with reference to Ricoeur).

Levin argues that unlike ordinary language, metaphor must "be construed before understanding can be achieved" (1988, p. 1). He argues that most theories of metaphor proceed by analysing the language[9] in order to identify what the speaker intends to convey about the actual world. Levin suggests that there is a logical alternative – that the metaphor can be taken as literally true, and that the world of the speaker can be seen as the abnormal. His approach distinguishes between metaphor in ordinary language and metaphor in poetry, and in the case of poetic metaphor he argues that there are practical benefits that accrue from an approach which accepts the metaphor literally, and instead seeks to understand the world being portrayed by the poet. Levin argues this is particularly true of Wordsworth.

---

[9] Metaphor is considered deviant language – perhaps that is why I am attracted to it.

A related concept that Levin introduces to operationalize his view of metaphor in poetry, is the notion of a 'higher sentence'; 'higher' in a linguistic 'deep structure' sense, where each poem is preceded by an implicit sentence: *I imagine (myself in) and invite you to conceive a world in which* ...Thus in the preceding poem we read

> *I imagine (myself in) and invite you to conceive a world in which*
> I gazed--and gazed--but little thought
> What wealth the show to me had brought:

Sometimes this sentence is included in the poem when the poem begins with a supposition, as in *Suppose...*, or *Imagine...*, or *When...* or *If...* . For example, in

> Supposing i dreamed this)
> only imagine, when day has thrilled
> you are a house around which
> I am a wind-   Cummings (1968)

it is often difficult to know what is poetry and what isn't. On the other hand here is another piece which is almost pure metaphor

> Words are weasels
> which bite and gnaw
> at the cake of knowing
> I can't bear to be without
> their squirming lively forms
> They take you over
> swarm everywhere
> till you are
> a crawling mass
> of words alone
>
> And after a period
> of scrabbling activity
> ripping and pulling
> they will abandon
> an empty shape
> a few well picked bones
>
> You appear alive
> but it is

>   the squirming mass
>   of little words
>   eating everything away

This was defined by the author as not a poem. It is from Miller Mair's book *Between psychology and psychotherapy: A poetics of experience*, which features some 78 pieces of writing[10] that Miller called 'short lines' (1989, p.87) that were "not intended as 'poems'" (1987, p. 88). But it has a title, *Words are weasels*, looks like a poem, and sounds like a poem. Here a poem is taken to be a piece of text that uses more than grammar and punctuation to structure it, devices such as rhyme, rhythm, and visual appearance.

Levin's notion of a poem being prefaced by the phrase *'I invite you to conceive a world'* also brings us back to PCP. Kelly too was fond of the 'invitational mood' (Kelly, 1964) who wrote *"suppose we regard the floor as if it were hard"*. *We approach the truth through the door of make-believe.'* (p. 152). Spence McWilliams in his paper 'Accepting the invitational.' (McWilliam, 1996) also emphasized this mood, while Mair, in his paper on metaphor, noted from a kellyian perspective "the invitational aspect of metaphor" (Mair, 1978, p. 262). Metaphor is very directly a device for communication between people. The invitational which is directed at the hearer or reader, invokes our commonality of construing, something that poets have been aware of as much as personal construct theorists. In a letter to the editor of Poetry magazine, Hart Crane (1966) wrote

> *There are plenty of people who have never accumulated a sufficient series of reflections (and these of a rather special nature) to perceive the relationship between a drum and a street lamp – via the unmentioned throbbing of the heart and nerves of a distraught man which tacitly creates the reason and "logic" of the Eliot metaphor ['Every street lamp I pass beats like a fatalistic drum'] ...If one can't count on some such bases in the reader now and then, I don't see how the poet has any chance to ever get beyond the simplest conceptions of emotion and thought, of sensation and lyrical sequence.*

Of course Crane here is also talking about the commonality of construing, the need for the audience to be able to incorporate new constructs into their construct system. A dramatic demonstration of this in a poetic context can be found in the Japanese poetic form, the *renga*, or as it sometimes known *haikai no kasen*. The Japanese poetic form most people are familiar with is the brief three line *haiku*. *Haiku* derived from the first 'poem' in a *renga* sequence, the *hokku*. The *renga* was essentially a social activity. One poet would

---

[10] 'Pieces of writing' is English-teacher talk for pieces of writing

compose the *hokku* [of a 5-7-5 syllable count]. The next poet would compose a further two lines [of a 7-7 syllable count] that was consistent with the first composition. Together the two would form a 31 syllable poem [a given form in itself, *tanka*]. However the next poet would compose another segment [of a 5-7-5 syllable count] which together with the preceding two lines would form a separate *tanka* poem. This poem would differ from the first, despite the overlap, and the sequence would have to follow rules of content and mood (as for *haiku*). The next poet (perhaps the first again) would then compose another couplet, and so on. The remarkable thing about this sequencing, is that any segment (construct) would be open to two construings. Ueda (1970) has provided detailed analysis of two renga by the Haiku master Bashō, showing the linkages and transitions.

To turn back to the individual however, as in the concerns of James Britton and William Wordsworth to consider the role of language in private rumination, Mair (1978, p. 261) describes metaphor, albeit metaphorically (and echoing an earlier quotation from Kelly[11]), as *"a means of entering the unknown through the gateway of the known"*, and pointed to Kelly's similar concern as to *"how man, from his position of relative ignorance, can hope to reach out for knowledge no-one has yet obtained"* (Kelly, 1977, p. 4). Metaphor, like language in general has a role in our own private explorations to construe and make sense of our world.

Poets, too, talk about their craft in this way. Thom Gunn the Californian-expatriate-British poet, describes a poet as *"mainly concerned at finding himself on a barely known planet in an almost unknown universe, where he must attempt to create and discover meanings."* (Gunn, 1985, p. 43) and *"What Duncan [another poet] has stressed is the importance of the act of writing. It is a reach into the unknown, an adventuring into places you cannot have predicted,."'* (Gunn, 1985, p. 193)

Mair, I think correctly, distinguished metaphor from construct, although I would not characterize the difference in the same way. He thought *"a construct seems to be a more abstracted notion than metaphor"* and *"more clearly delineated than metaphor"* (1978, p. 263) and for him, *"constructs often seem linear, directional, geometrical axes of reference which seem hard, straight, angular, intellectual, and 'digital'. Metaphor, on the other hand, often carries an aura of associations which are flowing, colorful, sinuous, sensuous, surprising, ambiguous, inviting, warm, rich, protean"* (1978, p. 264). Of course 'construct' has for Kelly and others [see Shaw & Gaines, 1992] geometric connotations, but all I can say is, who wants to choose 'construct'?

---

[11] *"We approach the truth through the door of make-believe"*

For me, metaphor seems to be a way of using constructs; either as a way of linking constructs in otherwise fragmented systems, or to represent other constructs which may incapable of verbal representation (such as core constructs). We should remember that the word 'metaphor' is from the greek, *metaphora*, which is in turn derived from *metapherein*, meaning 'carry over'.

An example of how metaphor may be used to involve core constructs, of which the poet might be aware and at the same time not be able to access can be found in Robert Lowell's talking about the writing of a poem

> I began to feel that real poetry came, not from fierce confessions, but from something almost meaningless but imagined. I was haunted by an image of a blue china doorknob. I never used the doorknob, or knew what it meant, yet somehow it started the current images in my opening stanzas. *[of the poem 'Skunk hour'.]*

> Nautilus Island's hermit
> heiress still lives through winter in her Spartan cottage;
> her sheep still graze above the sea.
> Her son's a bishop. Her farmer
> is first selectman in our village,
> she's in her dotage.[12]

At the other extreme (the contrast pole we might say) there is for poets an awareness of the constructs they apply

> Why did I laugh tonight? No voice will tell:
> No God, no Demon of severe response,
> Deigns to reply from Heaven or from Hell.
> Then to my human heart I turn at once.
> Heart! Thou and I are here, sad and alone;
> I say, why did I laugh? O mortal pain!

Here the poet engages in reflecting on his own actions, "Why did I laugh tonight?" In clinical construct psychology there is a reliance on the therapist to provide such reflection, although those of us who pride ourselves on our 'psychological-mindedness' or 'emotional intelligence' will readily claim that we regularly perform the same kind of self reflection that John Keats is engaging in here. Formally however personal construct psychology has paid little attention to this kind of construing. In one sense such reflective constru-

---

[12] Lowell (2003)

ing is superordinate to simple direct construing, in that the simple construal is a pre-requisite for the reflective construing

In the same way the use of irony similarly employs a superordinate construing over a simple direct construal.

> All the time I pray to Buddha
> I keep on
> Killing mosquitoes[13]

> What matter if I live on
> A tortoise lives
> A hundred times as long[14]

These two haiku are by the master haiku poet Issa. The haiku structure lends itself admirably to the contrast structure required by irony, although irony also abounds in western literature from Shakespeare to e.e. cummings. The second haiku is notable for another reason. It is from a collection entitled *Japanese Death Poems* (Hoffman, 1986). Traditional Japanese culture has always involved a social view of death, although there many examples also in western literature. For example the John Keats poem quoted above was written when he first suspected that he had tuberculosis [which eventually led to his death]. But personal construct psychology although it has pioneered research into the grieving and bereavement aspects of death, has had little to say about what kind of structures we might normally use in construing this eventuality. And as for love, that staple of poetry (even for Miller Mair), George Kelly (1977, p. 3) seemed to say it was too hard. Faced with his reconstruing of 'love' as 'dependency' or even 'hostility'; I have to say, I'm with the constructivist poet who said

> Ah, love, let us be true
> To one another! for the world, which seems
> To lie before us like a land of dreams,
> So various, so beautiful, so new,
> Hath really neither joy, nor love, nor light,
> Nor certitude, nor peace, nor help for pain;
> And we are here as on a darkling plain
> Swept with confused alarms of struggle and flight,
> Where ignorant armies clash by night.[15]

---

[13] From Hass (1994)
[14] From Hoffman (1986)
[15] Matthew Arnold, *Dover beach*.

Poetry thus can be seen as a personal construct activity, employing many of the devices we recognize as elements of Kelly's theory. However in some respects poets go further than constructivist psychologists in looking at those aspects of our lives that are complex and difficult, and employing very sophisticated construct systems such as irony and reflective construing, in making sense of these.

References

Arnold, M. (1867). *New Poems.* London: Macmillan/
Bannister, D. (1988). A PCT view of novel writing and reading. In F. Fransella and L. Thomas (Eds.) *Experimenting with personal construct psychology.* London: Routledge (pp. 509-514) (reprinted in this volume, pp. 12-16).
Bannister, D. (1977). The logic of passion. In D. Bannister (Ed.) *New perspectives in personal construct theory.* London: Academic Press (pp. 21- 37)
Bannister, D., & Fransella, F. (1971). *Inquiring man: The theory of personal constructs.* Harmondsworth, Middlesex: Penguin Books.
Boscolo, P., and de Bernardi, B. (1992). Writing as meaningful activity. *International Journal of Personal Construct Psychology,* 5, 341-353.
Britton, J. (1970). *Language and learning.* London: Allen Lane The Penguin Press.
Crane, H. (1966). From Mr. Crane to the editor (Harriet Monroe). In J.Scully (Ed.) *Modern poets on modern poetry.* London: Fontana. (pp. 167-172).
Cummings, E.E. (1968). *Complete poems.* London: MacKibbon & Kee.
Gunn, T. (1985). *The occasions of poetry.* San Francisco: North Point Press.
Hass, C (Ed.) (1994). The essential haiku: versions of Bashō, Buson, and Issa. Hopewell, NJ: Ecco.
Hoffman, Y. (1986). *Japanese death poems.* Tokyo: Charles Tuttle.
Hutchinson, T. (Ed.) (1906). *The poetical works of William Wordsworth. Oxford edition.* London: Henry Frowde.
Keats, J. (1956). *The poetical works of John Keats.* London: Oxford University Press.
Kelly, G. A. (1955). *The Psychology of Personal Constructs* New York: Norton.
Kelly, G. A. (1964). The language of hypothesis: Man's psychological instrument. *Journal of Individual Psychology,* 137-152. Reprinted in B. A. Maher (Ed.) *Clinical psychology and personality: The selected papers of George Kelly.* Huntington, NY: Krieger. (pp. 147-162).
Kelly, G.A. (1977). The psychology of the unknown. In D. Bannister (Ed.). *New perspectives in personal construct theory.* London: Academic Press, (pp. 1-19).
Levin, S. R. (1976). Concerning what kind of speech act a poem is. In T.A. van Dijk (Ed.). *Pragmatics of language and literature.* Amsterdam: North-Holland, pp. 141-160.
Levin, S. R. (1977). *The semantics of metaphor.*
Lowell, R. (1987). *Collected prose.* New York: Farrar Strauss & Giroux.
Lowell, R. (2003). *Collected poems.* New York: Farrar Strauss & Giroux.
Mair, M. (1977). Metaphors for living. *Nebraska symposium on motivation,* 1976, 24, 243-290.

Mair, M. (1989). *Between psychology and psychotherapy: A poetics of experience.* London: Routledge.

Miall, D. S. (1985). The structure of response: A repertory grid study of a poem. *Research in the teaching of English, 19, 254-268.*

Miall, D. S. (1988). A repertory grid study of response to poetry. In F. Fransella and L. Thomas (Eds.) *Experimenting with personal construct psychology.* London: Routledge (pp. 539-547)

Shaw, M., Gaines, B. (1992). Kelly's "geometry of psychological space" and its significance for cognitive modeling. *The New Psychologist,* 23-31.

Ueda, M. (1982) *Matsuo Basho.* Tokyo: Kodansha.

Haiku poetry: Escape from constriction

Sean Brophy

The escape referred to in the title relates to a small book of haiku poetry written in response to particular constricted circumstances in my life[1].

The preface of that book provided the core ideas of the chapter below. These tiny poems or haikus were written twice; the first time in my head while in the throes of a serious illness and the second time on scraps of paper as I punched in time during a long recovery in the autumn of 2003.

I had spent a week unconscious on a ventilator in an acute general hospital in Dublin, Ireland, now and then wandering in my mind in a surreal world of fantasy induced by hallucinogenic drugs. As I emerged into consciousness I experienced a sense of devastation never encountered before. I couldn't eat or drink. I was being ventilated through a tube in my throat, couldn't speak and could barely communicate with a painful, hardly legible, pencil scrawl that literally swam before my eyes. My body was a battleground, like the field at Waterloo, Napoleon's bacteria fighting for supremacy with Wellington's antibiotics.

My construing system was inadequate to the task of making sense of my circumstances. My emotions reflected the changes I was forced to experience. The events I was living through lay outside the range of convenience of my constructs. I could not predict from moment to moment and was gripped by anxiety. I sensed that my death was a near term possibility and I oscillated between the threat that this posed to my construing system and the peace I derived from my faith in an afterlife of my soul. I began to give up the fight, to question the meaning of a life under those conditions and the suffering I was enduring. I tried aggressively to enlarge the frame, to construe my suffering in a broader sense. Something triggered a memory of Viktor Frankl's book, *Man's Search for Meaning*, wherein he challenges thus:

> *Ultimately, man should not ask what the meaning of his life is, but rather he must recognise that it is he who is asked. In a word, each man is questioned by 'Life'; and he can only answer to 'Life' by answering for his own life. He can only respond to 'Life' by being responsible. Responsible-ness is the very essence of human existence.*[2]

---

[1] Sean Brophy. *Girl Through My Window* (Dublin: Rainsford Press, 2004).
[2] Viktor Frankl. *Man's Search for Meaning* (London: Hodder and Stoughton, 1987), p.111.

Frankl had helped me to apply the construct 'to live' versus 'to give up'. I had a choice, to choose life and be responsible for my life or to give up and declare my responsibilities over. The Choice Corollary suggests that we will choose the pole of a dichotomised construct that leads to a definition or extension of our construing system. I became aggressive and tried to elaborate 'to live'. So what was I responsible for that would give meaning to my life and how was I to deal with the suffering? I was responsible to my family, friends, colleagues and clients to contribute to their flourishing as human beings in their interactions with me. I was responsible for poems and stories not yet written, music not yet played, social occasions to celebrate life not yet held. As I faced the question from Life I chose 'to live'. From that point on my recovery commenced.

I reflected on my suffering and remembered Frankl again:

Whenever one is confronted with an inescapable, unavoidable situation, whenever one has to face a fate that cannot be changed e.g. an incurable disease, such as an inoperable cancer; just then one is given a last chance to fulfil the deepest meaning, the meaning of suffering.[3]

I remembered that I had consoled myself after the death of my partner Emily by recalling her anxiety at the thought that I might die first, which she would find unbearable. My suffering therefore had a meaning; I was relieving her of her suffering by surviving her and by her not having to witness my current distress.

The suffering of my illness was given further meaning when I resolved to accept the challenge to live; to live to write books, my spiritual children, to play music, and to be significant in the lives of those I touched. My pain and discomfort were unavoidable. My suffering was optional so I chose not to have it. I kept my mind on the main game, the life of the inner self, the life of my soul. I believed that everything in life was transient, even my body, but my soul was eternal. Months later I was to be reminded of that critical time when reading the following lines by the English poet, Shelley:

The one remains, the many change and pass;
Heaven's light forever shines, Earth's shadows
Fly; Life, like a dome of many-coloured glass,
Stains the white radiance of Eternity.[4]

---

[3] Frankl, op.cit, p.114.
[4] Percy Bysshe Shelley. 'Adonais: An Elegy on the Death of John Keats' (stanza 52), in Donald H. Rieman and Neil Fraishat (eds.). *Shelley's Poetry and Prose* (London: Norton, 2002), p. 426.

From that moment, when I relinquished suffering, the construct 'writing' became more permeable. I began to elaborate the self as a writer and to compose poetry in my head. For three weeks I lay in my bed staring at the ceiling, having all my needs taken care of by nurses barely half my age. I remembered a technique taught to me by Chris Thorman, a gifted psychotherapist, who tutored me while I was studying Personal Construct Psychology in London in 1987. Chris had reminded me of the philosophical notion of the 'I' as observer that did not identify with that which 'It' observed. As I lay in the bed I let my real Self, my 'I', float up to the ceiling and just observe the weakened body below. On one occasion I succumbed to a new infection and I spent a night fighting for each breath, telling myself I was not my body. I lay staring at a spot high on the opposite wall, trying to dispel feelings of anxiety, and intoning 'just this moment now, Lord, just this moment now, Lord', until a brilliant young doctor arrived. He made the right judgement call and alleviated my distress.

As my condition slowly improved, I was able to live in my head in a more detached distress-free way, and the poems began to come. I knew I was getting better when I began to force myself to write my thoughts on paper. After that it was effortless as I loosened my construing and dilated the world of my imagination, leaving the tightening craftwork until later. The days flew and eventually I was well enough to go home. I will forever be in debt to the nursing and medical staff of the Accident and Emergency and Intensive Care Units and St. Laurence's Ward in Beaumont Hospital, Dublin, who loved me enough to give me back my life, and to my family and friends who stood by me for days and nights for nearly three months.

So, the theme of my scattered fragments, that later metamorphosed into a little book of poems, was about love. I had received so much of it, and hopefully given some in return, that I felt competent to write about it. The fragments were in the form of Haikus, observations or recollections of moments in time as my construing system dilated in response to my need to escape constriction and then to return to constriction in the act of crafting these miniature poems.

Haiku is an unrhymed Japanese poem recording the essence of a moment closely observed in which the world of nature is linked to human nature. It usually consists of seventeen *Onji,* or Japanese sound symbols. English syllables are variable in length, and therefore it is possible to write Haiku in English in less than seventeen syllables, and without the restriction of the '5-7-5 line' formula. In addition, major developments in English language Haiku writing have led to adaptation of the common form focussed on nature to include an infinite variety of subjects and images including human relationships, sex and love as subject matter. I have remained with the classic format while experimenting with the subject matter. Technically, most of my poems would be called Renga or linked Haikus. Where the subject matter is concerned with subjects other than nature the genre is known in Japanese as Senryu.

However, as my fragments formed a pattern and my little book emerged I needed to set out my stall, philosophically speaking, before I started so that the reader would know where I was coming from. I have always liked the notion of the modern Christian mystic, Pierre Teilhard de Chardin, of the teleological, goal-directed nature of the universe. The universe is going somewhere; and I as an infinite though minute part of it am going somewhere too. He says: 'The world is still being created, and it is Christ who is reaching his fulfilment in it'.[5] Everything, every being in nature, carries the imprint of the Divine. We are, as it were, atoms in the body of the mystical and cosmic Christ.

I see myself, therefore, 'in the likeness of'[6] this Divine consciousness. My soul is like a mirror reflecting the stamp and impress of God's creating hand on me and in me, which draws me towards His ineffable light. I have been dropped into the world at a point in time, for what purpose God only knows for sure. My guess is that I am here to express who I am and I do this by using my gifts especially the gift of love for my own benefit and that of the world. The world in that sense is the other images of Divine consciousness represented by human beings and, at lesser levels of consciousness, by nature in all her manifestations. Teilhard de Chardin sees love as the working out of the creation:

Moved by the forces of love,
Fragments of the world seek out one another
So that a world may be[7]

This idea of love being 'the natural in between' oneself and others is supported by the Sufi poet, Rumi:

All the particles of the world
Are in love and looking for lovers.
Pieces of straw tremble
In the presence of amber[8]

Rumi uses an analogy similar to Teilhard de Chardin and could be seen to be anticipating modern day particle physics. The impulse towards the Divine is

---

[5] Pierre Teilhard De Chardin. *Writings in Time of War* (London: Collins, 1968), p. 60.
[6] Genesis 1.26-27.
[7] Pierre Teilhard De Chardin. *Le Milieu Divin: An Essay on the Interior Life* (London: Collins, 1960)
[8] Jalal al-Din Rumi. *The Essential Rumi* (trans. Coleman Barks and John Moyne) (San Francisco: Harper, 1995).

cellular, at the tiniest particle level of our being. Following Teilhard de Chardin and Rumi, we can say we are constituted as human beings to love. These particles (ourselves) cannot help loving; it is vital as oxygen to our lives. We are guided in our loving by the interests of the beloved (another particle), another reflection of the Divine. Love is the will to see the beloved flourish. This stands in contrast with love as manifest in attachment or possession.

Viktor Frankl comments on the meaning of love:

> *Love is the only way to grasp another human being in the innermost core of his or her personality. No one can become fully aware of the very essence of a human being unless he loves that person.* [9]

My previous two books of poems were evocations of love for my late partner, Emily. Standing back now, removed from the immediate trauma of her death six years ago, I can see that many of my sentiments and my sense of loss were due to feelings of attachment, not unlike the feelings of sadness expressed by Pablo Neruda in his 'Song of Despair':

> Oh flesh of my own flesh, woman whom I loved and lost
> I summon you in the moist hour, I raise my song to you[10]

My attachment to Emily was a form of pre-emptive construing requiring her presence as an implied subordinate construct. In choosing the pole attachment versus non attachment on this construct I was set up for grief because of her absence. As I gave up those feelings of attachment my grief dissolved and I was left with the pure love underlying them, which is indissoluble.

The essence of pure love was rendered real in my mind some time ago as I reflected on my thirty-five years of friendship with Emily and on various episodes in our discovery of each other. She could oscillate in her approach to life from displaying a childlike innocence at one moment to the wisdom of Socrates at another. On one occasion, I remember asking her what she saw in me. Perhaps I was fishing for compliments, or attempting to bolster a flagging self-image at the time. Her answer astounded me then and reverberates in my memory to this day. She gave an intake of breath and said: 'Oh! Your face, I see the Divine in your lovely face'. This was the most complete validation I could receive. In that moment I knew she loved me at the deepest most authentic level I could ever experience. It was not a love I could have or

---

[9] Viktor Frankl, op.cit., p. 113.
[10] Pablo Neruda. *Twenty Love Poems and a Song of Despair* (trans. W.S. Merwin) (San Francisco: Chronicle Books, 1993), p. 72.

possess, just an experience that was shot into my conscious awareness then and has not left me since.

As I organised the Haikus they patterned into three sections, **Love, Landscape** and **Life**. The first series of poems, **Love**, were expressions of love as celebrations of the beloved drawn from a range of different relationships including Emily and my parents Michael Joseph and Mary Frances. The opening poem, set out below, recaptured the philosophy of love outlined above. It was formed from recollections of moments in time during my relationship with Emily.

Love is...

Being present, in
That moment, you are the most
Important person.

Seeing the Divine
In your lovely face__
Your uniqueness.

Accepting your right
To be, my will for you is
Your will for yourself.

Without judgement, you
Are always doing your best,
With your reality.

Compassion, aware of
Frailty, being there for you,
Total commitment.

Encouraging you,
Showing you the sun, so you
Can attain the stars.

Overcoming your fears...
Enabling independence
And freedom to love.

Sharing together,
Celebrating each other__

Seeing us anew.

Listening to the
Stirring of your heart, quiet
Yearnings of your soul.

Filling each other
So much, there is nothing left
But our two names.

Beings in motion,
Creating our life, love lies in
Stillness between us.

Like two trees growing,
Roots slowly binding, serene
In each other's shade.

This poem elaborates what love is and it shows that love is not about attachment. Therefore, it is not about having in any real sense, whether having persons or things. We do not ever possess a thing, though we may be in possession of it at a given point in time. All we can do is experience the presence of others or things in our lives. Only through the giving of something, e.g. love, can we experience the having of it. Master Eckhart taught that to have nothing and make oneself open and 'empty', not to let one's ego stand in one's way, is the condition for spiritual wealth and strength:

People should not consider what they are to do as what they are[11].

In his classic book, *To Have or to Be*, the philosopher Erich Fromm juxtaposes the ideas of illusory *having* with authentic *being* as two different modes of existence[12]. By way of illustration, Fromm contrasts the experiences of the 19th century English writer, Tennyson, with those of the 17th century Japanese poet, Basho, when contemplating a flower they see while each of them was taking a walk. In his poem 'Flower in a Crannied Wall', Tennyson wants to have, needs to possess, the flower. He "plucks it roots and all". Basho, does not touch the flower. In his Haiku he just wants to 'see' it, to be at one in the moment with it, and through it to see the mind of God. The German poet, Goethe is seen by Fromm to stand between Tennyson and Basho. In his beau-

---

[11] Meister Eckhart. *Meister Eckhart: A modern translation* (trans. Raymond B. Blakney) (New York: Harper and Row Torchbooks, 1941).

[12] Erich Fromm. *To have or to be* (New York: Bantam Books, 1981), pp.4-6

tiful poem 'Gefunden' (Found), Goethe is attracted by a brilliant little flower and is tempted to pluck it but unlike Tennyson he is aware that this means killing the flower. He solves the problem when he lifts the flower with all its roots and surrounding soil and replants it in his own garden. Giving transforms having into being. By giving the flower its life Goethe manages to continue to have, that is to say, to experience it. And so it is with love, creativity, wealth and all the other features of our lives. To give is to be. If Erich Fromm had read the Irish poet, Patrick Kavanagh, he would have found a perfect example of Basho's and Goethe's thinking in Kavanagh's poem 'Primrose':

The primrose that lighted me to Heaven.[13]

Another example is the evocation of the metaphysical quality of flowers in Kavanagh's poem 'The One':

That beautiful, beautiful, beautiful God,
Was breathing His love by a cutaway bog.[14]

Goethe's concept of investigating nature is to see that the force of life is greater than the force of intellectual curiosity. As I dilated through my memory while still confined to bed I organised a second series of fragments into haiku poems later in a theme called **Landscape**. I tried to just observe and recapture moments when I was at one with elements of nature, and to experience the joy of that oneness. My intention was to remain true to the philosophy of not having any person or thing but to experience them as the unfolding of creation, rather than just 'clunking along' with poetic diction as the poet Mary Oliver[15] puts it. There is only One of us, and I am a particle of that One. I turned for my inspiration to books I had read, to Basho, and other Japanese Haiku poets[16], and to Patrick Kavanagh's poems 'March', 'April', 'After May' and 'October'. I had been inspired also by the poems of the Irish poet, Francis Ledwidge, my favourite, the English poet John Clare, and the Scottish poet, Norman MacCaig.

Ledwidge's 'June' is particularly lovely:

---

[13] Tom Stack. *No Earthly Estate-God and Patrick Kavanagh: An Anthology* (Dublin: The Columba Press, 2002), p.66.
[14] Tom Stack, op. cit., p.106.
[15] Mary Oliver. *A poetry handbook* (Orlando, Fla.: Harcourt Inc. 1994), pp. 87-88.
[16] Lucien Stryk and Takashi Ikemoto (eds.). *The Penguin Book of Zen Poetry* (London: Penguin, 1981)

> *Broom out the floor now, lay the fender by,*
> *And plant that bee-sucked bough of woodbine there.*[17]

I first encountered John Clare's poetry when listening to Nobel Laureate Seamus Heaney acknowledging that poet's gifts in a lecture some years ago. Clare was the poet of pastoral England before the industrial revolution led to the enclosure of commonages. Like Francis Ledwidge, John Clare engages the muse of the fields in his poetic endeavour in his poem 'To a Rural Muse':

> *Muse of the fields oft have I said farewell*
> *To thee my boon companion loved so long*
> *And hung thy sweet harp in the bushy dell*
> *For abler hands to make an abler song*[18]

I love reading Norman McCaig's poetry and listening to the poet reading his own work in his pronounced Scottish accent. He displays complete enjoyment in observing animals and landscape, for example, in his poem 'Praise of a Collie':

> *She (Lassie) flowed through fences like a sheet of black wind.*[19]

As I dilated away from the constriction of my physical circumstances, I harvested ideas from these and other poets, from the memories of years of travelling on five continents, from radio plays, films, photographs and paintings of nature. The brilliant landscape descriptions of authors like Ivan Doig's *'This House of Sky'*[20] and David Guterson's *East of the Mountain*[21] fuelled my imagination. Inspired by all these sources and memories I turned the moments in time of my life experiences into Haikus on nature. One example of a series of linked haikus is the poem Glenstal Abbey, that recaptures moments during a visit as guest of the Benedictine monks at their monastery in Co. Limerick in the mid-west of Ireland. This group of poems is set out below:

---

[17] Liam O'Meara (ed.). *Francis Ledwidge: The Complete Poems* (Newbridge, Ireland: Goldsmith Press, 1997), p. 108.
[18] Kelsey Thomas and Anne Tibbley (eds). John Clare: The Midsummer Cushion or Cottage Poems (Manchester: Carcanet, 1990), p. 3.
[19] Norman MacCaig. *Collected Poems* (London: Chatto and Windus, 1990), p. 318
[20] Ivan Doig. *'This House of Sky': Landscapes of a Western Mind* (Orlando, Florida: Harcourt Brace, 1978).
[21] David Guterson. *East of the Mountain* (London: Bloomsbury, 1914)

Glenstal Abbey

Glenstal Abbey rain
Rushes down drain pipe dancing
Into dropping well.

Blades of green grass
Scythe upwards towards the sky,
Shimmer in the breeze.

Apples ripening,
Dropping heavy from young trees__
September harvest.

Crystal raindrops rest
On mist powdered leaves__
Sedum flowers fall.

Bees drone, busy
Sucking nectar from a rose__
Honeyed lovemaking.

Monks chanting Compline…
Evening prayer signals rest
After joy of work.

This theme of oneness with all of creation was continued in the final pattern of fragments called **Life**. Here I returned to expressions of love and admiration for the actors who had played major parts in the drama of my life. Some of these people had passed on, but most of them were happily still with me on life's journey. Conversations in my head with my ghosts led to a happy phase of dilation. I roamed the corridors of my life and had encounters that brought me to a stunning awareness of the constancy of love. My late parents featured a lot as epiphanies re-entered my consciousness and resulted in several haikus. One of these groups of haikus is set out below:

Parents

My life line is a
Rolling river; my parents
Were its closest quays.

The silent shadows,
On the streets of old Dublin,
Point out their presence.

I miss my impish
Father, every corner
Of each days turning.

Mother crocheting...
Snow-flaking her cottage floor
With white lace flowers.

Old vellum letters,
Fast fading after these years__
Brittle as old leaves.

Reading and writing are acts of philosophy. If philosophy, the love of wisdom, is the art of being human, then Haiku, in a unique, albeit small way, shows what it is to be human. The Japanese poet Basho says we should:

Learn about a pine tree from a pine tree, and about a bamboo plant from a bamboo plant.[22]

With this injunction, Basho captures the notion of the oneness of existence, *le Milieu Divin* (the Divine Milieu) of Teilhard de Chardin[23], or what the physicist David Bohm calls the *'implicate order'* [24]. It is not enough to describe the person, object or scene but to connect with it, perceive its unique life and feel its feelings. In this way a poem forms itself.

In his book, *Haiku*, the poet R. H. Blyth has written:

A Haiku is the expression of a temporary enlightenment, in which we see into the life of things.[25]

---

[22] Cor Van den Heuvel (ed). *The Haiku Anthology* (New York: Norton, 1999), preface p.liv.
[23] Pierre Teilhard De Chardin, op. cit.
[24] David Bohm. *Wholeness and the Implicate Order* (London: Routledge, 1980).
[25] R.H. Blyth. *Haiku* (Tokyo: Hokuseido Press, 1949-1952), Vol.1, p. 270.

In this way the smile on a lover's face, the frost on a window, the gurgling of rain in a gutter, the patterns on a sycamore leaf, the ghost of a deceased parent come truly alive, become part of our lived experience, speak their own silent language.

In conclusion then, reading Haiku is to be acutely aware of what is happening right now in the writer's life. The dynamism and permeability of the writer's construing system is almost palpable. The range of ideas and experiences reveal a process of dilation limited only by the poets urge to capture images on the blank page. The sparseness of the chosen haiku form then reveals a capacity for constriction where a moment in time is tightly construed. Haiku crystallises the present moment for all time in a fragment on a page or in the leaves of a book, to explode later in the consciousness of the readers and, hopefully, to swell their hearts.

References

al-Din Rumi, J. (1995). *The Essential Rumi* (trans. Coleman Barks and John Moyne). San Francisco: Harper
Blyth, R. H. (1949-1952). *Haiku*. Tokyo: Hokuseido Press
Bohm, D. (1980). *Wholeness and the Implicate Order*. London: Routledge
Brophy, S. (2004). *Girl Through My Window*. Dublin: Rainsford Press.
Doig, I. (1978). *'This House of Sky': Landscapes of a Western Mind*. Orlando, Florida: Harcourt Brace
Frankl, V. (1987). *Man's Search for Meaning*. London: Hodder and Stoughton.
Fromm, E. (1981). *To Have or to Be*. New York: Bantam Books
Guterson, D. (1999). *East of the Mountain*. London: Bloomsbury
MacCaig, N. (1990). *Collected Poems*. London: Chatto and Windus
Meister Eckhart (1941). *Meister Eckhart: A Modern Translation* (trans. Raymond B. Blakney). New York: Harper and Row Torchbooks
Neruda, P. (1993). *Twenty Love Poems and a Song of Despair* (trans. W.S Merwin). San Francisco: Chronicle Books
O'Meara, L. (ed.) (1997). *Francis Ledwidge: The Complete Poems*. Newbridge, Ireland: Goldsmith Press, 1997
Oliver, M. (1994). *A Poetry Handbook*. Orlando, Fla.: Harcourt
Shelley, P. B. (2002). 'Adonais: An Elegy on the Death of John Keats' (stanza 52), in Donald H. Rieman & Neil Fraishat (eds.). *Shelley's Poetry and Prose*. London.
Stack, T. (2002). *No Earthly Estate-God and Patrick Kavanagh: An Anthology*. Dublin: The Columba Press
Stryk, L. & Ikemoto, T. (eds.) (1981). *The Penguin Book of Zen Poetry*. London: Penguin
Teilhard de Chardin, P. (1960). *Le Milieu Divin: An Essay on the Interior Life*. London: Collins
Teilhard de Chardin, P. (1968). *Writings in Time of War*. London: Collins
Thomas, K. & Tibbley, A. (eds). (1990). *John Clare: The Midsummer Cushion or Cottage Poems*. Manchester: Carcanet
Van den Heuvel, C. (ed) (1999). *The Haiku Anthology*. New York: Norton

EXPERIENCING MUSIC

Music and the person

Eric Button

Introduction

Music has been a big part of my life since I was about six years of age. Apparently I had shown an interest in the piano from early childhood and one day my parents took me into our local piano store and out of the blue bought me a piano – just like that! This was a very substantial financial commitment for my parents at the time and I shall forever be indebted to them for their generosity and foresight in making this sacrifice. Some fifty years on I still have a piano, as well as an electronic keyboard and derive much pleasure from playing. There's no chance of me making a living out of it, but it provides a welcome contrast from my work as a clinical psychologist and provides one of my main outlets for self-expression.

Around twenty years ago, I entered a phase where music began to take on a more central role in my life. For some years I had had regrets over not choosing to pursue music as a career. I would often say to others, and myself 'I wish I had carried on with music'. Eventually, I came to recognise that I didn't need to go on *wishing* and that I wasn't too old to start *doing* something. I thus began to 'elaborate' on the musical pole of my *psychologist-musician* construct, which led me into returning to piano lessons as well as starting tuition in musical composition. I also began exploring ways of combining psychology and music and the arts in general. One manifestation of that period of intensive musical elaboration was a paper and workshop I ran at the 6th International Congress on Personal Construct Psychology at Churchill College, Cambridge in 1985. For my workshop, I was very fortunate in being allocated the college music room, which housed a splendid grand piano and plenty of space for musical activity. Armed with the piano, various other instruments and the human voice, a group of us tried out a range of musical exercises as a way of exploring the role of music in personal construction. For me, this was a highly exciting and enjoyable experience, which I look back on with some nostalgia and I still have a cassette tape of the event for anyone who is interested in having a copy. The other record of this event is the paper (Button, 1988) subsequently published in the congress book (Fransella & Thomas, 1988), along with Ben-Peretz & Kalekin-Fishman's (1988) paper on applying personal construct theory to the interpretations of music shared by groups.

When Jörn Scheer approached me late in 2004 to tell me about his plans for this book and inviting me to contribute, my initial reaction was one of doubting whether I had anything new to say on the matter, having not published anything on music since the above article. He reassured me, however, that this did not matter and that a 'slight updating' of this earlier work would be possible. Having shared the musical stage with Jörn at the social event of another personal construct conference, it seemed like an offer I could not refuse.

I would like to begin by returning to my above paper, the ideas of which still seem pertinent today. Later in the chapter, I will introduce some reflections and further thoughts on the topic, with the benefit of twenty more years of experience and put in the context of music in the 21st century.

The Cambridge paper

To my knowledge there is no existing construct theory literature on music. Nor have I yet found any references to personal construct theory in the literature on music, but on delving in the latter one finds many echoes of a constructivist position. A major theme which runs through such writings is the importance of *form* in our appreciation of music. For example, Joseph Machlis (1979) states:

> *A basic principle of musical form is repetition and contrast, which achieves both unity and variety. The one ministers to man's joy in the familiar and to his need "for reassurance. The other satisfies his equally strong craving for the challenge of the unfamiliar.* (p. 47)

The business of construing is thus clearly at work in the musical context and presumably playing its customary role in our anticipatory processes. When a person listens to music he or she will thus be looking for similarity and contrast. One common way in which composers achieve this melodically is by the use of 'ternary form', which embraces Kelly's affinity for triads. Typically, there is an A-B-A or A- A-B-A structure in which a fairly short phrase (A) is heard with a pause, typically followed by its repetition (more or less identical). Next, a contrasting phrase (B) is heard, and finally there is a return to the original. Such forms are so familiar to most of us that we easily recognise the musical 'constructs', although, of course, we don't necessarily share the same meanings. In contemporary 'serious' music, however, perhaps because of it's very newness, the form is not thrust at the listener and the music requires more active construction on the part of the listener. Repetition-contrast remains as a basic principle, but it is less obvious and predictable, with irregularity of the essence, so much so that many people find it unpalatable. But art moves on with time and it would not truly reflect life if it only presented us with forms (or constructs) which we already know.

Musical experience, like all experience, can lead to what Kelly called 'elaboration', either through increasing *definition* or *extension*. From a musical point of view we may see choice exercised in a definitive way by the repetition of themes, rhythms, harmonies, and so on. Some repetition is indeed necessary for us to identify the theme, but typically in music, repetition is not identical. The basic musical idea is presented in a number of guises. In the development section in sonata form, for example, the principle themes are presented in a number of different keys, but there are a variety of other techniques of varied repetition, like differing pitch, rhythm, instrument, and so on. In all these cases, however, underlying features recur. Furthermore, in the case of sonata form this development is followed by the 'recapitulation' in which the basic theme is returned to in more or less its original form. This repetition with a difference can be seen to be analogous to non-musical action. For example, someone seeking to present a sporting image may engage in a variety of energetic or competitive pursuits, but which all seek to confirm the common theme of 'sporting'. I am suggesting, therefore, that a major role for much musical activity is in the *confirmation,* mainly of identity, but also of beliefs, values, moods, achievements, and so on; for example, 'l appreciate Bach', 'This is a sad day', 'I'm a jazz person'. Such confirmation is not just individualism but also has a social role in establishing or confirming what a group of people have in common. This is vividly demonstrated by national anthems, which remind us that our country still exists, what it stand for and that we are part of it.

But we would soon get bored with music that was entirely predictable. John Booth-Davies (1978), although making no explicit reference to personal construct theory, makes the point that 'It is this process of confirmation or disconfirmation of expectancies which is at the centre of musical experience' (p. 68). He goes on to assert, 'Listening to a tune is therefore not a passive process of mere reception, but one of active construction' (p. 82). Booth-Davies suggests that our musical preferences tend towards intermediate degrees of predictability or what he refers to in information theory terms as 'complexity'. In other words, music which is either too familiar or too unfamiliar will not be appealing - with the emphasis on personal interpretation as determining what is meant by familiar. This accords with our experience of even our favourite piece of music becoming less appealing if repeated too much. If we are not just trying to stand still in life, we will need some contrast: fast music may lead to the slower; sad songs at concerts are often followed by something cheerful; highly rhythmic music may be followed by more freely flowing music.

It seems to me, therefore, that there may be two broad kinds of way in which people use music. One is as a kind of confirmation: here we know what to expect, in fact we deliberately look for it - we dig out the record, we sing the song, we whistle the tune. In a sense there is a kind of reaching *back* - validating something we've been through before. In contrast, we may also wish to *reach forward* with the exciting prospect of 'extension' or broadening of our horizons. The pleasure perhaps comes from the anticipation of going somewhere new, something just beyond. So, are these two aspects as different as they seem? Perhaps not, since it is feasible that both alternatives are dependent on our degree of certainty/uncertainty: when faced with too much certainty we may look for something new from music, but following much uncertainty we may go back or stay with familiar music.

I suggest that such musical choices don't just stand in isolation and may reflect our efforts to make sense of things at a more general level. A healthy balance may be reflected by the ability to go back *and* forward with music at different times. In addition, he or she may be able to tolerate a range of different types of music. A person who has severely constricted his or her world, however, may opt for only one kind of music, perhaps reflecting a particular mood. One of my patients seemed to have chosen this kind of course: for her it was important to be *serious* and she steadfastly rejected any music which could be regarded as *frivolous*. I don't imply here that there is anything unhealthy about having musical preferences. To the contrary. At any point in time a person will be seeking to 'elaborate' or express some particular theme. Musically, this will mean that right now we may have a favourite song, composer, mood or style of music. At the same time, however, what we are receptive to musically now may not be the same tonight, tomorrow morning or next year.

This leads me on to the point that an essential ingredient of music is movement. Music is always going somewhere. This is most powerfully revealed in relation to the movement towards a climax. We often know what's coming but, much as in sex, it's the build-up that makes it all worthwhile. The musical content at the peak would have little effect without that which precedes it. Similarly, the musical climax needs to be followed by a coming down, and this may be in pitch, loudness or speed. Just as in life in general, of course, the climax forms just one small part of a piece of music, and we see continuous movement in a much more general and variable way. It is in melody that movement is most obvious with its succession of rises and falls, usually with some degree of pattern, so that one is often able to roughly anticipate where the music is going, although we are sometimes surprised, if not teased, by delays and diversions, all of which add to the experience of the music.

In emphasising movement we are inevitably drawn towards Kelly's 'Dimensions of Transition' and the question of emotion. Emotion is a controversial issue in music. Although there has never been a question about the emotional potential of music, there have been changing fashions in the extent to which composers seek to elicit it, as opposed to a more intellectual approach. Most current authorities on music, however, are at pains to emphasise that good music is not just about the evocation of 'the passions'. Not that emotion is unimportant in music but that it is a by-product of *form:*

> *Great music is great because of its beauty of form and because of the emotions experienced by listening to it, which are largely a function of its beauty of form. A piece of music by Mozart may pass through a variety of moods which will be reflected in the listener but his delight and excitement will be mainly derived from Mozart's masterly handling of the form. This is what makes Mozart a greater composer than Tchaikowsky.* (Bacharach and Pearce, 1977, p.21)

This rapprochement of the cognitive and emotional aspects of music is, of course, consistent with a construct theory approach. Furthermore, it is also known that although there is a certain amount of agreement about broad musical parameters influencing emotion (especially speed and pitch), wide individual differences in emotional response have been reported to the same music. Thus it is reasonable to suppose that the emotional impact of a piece of music is a reflection of how the listener construes it. The Kellian position, elaborated by Mancuso and Hunter (1983), is that emotion occurs when we fail to anticipate. I must confess to not being entirely happy with this position, since it seems to me that we often feel things when we anticipate having an expectation fulfilled. McCoy (1981) touches on this when she states "positive emotions are those which follow validation of construing. Negative emotions follow unsuccessful construing" (p. 97). To my mind, however, each of these authors overemphasise the role of validation *after* an event is construed. What *seems* to me to be the crucial aspect is a degree of *uncertainty* as we *anticipate* some change in what we can expect. Take, for example, the lover (or potential lover) who carefully selects a record to set the scene for what he or she hopes to follow. I argue that it is because there is an element of doubt surrounding this situation that these preliminaries are gone through: I wonder if we all take this amount of trouble once the relationship appears to be confirmed.

A comment that has been made repeatedly about the emotional aspect of music is its link with associations from the past. When music from the past evokes some sort of emotion in us, I suggest this is because the events which surrounded this music were associated with a degree of uncertainty. It is also possible that musical past can create an emotional response in the present because of the doubts it casts on our present construing. Like me, I'm sure you've sometimes had an uneasy feeling when listening to music of the past which perhaps creates 'threat' by reminding us of constructs we thought we'd outgrown.

Another way of looking at such uncertainty is in terms of *transition*, a concept central to Kelly's view of emotion. Within a piece of music there will be a number of points of change, where the music moves from one set of expectations to another. At these points, such as the junction between movements of a symphony, the listener is in a state of transition requiring a change of expectations. Sometimes the change is extremely abrupt and startling if not disturbing, but more commonly the composer eases the listener into the new mood or theme. It could be argued that it is at times of transition that the vulnerabilities of a person's construct system are most exposed, and there may be therapeutic potential in using music as an indirect way of tackling such difficulties. By experimenting with the experience of changes in musical key, speed, loudness, and so on, a person may become more prepared for transitions in his or her life in general.

Much of what has been discussed so far has revolved around the personal, individual act of listening, performing or composing music. At the social level, I have already referred to the way in which anthems have a role to play in validating a national identity, values, and so on. But music does not just symbolise a nation: take, for example the protest songs of Joan Baez, rugby songs, *Auld Lang Syne*. There are numerous instances of this kind, all of which perhaps illustrate Kelly's Commonality Corollary. Like individual behaviour, we can regard group music as forming an elaborative choice - to extend or to define. A group may be emerging or expanding, and in such circumstances music seems to suggest where the group is going or it may be that the group is wishing to remind itself and others what it is. This was dramatically expressed in the recent British miners strike[16] by the theme tune *Here We Go*. It is my contention that there is an audience for much of our behaviour and the group which sings together seems to be both defining the group but also stating who is not part of the group, so that music can be at the forefront of conflict between groups, as vividly evidenced in war.

It can be argued, however, that the most fundamental feature of being social is the ability to enter other people's worlds - to construe their construction processes in Kellian terms. Therapeutic interventions such as Landfield and Rivers' (1975) Interpersonal Transaction Group, explicitly attempt to improve this aspect of a person's construing in their use of techniques like 'rotating dyads'. Music could easily be utilised in this kind of context by inviting the participants to find out about each others' musical experience. For example, the persons in a dyad could be asked to share with the other their favourite song or some other piece of music. Later, they could move on to more differentiated features like each being asked to give an example of a sad, frightening or exciting piece of music. This could be extended to 'music

---

[16] The miners' strike referred to was a major piece of industrial action and confrontation with the government headed by Margaret Thatcher. It ran for around a year between 1984 and 1985 and at times there were violent confrontations between the police and the striking miners. The song *Here we go* was a frequently heard rallying cry sung by the miners and in my recollection came to symbolise their cause.

that most represents the way you feel right now' or 'the way you hope to feel by the end of the session'. Both the experience of similarity and difference of musical construction could contribute to an improved ability to understand other people. In the experimental workshop I ran with about twenty people at Cambridge, we began with dyadic experience and later moved on to group exercises, and I shall never forget our ending with a group Amen, which I think demonstrated that we had been able to come together as a group through music.

Having reached Amen I should probably stop, but I would like to add a final comment. I have tried to demonstrate ways in which our musical experience reflects our construing processes in general. It seems to me that we may learn a lot about psychological processes by exploring how people relate to music. I would also like to encourage those involved in helping relationships to experiment with music. It could help ... it could also be fun!

Music and personal constructs re-visited

So, twenty years on, what more can be said? Well, from a personal point of view, my mid-life aspirations to combine an interest in music with my professional role as a clinical psychologist have not exactly blossomed and I can't claim to have made any further inroads into the literature in this area. Nevertheless, I continue to dabble in music and often make use of it as a medium for encouraging clients to elaborate their construing. At a societal level, music seems to be as important as ever, as evidenced by the huge global success of the *Live Aid* and *Live Eight* concerts. With the rapid advances in technology that have occurred, we now have potentially instant and constant access to an immense range of music, with an explosion of genres, much of which seems directed towards young people, for whom music seems to almost universally play a key role in defining who they are and what they stand for. Indeed, Leming (1987) found that 81% of young people say that music is an important part of their life and has influenced how they think about important issues. Green (1999) argues that music offers a powerful cultural symbol, which aids in adolescents' construction and presentation of self. At the other end of the lifespan, Odell-Miller (1995) describes how music can be used as a kind of reminiscence therapy with elderly patients. Music also has immense significance in death and in recent years I have been to more funerals than I would have wished and have found nothing in life more poignant than the hymn singing which is an essential part of our farewells to our loved ones.

Personal construct literature 1985-2005

I recently carried out a literature review to see if there had been any further applications of personal construct theory/methods to music during the past twenty years. A handful of studies were identified, all of which had explored personal constructs in relation to some aspect of music. Three studies concerned music therapy: Hoskyns (1988) used a music therapy grid to investigate how adult recidivist offenders perceived music therapy; Aldridge and Aldridge (1996) and Meadows (2002) both used personal construct methods as a tool for exploring therapists' construing. A further two studies were related to musical performance (Thompson et al ,1998; Tobacyk & Downs, 1986), the latter study demonstrating that a measure of Kellyian threat predicted increased scores on a measure of musical performance anxiety. For me, the most intriguing study was carried out by Frey and Adams-Webber (1992) who used music as a means of mood induction in a study of self-other construing. By comparing grid indices in a 'neutral' condition and when listening to music that made them feel good, subjects showed more positive judgements of self and others in the latter condition. Fay Fransella (2003) also reviewed applications of personal construct psychology in the world of music. In addition to the above papers from the Cambridge congress, she refers to Butler's (1995) work on stress and the performance of music students, as well as Blowers & Bacon-Shone (1994), who looked at methods for detecting perceptual differences in jazz. Such studies provide some modest evidence for the potential of personal construct theory for aiding our understanding of the role of music in our lives, but it is perhaps disappointing that such applications remain on a very small scale. Within the academic field of the psychology of music, personal construct psychology hardly ever receives a mention, whereas in the above literature search I found almost two thousand references linking cognition to music.

Music and the person

The title of this chapter reflects my perspective as a clinical psychologist, working with the very personal worlds of clients in distress. Through many years of research and clinical practice mainly in the field of eating disorders (see e.g. Button, 1993), I have little doubt that how people view themselves (their *self-image*) plays a very important part in determining their well-being. I have found personal construct theory to be a useful way of making sense of the processes which contribute to our self-image and the problems which arise when things go wrong. There are many complex concepts contained within the theory, but it is the emphasis on the unique way in which each individual interprets their experience which strikes a chord with me. It is a simple truism, however, that no man is an island and this act of constructing and reconstructing our self-image occurs *to varying degrees* in a social context amongst other people also busily construing themselves and each other. It is hard to get by in life without other people and at their best others can nurture, complement and enhance our view of ourselves. On the other hand, in our efforts to validate our own view of the world, we have the potential to be highly controlling and lethally destructive to each other. As a clinician, my task is to help clients negotiate this minefield by developing a wider range of avenues for constructing their own self-image and at the same time getting better at dealing with the multitude of other people's constructions they may encounter.

So what does all this have to do with music? Well, quite simply music can be an important modality in which a person may have come to define themselves as a person. This point is expressed aptly by the sociologist DeNora (199, p. 50), who argues that "musical materials provide terms and templates for elaborating self-identity", citing a respondent in her study who preferred "juicy chords" as like "me in life". Access to a person's musical constructs may thus help us to understand them as a person. This can be particularly true in a clinical context, where the individual has verbal communication difficulties or may be reluctant to talk about themselves in a more direct manner. Button (1993) exemplifies this:

> *Catherine was extremely wary when it came to self-disclosure. But she had indicated that listening to music was one of her main sources of pleasure. It seemed to her therapist that exploring her musical construing might offer a relatively safe way of relating more comfortably. But when she was asked what kinds of music she had, she would only say that it was "broad-ranging". Giving specific examples was far too risky for her and even with friends she would be reluctant to share her musical tastes. She was therefore unwilling to talk about particular pieces of music with her therapist. Some months later, however, she had loosened up somewhat and told her therapist of a friend visiting and of letting her see her record collection. Although very apprehensive about this, she had felt sufficiently reassured by this experiment in sharing to go so far as to extend the sharing with her therapist. Other sharing seems to have followed in its wake.* (pp. 67-68)

In adopting a personal construct approach to such exploration with people, one could apply repertory grid technique (e.g. Fransella & Bannister, 1977), in which the 'elements' for construct elicitation could be anything from pieces of music, composers/performers, to occasions in one's life where music has been important. It is not necessary, however, to be constrained by using grids and one technique for exploring a person's musical constructs, with which I have sometimes played, is based on a very well-known British (BBC) radio programme called *Desert Island Discs*, which was devised by Roy Plomley in 1942. For the benefit of non-British readers, the basic format of this programme is that a well-known person is invited to share with the programme's presenter eight pieces of music (more precisely records), which he or she would choose to take with them if stranded alone on a desert island. Excerpts from these pieces of music are played on air, interspersed with a conversation reviewing the person's life and the significance of the pieces chosen. At the very end, they are asked if they could just take one, which it would be. This is a very simple, fun exercise anyone could try, but it can also be particularly useful as a more formal way of eliciting a person's constructs both about music and more indirectly about themselves in general. There could be many variants on this theme, but the key thing is that the person chooses the music themselves, which should help ensure that the music is meaningful to them as a person.

Caveat

Writing about music seems to me to be a very dry business and a whole library of books on Mozart would be about as useful as reading a manual on sex. You have to experience it.

References

Aldridge, D. & Aldridge, G. (1996). A personal construct methodology for validating subjectivity in qualitative research. *Arts in Psychotherapy,* 23, 225-236.
Bacharach, A. L. & Pearce, J. R. (eds.) (1977). *The Musical Companion.* Revised ed. London: Gollancz.
Ben-Peretz, M. & Kalekin-Fishman, D. (1988). Applying PCP to constructs related to music. In Fransella, F. & Thomas, L. (Eds.) *Experimenting with personal construct psychology.* London: Routledge & Kegan Paul.
Blowers, G. H. & Bacon-Shone, J. (1994). On detecting the differences in jazz: a reassessment of comparative methods of measuring perceptual veridicality. *Empirical Studies of the Arts,* 12, 41-58.
Booth-Davies, J. (1978). *The psychology of music.* London: Hutchinson.
Button, E. J. (1988). Music and personal constructs. In Fransella, F. & Thomas, L. (Eds.) *Experimenting with personal construct psychology.* London: Routledge & Kegan Paul.
Button, E. J. (1993). *Eating disorders: Personal construct therapy and change.* Chichester: Wiley.
Butler, C. (1995). Investigating the effects of stress on the success and failure of music conservatory students. In *Medical problems of performing artists.* Philadelphia, PA: Hanley & Belfus.
DeNora, T. (1999). Music as a technology of the self. *Poetics,* 27, 31-56.
Fransella, F. (2003). New avenues to explore and questions to ask. In Fransella, F. (Ed.) *International handbook of personal construct psychology (pp. 447-454).* Chichester: Wiley.
Fransella, F. & Bannister, D. (1977). *A manual for repertory grid technique.* London: Academic Press.
Fransella, F. & Thomas, L. (Eds.) (1988). *Experimenting with personal construct psychology.* London: Routledge & Kegan Paul.

Frey, R. & Adams-Webber, J. (1992). Mood-related changes in construing self and others. *International Journal of Personal Construct Psychology*, 5, 367-376.

Green, L. (1999). Research in the sociology of music education: some introductory concepts. *Music Education Research*, 1, 159-169.

Hoskyns, S. (1988). Studying group music therapy with adult offenders: research in progress. *Psychology of Music, Special Issue*, 16, 25-41.

Landfield, A. W. & Rivers, P. C. (1975). An introduction to interpersonal transaction and rotating dyads. *Psychotherapy: Theory, Research and Practice* 12, 366-74.

Leming, J. (1987). Rock music and the socialisation of moral values in early adolescence. *Youth and Society*, 18, 363-383.

McCoy, M. (1981). Positive and negative emotion: a personal construct theory interpretation. In H. Bonarius, R. Holland & S. Rosenberg (eds., *Personal construct psychology: recent advances in theory and research. Macmillan:*London.

Machlis, J. (1979). *Introduction to contemporary music.* 2nd ed. London: Dent.

Mancuso, J. & Hunter, K. (1983). Anticipation, motivation, or emotion: the Fundamental Postulate after twenty-five years. In J. Adams-Webber and J.C. Mancuso (eds.), Applications of personal construct theory. Toronto : Academic Press.

Meadows, A. (2002). Gender implications in therapists, constructs of their clients. *Nordic Journal of Music Therapy*, 11, 127-141.

Odell-Miller, H. (1995). Approaches to music therapy in psychiatry with specific emphasis upon a research project with the elderly mentally ill. In Wilgram, T., Saperston, B. & West, R. (Eds.) *The art and science of music therapy: A handbook.* (pp. 83-111). Langhorne: Harwood Academic Press.

Thompson, W. F., Diamond, C. T. P & Balkwill, L. L. (1998). The adjudication of six performances of a Chopin etude: A study of expert knowledge. *Psychology of Music*, 26, 154-174.

Tobacyk, J. J. & Downs, A. (1986). Personal construct threat and irrational beliefs as cognitive predictors of increases in musical performance anxiety. *J. Personality & Social Psychology*, 51, 779-782.

Construing sounds, constructing music and non-music

Devorah Kalekin-Fishman

In talking about music as an event, I assume that it is useful to look at music as a collaborative consensual phenomenon. With this in mind, it is possible to eschew analyses of possible and probable affect that attends listening to, or making music, in favor of examining music as it is contextualized. Acquiring the notion that certain families of sound configurations should be construed as music is possible because there is a deliberate investment in constructing a consensus through replication and validation. This is supported by Mead's theory of symbolic interaction (a theory that accounts for how individual selves are shaped by the development of shared meanings through interaction). The theme of this paper is, then, that the construal of sounds as music (a) is a consequence of exposure to replicable events that are deliberately constructed; and (b) in those events, the meanings constructed include construals of both music and non-music.

I will first reflect on work I was partner to twenty years ago, pointing out weaknesses I subsequently realized. Then I will describe a context where music is constructed – Israeli kindergartens; finally, I will discuss the basis for the shared construal of music in PCP terms.

From retrospect to prospect

A concern with music as a contextualized event is not self-evident. People who write about music usually take it for granted that, like their readers, they know what music is and what kinds of effects it is likely to have. Given such certainty, it is possible to 'use' music to work on group process (Button, 1988), to uncover the social qualities embedded in music, or even to apply principles of well-known musical forms to anthropological analysis (Levi-Strauss, 1963). This reification of music is evident in the chapter we wrote on 'Applying PCP to constructs related to music' (Ben-Peretz & Kalekin-Fishman, 1988), which appeared in the book edited by Fay Fransella and Laurie Thomas on the basis of papers presented at the 1985 PCP Congress in Cambridge. Taking the recognition of sounds as music for granted, we had no doubts about the fact that music can be taken for granted, so our interest then was to set up a theoretical description of how rep grids could be used for learning about the constructs people attach to (what everyone knows as) music. In another article, which reported on an experiment in which we used rep grids to elicit students' construals of music (Kalekin-Fishman, Bruen &

99

Ben-Peretz, 1986), we realized that Mead's model of socialization "explains how data elicited by the repertory grid, or any other methodological translation of PCT, represent the range of constructs for the group reality in a determinable socio-cultural context." In a word, aesthetic phenomena, which are cultural products, can be understood as a domain of group reality. The experiment we carried out, however, did not actually make use of this insight. At the time, we assumed that songs that were broadcast on the radio, a type of virtual scene, were units that everybody could identify as music. I later realized that we were taking far too much for granted. In a student body about 20% of which had Arabic as a native tongue, and another 20% consisted of recent immigrants to Israel, we did not ask about leisure activities, nor did we ask general questions about artistic, or musical taste for that matter. Nor did we try to find out about the students' early experiences of music. We had no inkling of how familiar the students were with the music we played for them, or of what their tastes were and, indefensibly, in choosing the elements, we were imposing our own stereotypical construals. Because the type of experiment we performed was insensitive to the shades of individuality that come into play in construing music, it is patent that an issue which is both logically and experientially prior should have been our starting point. When all is said and done, what types of sound-clusters are construed as music? And how do people come to agree on that?

Considering the extensive distribution in the media and in the concert hall, of varieties of sound called music, its problematization is increasingly pertinent in the framework of PCP. Evidence is manifold of both an impressive expansion in musical taste, on the one hand, and a tightening of local biases, on the other. Thanks to the globalization of the media of mass communication, audiences in the west are exposed to diverse types of compositions and performances that were once anathema to self-righteous cultivated music lovers. Exotic compounds of sounds are now accepted as 'world music'. Similarly, in local settings, music that for long was considered 'lowbrow' and unworthy of attention, music such as jazz, swing, disco, dance music, is now served up in festivals and on concert stages. How can we account for this growing tolerance for what was unknown and the object of distaste not too long ago? On the other hand, while professional composers of serious music in all genres extend their control of sounds as resources in their work, the products are not always accepted as belonging to music. Audiences do not hesitate to demonstrate repugnance for compositions that are based on unfamiliar musical idioms. While throwing ripe tomatoes at the performers (e.g., Stravinsky's *Rite of Spring*) has apparently gone out of fashion, concert-goers react by leaving early, or simply not buying tickets to programs that propose enjoyment of serious 'new' music. Still, this, too, is part of a process familiar in the history of European music. In every generation, a great deal of serious music has had to battle its way to acceptance. Examples range from the symphonies of Beethoven to Schönberg's Verklärte Nacht, not to mention experimental pieces such as the once astounding but already tame, 'Pacific 232' of Milhaud. The fact that there are such wide differences not only in people's tastes, but in their recognition of what can be called music, suggests that some 'matrix of decision' is involved, and that matrix is apparently taught and learned.

As noted, my hypothesis is that the construal of sounds as music is consequent on the experience of constructed contexts. The basic questions that have to be dealt with by a constructionist psycho-sociology of art are, then, to my mind:
- What is it that people construe as music?
- How are construals of music linked to constructed experience?
- What constructs shape the context?
- What in the context may be co-opted into a personal construal of music?

Although these questions could be treated as issues in neuro-psychology, they have a clear affinity to concerns of the broadening field of the social science of music. Abundant evidence of radical shifts in contemporary tastes is probably why numbers of such studies of music have grown significantly in recent decades. Philosophers and researchers – ethnomusicologists, semiologists, and sociologists, who are elaborating analyses of the arts, are proposing insights into the role of music in society and the role of society in music. Although there is still "no coherent field of music sociology" (Peterson & Dowd, 2004), the 2004 issue of *Poetics* devoted to 'Making music sociology' includes articles on the production of music (Dowd, 2004), on 'Intersections of form and content' in musical tastes (Sonnett, 2004), as well as historical perspectives (DeNora, 2004), and a discussion of ethnographic research in the service of music sociology (Grazian, 2004). The sociologists' debates tend to expand on the work of Adorno (1999), centering on how social processes impinge on music, and, rarely, how music affects social processes. To do this, they, too, for the most part, take it for granted that recognizing music is somehow a natural phenomenon. None of the papers in the journal actually problematizes music as such.

Still, there are slots where fundamental questions can be raised. One appropriate slot is to be found in the groundbreaking 'music scenes perspective' proposed by Bennett (2004). Relying on the dynamic approach elaborated by Straw (1991), Bennett (2004, p.225) explains that *"scene constitutes a far broader and more dynamic series of social relationships than those considered in the context of [earlier definitions, such as] subculture or ... community; ... scene memberships are not necessarily restricted according to class, gender or ethnicity, but may cut across all of these."* Most important for my purposes here, Bennett explains that *"scene ... offers the possibility of exami-*

ning musical life in its myriad forms, both production- and consumption-orientated, and the various, often locally specific ways in which these cross-cut each other" (Bennett, 2004, p. 226). His analysis goes on to relate to local, trans-local and virtual readings of scene. In this paper, I will be looking at the local reflection of a trans-local educational scene, the construction of music as it is produced and consumed in (Israeli) kindergartens.

Realizing the need for definitions

The kindergarten was a context that I knew well, yet chose to ignore when I planned the above-mentioned research with my colleagues. After a period of five years during which I had spent time doing observations and listening to what was going on in different kinds of Israeli kindergartens (state-Hebrew-speaking, state-Arabic-speaking, state-religious, Jewish, private-religious, Christian), and trying to figure out what I had seen and heard; I had come to the conclusion that children are "carefully taught" to recognize music, and non-music. Although at the time, I did not have the vocabulary to generalize my intuition, I actually wrote about the kindergarten as the *scene* where consensual meanings, including a consensual interpretation of what sounds are to be construed as music, was imparted. In this presentation, I want to emphasize how the construction of events as music was done in the kindergartens I observed and what I think can be learnt from that.

When I first set out to observe kindergartens, I formulated my goal as trying to describe how music functions as educational material. I had initially chosen that topic for my dissertation because as a former teacher of music and of English as a second language, I thought that I knew enough about music, about children, and about schools to collect data that I could analyze easily. Moreover, having seen my own children in kindergartens at different times, it was my impression that in the kindergarten, teachers used music to convey specific educational communiques. Since most of the music dealt with in kindergartens was attached to words, it was clear that the words of the songs taught were the bearers of officially sanctioned values and saturated with cultural messages. Basically, even though I was not satisfied with the aesthetic standards that were implemented, I had a preformed idea that music taught in kindergartens was not only a foundation stone of children's education in the arts, but was also related to the serious task of imparting axioms of moral education. Spending time as an observer taught me how unsafe it is to rely on impressions, even those of an involved parent. When I examined my recordings of kindergarten events and my written notes, I was astounded to discover that what the kindergarten teacher (and any reasonable person in the community including myself) defined as music turned out to take up no more than five [sic!] percent of the time that children spent in the kindergarten. This primitive finding freed me from my fixation on recognized songs and melodies. Instead, I turned my attention to what the recordings and the notes were telling me about the rest of the morning. The story was a complex one about constructs: collating evidence of how music is constructed and drawing conclusions about how sounds are construed.

Looking at all the recorded sounds, I found that by analyzing them according to qualities used for describing music: dynamics, rhythm, range, degrees of connectedness (legato / staccato / portato), and so on, I could derive a minimal 'behavioral' definition of music as production. While the characteristics noted here can be located in every kind of sound – language, clanking, thunder – events that teachers constructed as music had two specific sonal constructs: intentional pitch and / or intentional rhythm.[17] This discovery means that the production of music is accomplished through an identity between a performer's intention and her anticipation.

Teacher thinking and teaching practice

Teacher practice is the outcome of teacher thinking – the active construction of what is implied by a teacher's construals. Yorke (1987, p. 35) suggests that teacher thinking can be understood as a complex of "belief systems, strategic planning, and tactical adjustments". In his theoretical interpretation, classroom events take shape as proactivity when the teacher implements elements from the strategic plans (intentions, anticipations). Confronting inevitable unintended elements in the realization, whether contingent on her own behavior or on events extraneous to her behavior, she makes tactical adjustments (Yorke, 1987, p. 43).[18] In kindergartens, the teachers are in control. It is, therefore, safe to say that their actions (constructions) are realizations of their interpretations (construals) of the required curriculum. From the point of view of the children for whom those constructions constitute the kindergarten experience, the process is reversed. Exposed to actions that embody the construction of music, they are educated to anticipate what they should construe as music. While the construal is holistic and spontaneous, constructs are discoverable only in retrospect upon reflection. In constructing events to be construed as music, the reactivity of the children is the basis for the tactical adjustments the teacher may make, and, as I will point out later, provides an indication of how stable the children's construals of music are likely to be.

---

[17] In the framework of this paper, I do not have the space to present a detailed analysis of the kindergarten music in terms of the strictly musical qualities, such as musical modes, diapason, form, the relationships among the parts of the songs chosen, the relationship between the musical sounds and the words, and so on.

[18] Yorke goes on to show that teachers may assimilate the invalidations that burgeon in these events, leaving intact the core constructs that govern their belief system, but they may accommodate to them by revising core or peripheral in at least one significant way. Following through on this insight is beyond the scope of this paper.

Constructing music – building a construal of music – the emergent pole

In the kindergartens I observed, the agenda was carried out daily with specifically-named activities distributed on a timetable that covered all of the children's apportioned time at school. Although music was integrated into the kindergarten day regularly and all the kindergartens made time for songs, music was not delineated as a discrete activity in 11 of the 12 kindergartens I looked at. Only in the twelfth, was there actually an activity that was given the name, *music*. This is not to say that in the others, music was introduced haphazardly. Without taking up very much of the schedule, small doses of music did turn out to be part of everything that went on in the kindergarten. Teachers made clear what was to be construed as music by embedding it in different kinds of activities as the program required, by consistently constructing it as an aspect of action. Here are some examples.

There were three types of kindergarten events where music played a significant role.

1. Music was used extensively as a marker, a non-activity that signaled the end of one item on the schedule and the beginning of another. In the first activity of the morning, for example, an activity called 'the meeting,' the kindergarten teacher usually provided a story, or a game related to a pedagogical theme and the children were asked to tell about interesting things that had happened at home. Between the teacher's opening sally and the children's stories, the teacher sometimes led the children in a song they all knew. The end of the meeting was similarly signaled by singing. 'Music' was constructed to indicate that the meeting would soon be over and the children would be able to disperse to the various tables set up with materials for 'work'.

2. During the period of my observations, there was a slot for learning songs. This was a distinct activity only on the day of the week when the teacher of eurhythmics led the children in prescribed movements, handed out simple percussion instruments for them to play, and taught new lyrics. In the everyday schedule, practicing the new song was sometimes part of the scene of 'work'. While children were working at making plasticene figures, or at drawing, or at playing house, or building with blocks, the teacher was likely to begin humming a melody, and singing the words, expecting the children to join her, but this was not obligatory.

3. In the one kindergarten where there was a scheduled activity called 'music', its realization was exposing the children to recorded music. Well-known pieces of the kind that is usually included in elementary courses of

'music appreciation' were played as background while the children ate their sandwiches during their 10:00 o'clock snack.

Locating music in the agenda is, of course, only part of the story. Most significant is the mode of its introduction. In constructing musical events, the kindergarten teacher and the eurhythmics teacher as well, underline a message that has the widest connotations for the children's school career. Like many important fabrications, music can be produced only with management and control. The teachers regulate tones and rhythms, but also the positions of the pupils and their relationships with one another. Thus, learning to construe an interlude, or a part of an activity as music includes not only the experience of singing with the teacher, but also the experience of using the body in rigidly specified ways. Singing at the margins (between two items on the agenda) was done with arms folded across the chest, faces toward the kindergarten teacher, and feet flat on the ground. Singing during a eurhythmics lesson was similarly done in a highly specified way – singing to the accompaniment of an accordion and stepping in a required percussive rhythm. In the kindergarten with the activity defined as 'listening' to music, children were required to eat while sitting without making a sound in their fixed places at the tables. A norm that teachers insisted on was the rule that music precluded interaction of any kind. Listening meant not saying a word. When singing was going on, children who looked at their neighbors, or wiggled in their seats were taken to task for 'not participating'. Children who did not sing along while 'working' were also informed that they 'really should' mend their ways.

In sum, performances of music were framed in particular uses of the body and enforced as a collective undertaking. Thus, in all the events that the teachers constructed as music, children showed that they were construing the situation correctly by doing all the required actions together at all costs. They were careful to observe all the rules for using the body, as well as the rules governing pitch, rhythm, and the exact words in any song the teacher initiated. Interestingly enough, given that the organizational rules were observed, there was next to no monitoring of the aesthetics of the performances. Togetherness meant that the sound was often unrefined; the very coarseness was assumed to be a sign of 'energy', and being energetic was a clearly constructed aspect of doing music. Silence could be part of a song, or a permitted interlude, as in songs that were taught as games with accompaniments. Even though the name, music, was almost never mentioned, the slots for its appropriate performance were clearly indicated and inscribed in apt action – or inaction. In Kelly's terms, the production of music – its creation, performance, and dissemination (Dowd, 2004) – is taught in kindergartens as a set of activities that shape music as a richly contextualized type of event.

Constructing music – building a construal of music – the submergent pole

Music in the kindergartens that I observed was always created 'someplace else' and brought into the kindergarten as a pre-formed entity. Diffusion was the responsibility of the teacher and discretion in these matters was not granted the children. Where music was intended, activities that involve people as performers or as audience define not only the relevant but also *the irrelevant* interpersonal relationships (cf. Kelly, 1955, p. 721). Under no circumstances did teachers leave opposite poles of the matrix to speculation. The kindergarten teacher reinforced her construction of music by invalidating deviations. These were of two kinds. Children whose performance of the institutionalized pitches or rhythms was inaccurate, i.e., not consonant with what the class as a whole was directed to perform, were corrected. They were told sharply not to sing 'false notes' or to be silent. Mistakes in words were also corrected; this, however, was done often with an indulgent smile. Children, who wanted to whisper while eating to a background of recorded music, were reminded of the law that "there is no talking while we are having a meal." Thus music was recognized as part of the general limitations on how meals are done in the kindergarten.

On the other hand, it behooved the kindergarten children *not* to observe the rules for production when the slot for music was not available. Children's spontaneous play with sounds, the production of self-initiated music, i.e., solo performances based on intentional placement of pitches, intentional repetitions of rhythmic motifs, or improvisations with several participants, was curbed. Children's designs of planned pitches and planned rhythms were dispatched as 'noise' or 'rowdiness'. Sometimes, a child raised his voice forcefully on intended pitches while the item on the agenda was working or playing. Groups of children, who were sitting together at a table, tended to experiment in concert with different kinds of sounds or with different rhythms. The extemporizations were scotched. Several teachers had a reproach to hand. They reminded the children that such sound play showed that they were "too happy over there". Their anticipations and intentions were clearly marked as 'non-music'.

Norms of collectivism and submission

As noted earlier, my plan to explore the dissemination of music in kindergartens was disappointing in terms of quantity, but turned out to be richly indicative of institutional and normative constructs. The constraints imposed on the children's performance of music defined the limits of the event, the range of convenience of the matrix to be identified as music, the construction of sociality that was appropriate, as well as the basis for anticipating replication. In their induction into the framework of formal learning, children are not being taught to create music; they are being taught to submit to it. Collectivism and normative pacification seem to delineate the symbolic boundaries of the experience and its affective charge. This construal belies the myth that learning music is important because it provides children with access to a free, unconstrained, creative act. The events signaled as music were burdened with uncompromising verbal and non-verbal constructs.

Beyond acknowledging that they were being noisy, the children were not encouraged to construe what the teacher considered random sounds, as music. Sounds, however, fill the kindergarten space throughout the day. As people who visit kindergartens well know, they are bustling places. If and when they are not silenced deliberately, children naturally make sounds. They are constantly talking to friends, picking fights, deciding on games, explaining their point of view, laughing, and shouting. The objects that are available in the kindergarten are part of the general hum; there are thuds, swishes, clinks, and clatters that intersect with the human sounds. Adult voices often envelop the whole, usually giving instructions, praising or scolding, appealing or admonishing. In many kindergartens, sounds from the street – planes overhead, cars, motorcycles, people calling to one another – penetrate as well. This combination and recombination of sounds constitute the soundscape (Schafer, 1969) in which children and adults function throughout the kindergarten day. This is an inescapable setting. While eyes can be shut against undesirable sights, noses pinched shut so as to avoid smells, and the senses of touch and taste need not be activated; ears cannot be shielded without making great efforts and sounds cannot be screened out. Except when checked by some special directives, the soundscape is integrated into the kindergarten experiences that are, I dare say, most interesting. The apparently random soundscape is the background for creating friendships, for setting up dramatic play, for warm to heated interaction. In activities such as doing crafts or playing in the yard, children are given permission to talk, to climb on equipment in the yard, to build with only the presence of adults to remind them that there is a kind of barrier to complete 'freedom'. Thus, the general sonal setting provides the basis for some additional distinctive materials that undoubtedly moderate the assumption that only sounds that are constructed as music can be construed as such.

By contrast with the relative freedom of the uncontrolled soundscape, the use of music in the kindergartens I observed could be characterized as the acme of control. The introduction of songs, or the use of musical instruments, or the playing of records marks a drastic regulation of the soundscape. When activities to be construed as music are introduced, the free soundings, like the free movements, are constrained to fit into the constructed patterns of performance described above. How the whole package of relevant and officially extraneous configurations of sounds are perceived and interpreted to combine with the sounds officially constructed as music is likely to have an effect on what, after all, each individual will be capable of construing as music in the long run. Sharing the experience of a mass of sound events, children often hear the 'free' soundscape intermixing with the configurations of sound constructed as music. The proactivity of the kindergarten teacher constructs music as an event. The reactivity of the children in and to those events imposes modulation. In Yorke's terms, the children's sonal proactivity seems to evoke a 'defensive' strategy of invalidation in the teacher, and that strategy may evoke renewed shapes that are mutually validated by the children in the context of all the deliberately constructed and peripherally produced sounds.

Concluding remarks

Because of the complex construction of events in the kindergarten scene, acquiring a construal of music is acquiring a system of constructs that range from superordinate constructs of production (constructs pertaining to design), such as: controlled, collective, uniform, to subordinate constructs (constructs pertaining to performance) such as correct, convergent, immediate, along with an array of non-verbal construals of what these mean in relation to the body. Non-music is a conglomerate of the unrestricted, the individual, the inconsistent – often denoted as the contradictory. When children enter into the creation of these sounds with what is construed as superfluous enthusiasm, they are called to task and their sounds invalidated as mistaken, inconsistent, mistaken, divergent and delayed in their individualism. Some of the sounds produced are officially marked as extraneous and are derogated to the level of the to-be-ignored, the non-existent.

The fact that music is a shared cultural construction is not a chance phenomenon. Examining the kindergarten scene, we learn that children are initiated into the culturally desirable mode of constructing and construing music through replicated performances that govern the types of anticipations that the kindergarten teacher, on her state-defined mission, intends the students to develop. This is done through on-going monitoring. As to the sounds to be construed, those that do not fit in with the planned construction can be derogated (children are scolded) and ignored so that they may be excluded from the frame of music. The pedagogical assumption is that children will anticipate such structures as irrelevant constructions that combine into 'non-music'. But teachers can only monitor externalized performances; they cannot monitor the processes of consumption. Observations demonstrate that sounds (like freedom?) are in fact indivisible. Moreover, they are anticipated and mutually validated by the children among themselves (cf. Mead, 1934). From the point of view of PCP, this is the loophole that teachers can never stop up. Thus, what construal of music children actually take out of their consumption of kindergarten experiences cannot be defined exhaustively. From the compendium of sounds – some generated by the children themselves, some impinging on the kindergarten from the world at large, the macro-system that has chosen the kindergarten as the portal to society – each individual has opportunities to cut out the intricacies, sonal and performative, that in her perception are to be construed as music, and those that are negative evidence. Over the years of the children's careers as students, and beyond that, over a lifetime, their personal constructs are put to the test over and over again until eventually what can be called music and how singers, players, and audiences perform it is negotiated and renegotiated, often yielding diverse channels of musical expression. Considering that construals of music and non-music are important at the foundation of formal institutionalized education, the issues that arise in the course of those negotiations, the forces exerted, the changes undergone, the mechanisms of diversification implicate the convolutions of macro-society.

A personal construct psychology view of the construal of music and non-music provides a foundation for unraveling the webs of relationships that are ultimately the stuff of a psycho-sociology of music, an approach that can construe foundations and trace the interweaving of constructs, their validations, and their institutionalization as anticipations of music as a domain of shared consumption and a shared taste.

References

Adorno, T. W. (1999). *Sound figures.* Stanford: Stanford University Press.
Bennett, A. (2004). Consolidating the music scenes perspective. *Poetics, 32:* 223-234.
Ben-Peretz, M. & Kalekin-Fishman, D. (1988). Applying PCP to constructs related to music. In: Fransella, F. & Thomas, L. (eds.) *Experimenting with personal construct psychology.* London: Routledge & Kegan Paul, pp. 515-530.
Button, E. (1988). Music and personal constructs. In: Fransella, F. & Thomas, L. (eds.) *Experimenting with personal construct psychology.* London: Routledge & Kegan Paul, pp. 531-538.
DeNora, T. (2004). Historical perspectives in music sociology. *Poetics, 32:* 211-221.
Dowd, T. J. (2004). Production perspectives in the sociology of music. *Poetics, 32:* 235-246.
Grazian, D. (2004). Opportunities for ethnography in the sociology of music. *Poetics, 32:* 197-210.
Kalekin-Fishman, D., Bruen, H. & Ben-Peretz, M. (1985). Perception and interpretation of vocal music: Constructs of social groups. *International Review of Aesthetic and Sociology of Music, 17*(1): 53-72.
Levi-Strauss, C. (1963). *Structural anthropology.* New York: Basic Books.
Peterson, R. A. & Dowd, T. J. (2004). Making music sociology: An introduction. *Poetics, 32:* 195-196.
Schafer, R. M. (1969). *The new soundscape.* BMI Canada: Universal Edition.
Sonnett, J. (2004). Musical boundaries: Intersections of form and content. *Poetics, 32:* 247-264.
Yorke, D. M. (1987). Construing classrooms and curricula: A framework for research. *British Educational Research Journal, Vol. 13,* No. 1: 35-50.

Living with jazz: Construing cultural identity

Jörn W. Scheer

It is common knowledge that music has been an important part of civilisation since early on, be it for sacred purposes or mere entertainment. Until 100 years ago, people had to go somewhere to hear music; music was always performed live. Since the advent of the phonograph and the radio, music could be consumed and enjoyed on a mass scale, and anywhere, even at home. But only in the last few decades, with cassette recorders, CD players, and, most recently, digital players like the iPod, music is virtually everywhere, and all the time. Isn't it surprising that this has not caught the attention of people within Personal Construct Psychology (PCP)?

Without delving into the question of what music *is*, we can see that people have different 'tastes' in music: some like classical music, some prefer listening to jazz, many, in fact most, enjoy listening to pop music of different kinds. I would argue that 'musical preference' is too weak a term: for some, the music they like becomes a constituent of their self-construal.

When two people meet at a PCP conference for the first time, the usual opener is: *How did you get involved with PCP?* When two people who love jazz meet for the first time, the usual opener is: *How did you get involved with jazz?* PCP and jazz must have something in common. Probably, that both are 'disciplines' that minorities are involved in. In 1973, for instance, 75 percent of records sold in the United States were rock and similar music, 6.1 percent was classical music, and 1.3 percent was jazz (Hobsbawm, 1998). I don't dare make a guess about the percentage of people with an interest in PCP of the relevant sample of society. As disciplines, both are outside the mainstream, and also somehow 'in between': Jazz between popular music and classical music, PCP between quantitative and qualitative approaches, or between behaviourists and psychodynamists…

With this in mind, I was always intrigued by questions like: How does one become a PCP person? How does one become a jazz fan? We know what PCP is. But what is jazz? When you ask around you will hear that to many people jazz means 'Louis Armstrong singing *Hello Dolly*' or 'Glenn Miller and the *Sun Valley Serenade*', or, more advanced, Dave Brubeck's *Take Five* or the music of Oscar Peterson. Or recently: Norah Jones the singer. But does anyone remember Duke Ellington? Or Charlie Parker? Or John Coltrane? Or all those other jazz performers who make all these dissonant noises?

I shall now report a case study, the case being myself. And to emulate qualitative research methods, I shall conduct an interview with myself.

*

Jörn, you have been involved with Jazz since 1957, with PCP since about 1985, but apparently it took some time before you tried to connect your 'me as a jazz person' with your 'me as a PCP person'.

Yes, when I started to think that the range of convenience of PCP could be extended beyond the Big Three Cs: *Counseling*, *Consulting*, and *Curriculum*, I thought that it would be a good idea to start with myself, not because I think I am of prime importance, but because, to paraphrase George Kelly, I am what (or whom) I know best – including of course self-deceptions and the inevitable errors of judgment attached to them.

Well then, how did you get involved with jazz in the first place?

It was in 1957 when I was 16 that a friend, Karl, happened to lend me a couple of 45 rpm records, among them one with the widely unknown *Fernando Arbello's New Orleans Jazz Band* and one with the well-known *Charlie Parker Septet*. I remember these recordings well because on another occasion that year I had lectured someone about how all the dynamics and richness in sound structures that allegedly where characteristics of jazz can be found in Beethoven already. I had actually been aping my older brother, and now Karl's records proved me wrong.

Did that come out of the blue or had the way into jazz been paved somehow, for instance in your family?

My parents listened only to classical music, and they even thought operettas to be somewhat shallow. But among their records I found Débussy, Bizet, Ravel, Saint-Saëns, Strawinsky, Hindemith, and I liked them. I suppose that was a kind of foundation for my interest in jazz although I was certainly not pushed into it. Music lessons at school that included modern music may have been another source.

Wasn't jazz part of the youth culture of the time?

There wasn't really a 'youth culture' then, at least none that was defined by musical preferences as it is today. In our country, Germany, it was the time of social and economical consolidation after the war and young people were part of it rather than in opposition. There were two kinds of music, though, that had their followers primarily among young people: a more proletarian variant, mainly 'white' rock'n'roll as played by *Bill Haley and the Comets* which actually did accompany some street-fighting of 'rebels without a cause' and jazz: that is to say, traditional jazz, Dixieland or New Orleans jazz that had already had its revival in the United States in the Forties. We listened to touring Americans such as veteran *Kid Ory* and to European or local bands. Jazz was more popular among high school kids but not exclusively so: my friend Karl was to become a bricklayer. Older people preferred 'swing' music: *Glenn Miller* or *Benny Goodman*, the music of the guys that liberated us from the Nazis.

What was it then that got you hooked onto jazz?

I think, apart from musical aspects, it was the liveliness. To us, classical music seemed stiff, you wore suit and tie when you went to a concert, there was no obvious delight in listening, it looked like a kind of duty. When listening to jazz you could move, sway, smile, applaud when you felt like it while the musicians went on playing; it all seemed so relaxed. Also, the music was improvised–visibly *produced* on location, not *re-produced*, like classical music. You were witness to the actual creation of music. Also, distancing oneself from the taste of the parents' generation was probably part of the fun. And jazz was the music of the oppressed Black Americans, and included 'Negro Spirituals' and Blues which we tried to emulate. So it was certainly an emotional relationship–always the case with music. But this music talked to us in a special way, and made us tap our feet and snap our fingers, so quite definitely there was a psycho-physical dimension involved.

Are there musical specifics that might have caused this effect?

The so-called swing rhythm or swing phrasing is part of what created this liveliness. Most music is played 'straight', be it classical music, rock-pop music or Latin American: an eighth note is an eighth note and a quarter note is a quarter note. In swinging jazz it is different. The first of two eighth notes is played longer than the second one, almost double which causes an implicit triplet effect: the first note is played like the first two of a triplet, the second as the last. This phrasing goes without saying (or writing). In traditional jazz, this phenomenon was more pronounced, and it sounded more like a syncopated note, with a 'dotted' quarter note, followed by a sixteenth. Then the quantitative relation of two eighth notes was like 3:1 (Coker, 1964). That's why some people think that jazz is 'syncopated' music. To jazz buffs, this now sounds antiquated or corny.

I believe that this triadic, triolic, or triplet phrasing, or 'swing feel' is what attracts people like myself to jazz. It produces a sense of forward movement, sometimes apostrophised as 'drive'. But there is also something in the harmonics or chords that define the musical material used for improvising. I remember that after listening to the late night radio programmes of the *Voice of America Jazz Hour*, my friend and I used to listen to one particular spot in a John Coltrane recording (a tune called *Alabama*) again and again; it was mainly a downward interval and later I discovered that it was a 'flatted fifth' (meaning an interval) – a characteristic element of bebop music. Why we perceived this (and other such specific effects) as so moving...I have no idea.

Apparently this music attracted many young people in the Fifties, but that did not last?

That is true. Many did not follow up with especially the further developments of jazz beyond Dixieland and Swing: Bebop, Hardbop, Cool Jazz, Free Jazz and so on. This indicates that the Dixieland craze in the Fifties was mainly a social phenomenon. Real jazz as such was always an issue for minorities, and it was the same in the US. Among my friends it was always only a handful of people who were interested in jazz. I am not counting those who listened to musicians who had left the musical ghetto of jazz and appealed to a wider audience, such as Louis Armstrong, Dave Brubeck, Oscar Peterson or, at times, Keith Jarrett or Chick Corea, or recently Wynton Marsalis.

We'll get back to that later. If it was not family tradition–maybe it was opposition to family values that got young people interested?

Maybe in some cases – but that would probably not have lasted beyond the traumas of growing up. My parents were of the liberal sort and bought me jazz records from their record collectors' club, and hoped that my nervous system would not be affected lastingly by these ugly noises that they considered to be health hazards.

And was there room left to appreciate other forms of music?

There was, but classical music was never as important for me as for many people with a similar bourgeois background. I rather liked 'pre-classical' and, as mentioned above, 'post-classical' music. Besides, I enjoyed folk music, like Greek or Jewish music, or 'chansons' à la *Juliette Gréco* or *Georges Brassens*. But jazz did inoculate me against Seventies pop music.

Did this enthusiasm for jazz make you wish to make music yourself?

Strangely enough, not. I learned to play chords on a guitar to accompany friends singing folk songs and had piano lessons for a few years, but it did not occur to me to learn to play jazz. Maybe I found it too difficult or requiring hubris to attempt playing myself.

However, many years later, I started thinking about what kind of instrument would suit me, with no practical intentions whatsoever. The image of an alto saxophone rose in the back of my head – only in theory, of course, not seriously. How could I risk spending thousands of dollars without knowing whether that would make sense? Anyway, someone lent me an alto, showed me how to get sounds out of it, and the end of it was that I got myself a tenor saxophone – a *Selmer 80 Super Action Serie II*, found a teacher and took my first lessons – at age 46. That changed everything.

Didn't the memories of the dreaded piano lessons turn you off?

No, because the lessons were quite different right from the beginning. My teacher played me a Charlie Parker tune (which of course I knew), I had to repeat it and vary it a little bit. Then came some technical exercises, breathing, and scales. That was fun. Then came the theory. And, surprise, that was fun, too! I had known that there are things like 'major' and 'minor", and that they sounded different. Now I learned that there were different kinds of 'minor': Aeolian, harmonic minor, melodic minor, mixolydian and many more, and how they were related.

To give an example: Between all the keys on a piano (blacks and whites) there is a half note step. If you play only the white keys, starting from the C, the first two steps are a whole note long, then a half note, three whole, and one half. That's C major. Now if you start with the A, there is one whole note, then a half, and so on – it is the same white keys, but it sounds different: A minor. Now if you include some of the black keys, the half note steps are in different places of a scale, yielding a different sound attached to each so-defined scale. If you start with a half-tone step – you get this Spanish, Flamenco type sound, if you add a three-half-note step between note two and three – it is Arabic minor, and it sounds like you were in a harem. It was like a revelation. Then I learned chords, and chord succession patterns, so-called changes, and all this constitutes the musical material that an improviser uses.

Sounds pretty complicated!

It sounds more complicated that it is in practice. But it's true, it is quite a lot of musical raw material that a player has to learn and must be able to use almost intuitively. But the most dramatically appealing thing for me was that it gave me a key that opened a musical kingdom. Or to use a different metaphor: I felt like an explorer with a roughly drawn map entering uncharted territory...although of course explored by generations of jazz musicians before. The end of the story – of this story – is that I ended up playing in a jazz big band for the last fifteen years.

It seems like the musical hobby has an important role in your life?

Well–I am a bit reluctant to call it a 'hobby' like collecting stamps or growing roses. And I think it is about more than musical preferences. It may sound a bit over the top, but for me, jazz constitutes a prime part of my aesthetic or cultural identity, comparable to other art forms I identify with, but perhaps even more so because of the psycho-physically 'holistic' character of it. If I try to outline the philosophical term of the 'lived world' for myself, than jazz is an outstanding pillar of that world.

I'm wondering how it is possible that music that is rooted in the lives and times of slaves toiling in a different era, in a different cultural environment is so central in the life of someone living in Central Europe at the turn of the 21st century?

Good question! The answer is that the development of musical preferences and identifications is not strictly determined by the socio-cultural environment. Many African Americans don't care for jazz, a black person in the US is not necessarily a jazz lover. And in Europe not everyone loves classical music. Of course, the origins of jazz can be, and have been explained in sociological categories, and rightly so. And in my view, jazz is the only real contribution to world culture that America has given to us non-Americans. But what counts is whether an individual accepts such a present. It does not impose itself forcefully like Hollywood films or pop music. I believe that in a way, one *chooses* to become what then can be termed 'a jazz person'.

Is that really a conscious choice? Isn't it rather in a 'pre-reflexive' way that the individual's 'lived world' develops? Soaking in a variety of influences, from parents to school, to peers, to partners?

Certainly the 'agents of socialisation' play their parts, and you have to be exposed to the music in question in the first place. And the 'spirit' of an era may be involved, too. But I think that does not explain enough. At some stage, you *decide* that something does not become an episode but becomes a part of, yes, one's *self*...becomes integrated in one's identity. There are 'existentialist' ways of describing this act of incorporation, ultimately an act of designing oneself. A constructivist would call it *construing* oneself. As for me, at some point in time, a long time ago, I have construed myself as 'a jazz person'.

But certainly not only as a jazz person?

No, the construal of oneself is a complex process that includes many other sectors. If you had asked me, for instance, *how did you become involved in trade union activities?* that would have been another long story, beginning perhaps with how I did a poll in my class in high school about the forthcoming federal elections in Germany in 1953, followed by other episodes that contributed to my defining myself as 'a political person'. And so on.

I notice that the definition of identity, or as you say, your self construal, is often connected to episodes, events, or stories!

This is probably due in part to the opening question. But then I also think that in fact the process of construction of one's self, also called the development of an identity, arises from *events* and their repetitions, our reactions to them, our ways of dealing with them, thus from experience and what we make of it...in other words, from the *meanings* we attach to them. Describing them than may easily take the form of telling stories. In fact, the term 'psychology as story-telling' has been coined by a constructivist psychologist, *Miller Mair* (1988). I like that because it includes the *processes* as well as the *activities* of construing, the designing that occurs in the development of identity: *Identity as a piece of art!*

Thank you for sharing your personal constructions about your musical self!

*

Do we know more now about *why some people like jazz and most don't?*

A content analysis of my little auto-interview might give some hints. But some of the aspects mentioned are not specific to jazz. For instance, a psycho-physical involvement or arousal certainly also occurs when listening to marches, church music, and other 'awe-inspiring' musical experiences. If someone is confronted with this at a crucial point in time, in an environment that is important for her or him, or in a relationship that matters, it may become the nucleus of more than a mere preference, it may become part of one's cultural self.

If there is one thing special, then it may be a specific tension between anticipation rooted in past (musical) 'events' and new experience that is at the core of improvised music. Jazz musicologists have written about that, but Eric Button (another constructivist psychologist) finds the relationship between the *known* and the *new* crucial in any music (2006). If we hear only what we know we get bored; if we hear only new, never-heard sounds we are irritated or confused, even threatened. Listening to jazz, we are taken on an adventure trip, but we can be assured that in the end we will be taken back home safely. Given the focus on improvisation in jazz, maybe jazz persons are more on the 'enjoy new experiences in music' pole if we think of a bipolar dimension! Rather than wanting to have their anticipations validated– maybe they find 'joy in invalidation'!

Jazz is music appreciated by a minority. But this is, perhaps paradoxically, an international, overarching minority: there exists a worldwide virtual scene of jazz buffs. And some minorities are, or consider themselves as, a kind if elite. But a minority group (or an elite group) like the jazz scene is a context that one is *not born into* (like in an ethnic community), or *forced into* by others (like a group of migrants), and it is not a group defined by *social-economic* criteria (like social classes) or *family background* or by *achievements* (like some academic circles). To join the jazz community you *decide* to become part of it. Does that sound familiar to a member of the tiny worldwide PCP community? And maybe that brings us closer to the common ground of PCP and jazz: At the philosophical core of personal construct theory is what Kelly (1955) termed 'constructive alternativism', inviting us not to take for granted what we seem to know, but to always consider the creative exploration of alternative constructions – and isn't that what jazz improvisation is about?

There are many ways of defining one's identity, of construing one's self. Music is only one of them. If constructs about music become constructs about self, then they become *core constructs*. And to quote another of Miller Mair's terms: together with others, they form the *community of self* (Mair, 1977). And as in any community, there are neighbours. There are neighbours that get on with each other, in my case the 'political animal' (or *zoon politikon*), a 'runner', a 'bike-rider', a 'writer-storyteller', a 'bird-watcher' and a variety of others. And we know our opposites: the a-political petty bourgeois, the couch-potato, the city-slicker…

And as in any community there are neighbours in our community of selves that we are quite unhappy to share a fence with. But that would be stuff enough for another interview.

References

Button, E. (2006). Music and the person. In this volume, pp. 86-96.
Coker, J. (1964). *Improvising jazz*. New York: Simon & Schuster.
Hobsbawm, E. (1998). Jazz since 1960. In E. Hobsbawm (1998). *Uncommon people*. (274-280). New York: The New Press.
Kelly, G. A. (1955). *The psychology of personal constructs*. New York: Norton. (Reprinted in 1991, London: Routledge)

Mair, M. (1977). The community of self. In D. Bannister (Ed.). *New perspectives in personal construct theory*. London: Academic Press.
Mair, M. (1988). Psychology as story telling. *International Journal of Personal Construct Psychology*, 1: 125-137.

SINGING

Becoming a singer: PCT and voice

Vivien Burr

In this chapter I reflect on my own experience of 'becoming a singer' as a case study to explore some of the issues around reconstruing the self that are demanded in performance. I will argue that, for many people singing in front of others brings to the fore issues of self and identity that may be problematic. Performing the identity of 'singer' additionally demands the projection of a certain kind of self image. This means that becoming a 'singer', and especially one who performs in front of others, demands some reconstrual of self that may involve tension with core constructs. Furthermore, this reconstrual involves not just mental and behavioural adjustments but a 're-education' of the body.

I have been singing since I was a child, in school choirs, singing along to radio songs, and entertaining myself as an only child. As an adult, I have been singing and performing as a member of a choir, and also performing solos and duets as part of our concerts, for about twenty years. But although I have often sung/performed, in an important sense I was not a singer. Performing/singing does not make one a singer. It seems to me that I might now *just* be becoming a singer, but it is important to emphasise that this is not in any direct way related to my expertise or the quality of sound that I produce.

Like many performers, even most, I am simultaneously compelled to perform and wracked by nerves at the thought of it. 'Performance anxiety' is a topic that has usually been addressed from the vantage point of cognitive behaviourism, and with some success.

So in performance anxiety, like social anxiety, we imagine harsh judgements being made about us by our audience: we imagine that in others' eyes we are not intelligent enough, not good-looking enough, not articulate enough.

But I want to argue that our anxiety has rather more to do with identity and self-construing rather than our constructions of others' perceptions of us, although these are of course related. And 'voice' of course does raise issues about identity and self. Jonathan Rée (1999), in his book about deafness entitled 'I See a Voice', says:

> There is nothing more personal than voice. Shyness about using your voice in public- speaking out, screaming, singing, even just saying your own name- is probably the most elementary form of self-consciousness...It is as if your voice were as private and vulnerable as your defenceless, naked body. (p. 1)

He traces the connection between voice and selfhood back through the centuries, through the 19th century philosophy of Hegel, back to Renaissance metaphysics, finding a long-standing idea that the voice is connected with the soul, spirit or inner subjectivity. Furthermore, he points out, our voice is carried by the breath, so can easily be taken as "a kind of messenger despatched from our soul" (p. 9), so as the "breath of life" the voice is seen as expressing inner subjectivity.

But our voice is also meant to be heard. As Rée points out:

> *But voices are also destined for other people: you speak, primarily, to be heard. And the idea of being heard, of possessing a voice or having it neglected or denied, of seeking, vindicating, giving or offering a voice - the voice of the people, the voice of God - nearly coincides with that of human and civil rights.* (p. 1)

So through the voice we both desire to be heard but fear what we might reveal. The fear of self-disclosure seems particularly strong where singing is concerned. Whereas we tend to think of those who dislike speaking up in public as perhaps unusually shy, we accept as quite normal a reticence to sing in public and wonder admiringly at those who feel able to do this. The point is well illustrated by the acclaimed Season 6 episode of the cult TV series *Buffy the Vampire Slayer*, 'Once More With Feeling'. The episode takes the form of a musical where the characters, under the influence of a magic spell, were forced to sing their innermost thoughts, revealing secrets they wished to keep concealed from their friends and lovers.

On the face of it, singing in public should be no more anxiety-provoking than speaking in public. It is simply using the voice to communicate by different means. Our speaking voice is familiar to us, and revealing it to others is not usually an issue, so that nerves about 'public speaking', I would argue, are more usually about *what* we say than the voice we use to say it. But to most people singing is more terrifying. Whereas we think of our speaking voice as a vehicle we use to express who we are, we think of our singing voice as a *quality* of who we are, like the shape of our nose or the size of our feet. One's singing voice, is unmistakably personal, it may be unfamiliar even to us, hidden, uncertain, perhaps even shameful. When we sing, we feel naked in others' eyes. We feel we are revealing something fundamental about ourselves, like our naked body, and fear the ridicule this may bring. In a recent television programme broadcast in the UK called 'Facing the Music' a young woman who had once loved to sing had somehow lost her 'confidence' and asked for the help of experts. Her goal was to sing a very special song to her fiancé, family and friends at her engagement party. However, at first she literally could not 'face' her trainers, and could only sing if she faced a blank wall rather than her human audience.

But in performance one is not only oneself but is also projecting at least one, probably two, other personae. As an actor or singer, one must of course project the feelings of the character or sentiment of the song. But one must also project the identity of actor or singer. To the extent that lecturing is a performance, this makes sense of the anxiety I felt at 'becoming a lecturer' many years ago. It was about 'being a lecturer' in the eyes of students, when I could not claim this identity in my own eyes. Overcoming this was not just about rejecting negative thoughts about what others might be thinking about me, about gaining confidence in my ideas and my ability to communicate them, and not just about practice, although it did of course involve these things to some degree. It was primarily about the gap I perceived between my self and those qualities that I took to be included in what it meant to be a lecturer - to have a solid and extensive knowledge base, ready at my fingertips, which would enable me to speak with authority and assurance on topics in my area of expertise, and therefore to command the respect of my students. These things I certainly did not feel I possessed - and still do not, but it no longer seems important, and that has of course to do with my reconstrual of what it means to be a lecturer. My lack of 'confidence' was not the absence of a vital personal quality. Confidence here was identical with a sense of being what one purports to be.

It is not surprising, then, that *singing* in public raises so many issues around self and identity, around construing oneself. Performance anxiety, in my view, is not only to do with the fear of what others will think of you, what judgements they will make about you, but also, perhaps primarily, about the fear of being unable to convince others of the identity we are performing, to not 'be a singer' in people's eyes, to be an embarrassment to ourselves and others. Here, I think the work of Erving Goffman (1967) on embarrassment is particularly helpful. He was writing about social interaction, but I suggest that performance is just a peculiar kind of social interaction, a special case. Goffman says:

> *Embarrassment has to do with unfulfilled expectations...Given their social identities and the setting, the participants will sense what sort of conduct **ought** to be maintained as the appropriate thing, however much they may despair of its actually occurring...During interaction the individual is expected to possess certain attributes, capacities, and information which, taken together, fit together into a self that is at once coherently unified and appropriate for the occasion...At the same time he [sic] must accept and honor the selves projected by the other participants. The elements of a social encounter, then, consist of effectively projected claims to an acceptable self and the confirmation*

of like claims on the part of the others. (p. 105-106, emphasis in original)

Incidentally, Goffman points out that embarrassment is not just the preserve of the individual performer, but is also felt by the audience who recognises that the performance has broken down and the claimed identity threatened, thereby threatening their own identity as audience:

When an event throws doubt upon or discredits these claims, then the encounter finds itself lodged in assumptions which no longer hold. The responses the parties have made ready are now out of place and must be choked back, and the interaction must be reconstructed.

So conceptualising performance anxiety as simply a version of social anxiety does not adequately capture the way that self concept is implicated. For most of us, a public performance of some kind involves a quite different sense of self to what we are used to. It involves a shift in core construing and as such is, unsurprisingly to PCT thinkers, potentially threatening. The singer, like any other actor, must convince themselves if they are to convince others. The provisional aspect of construing was exhorted by Kelly, and the performance is in Mair's (1976) terms a 'passionate pretence' (p. 275). Although at some level we must not lose sight of the provisional and transitory nature of our construing, nevertheless we must passionately engage in living our present construction. I have used this metaphor many times when teaching PCT to students and think it wonderfully encapsulates the principle of constructive alternativism. We have to passionately believe our construction to give a convincing performance. And so the singer must in their role as character and as singer avoid a feeling of pretence. Like the hypnotised person (Burr and Butt, 1989) they must temporarily inhabit an alternative world and 'not notice' the cues which remind them of their 'real' self.

But this reconstruing cannot be conceptualised as manifesting only at the mental and emotional levels. Salmon (1985a; 1985b) has pointed out that the body, and particularly the body's expressiveness, is immensely important for our sense of self, and I have spoken elsewhere (Burr, 1995; 2001) about how important aspects of our construing are manifested in our embodied activity, arguing that construing is both a mental and a physical endeavour and that we construct ourselves through our bodies as much as through what we think or say.

Phil Salmon had insightful things to say about voice and embodiment from a PCT perspective, and reflected on her own personal experience of voice in both her autobiographical and creative writing. In part my motivation for writing this paper has come from the numerous communications I have had with her on this subject over recent years. In her book 'Living in Time' (1985a) she points out that:

> *Each person's embodiment represents a unique linguistic source- is a unique speaker of the language. Fundamentally, the way we hold ourselves, the way we physically move, conveys, carries, bespeaks our own particular ways of reacting, of feeling- it tells how we position ourselves towards our lives. Bodily stance is, perhaps, the very clearest expression of our personhood.* (p. 95)

I want to now elaborate on one particular aspect of this that I think is important for understanding performance anxiety and performing as a singer in particular. Singing is acting. To perform a song convincingly, one must be the character whose words one is delivering or one must take into oneself the position or perspective of someone who might deliver them. Rather like the fixed role (Kelly, 1955) sometimes used in PCT approaches to therapy, this means adopting not only the mental attitude of the person one is trying to be but adopting their physical attitude also. The singer, like the actor, must convey this construing through the body as well as the voice.

But as well as conveying the construal of the world demanded by the song, as I pointed out above, the singer must also adopt the role of the singer and perform this convincingly at the same time. Now, to the extent that roleplaying is not pretence but rather an elaboration of some aspect of self, or some member of our 'community of selves' (Mair, 1977), this is a complex task and requires that we can find the singer and the character within us and convincingly perform both. And as we so often find in everyday life, we may convince ourselves and others with our words, but our bodies seem to wilfully betray us.

I will illustrate the point with a brief personal anecdote. Novice singers are inevitably corrected by their teachers with regard to their 'bad habits', and every singer knows the lessons that are for them personally very hard to learn. I would argue that, largely, these lessons cannot be learned by the application of thought alone or even primarily; they concern embodied construing that has become sedimented (Butt, 1998) since our earliest days. People who know me will not be surprised to hear that I am constantly told by my singing teacher that I am 'trying too hard', and that if I took a more laid-back approach to singing and put in less effort I would sing better. On one occasion I took part in a local music competition, and after performing in the French Song class, the adjudicator had some important feedback for me. I was trying too hard. But on exploring the meaning of my 'trying too hard', it seemed that this was part of a bigger issue of self-construing, and was manifested in my bodily posture. It seems I was trying to bring the audience into my performance by mentally (and therefore bodily) approaching them, meeting them more than half way in the 'performance space'. My posture, instead of being perfectly erect and balanced, was bent forward, which also had the effect of inhibiting my breathing. My body said that I was going to bring my horse to the water and hope that he drank! This, I was told, was not the correct attitude for a singer. The performing singer must instead assume a sense of self-importance, almost an arrogance, a regal frame of mind which demands and assumes that the audience will travel the distance across the performance space for the privilege of hearing them.

I realised then that I would never 'become a singer' unless I could, at least for the time-limited experience of performance, reconstrue myself in this way. But of course this is easier said than done, and you could say that presently it is a work in progress. Phil Salmon also noted the reluctance of the body to be coaxed into new ways of construing self and world:

Whether through massage, the Alexander method, or the techniques of biofeedback, the exploration of one's own embodiment brings with it unexpected and remarkable discoveries about one's own personal feelings, personal reactions. In noticing how your shoulders, through what seems to be their own volition, habitually position themselves in a particular way - a way which is obstinately resistant to your attempts to hold them differently - you begin to glimpse something of your own intimate experience. The way you hold your shoulders seems to have to do with a profound resolution, on your part, to stay in charge of things, to avoid, at all costs, acknowledging weakness and vulnerability. You notice that their position seems particularly rigid and fixed in situations where you are under stress, where it is especially difficult to maintain your sense of being in control. (pp. 99-100)

The concept of 'sedimentation' (see Butt, ibid) has been used to refer to our mental and behavioural habits. But as a physical metaphor it is even more applicable to the world of embodiment. If our construing is sedimented, and our bodies are 'obstinate', reconstruing ourselves is about cajoling or training the body out of its set ways. This is physical, and like trying to remove the lines from our faces that are the traces of our lifetime's habitual stance to the world, we may be only partially successful; there is no analogy for the face lift when it comes to psychological reconstruction. To become 'set in our ways' is physical as well as psychological and may be even harder to undo as the body comes to *be* the shape of our psychology over the years. The shoulders that have been habitually held in a protective, enclosing posture for thirty years cannot suddenly open out with the desire to become more 'confident'.

I have considered in depth only the issues relating to performance with respect to the performer. But added to this must be the social world in which this performance takes place. One cannot be a performer without an audience to perform to, just as one cannot be a teacher without students. And these others must play their part in allowing the identity of performer to be constructed. I cannot 'be a singer' if others will not legitimate that identity.

Phil Salmon surely speaks for us all when she says: "The experience of seeing ourselves in action, on someone's home movie, or of hearing our own tape-recorded voice, is usually little short of traumatic" (ibid, p 97). This trauma is surely the realisation that the person we believe ourselves to be and so desperately need to be legitimated and validated by others, is perhaps not the person that others see. When we suddenly see ourselves as we believe others must see us, the rug is pulled from under us. It is a curious feature of performance anxiety that it can be harder to sing before sympathetic and supportive family and friends than in front of an audience of complete strangers. But this makes sense if we regard performance anxiety as more to do with our identity as performer than to do with evaluation apprehension. Those close to us know us in too many other roles and identities, as mother, daughter or wife, as co-worker, tutor or friend. When we perform to them, we ask that they put aside all their previous knowledge of us and see/validate only the performer. Goffman says:

> *To experience a sudden change in status, as by marriage or promotion, is to acquire a self that other individuals may not fully admit because of their lingering attachment to the old self. To ask for a job, a loan of money, or a hand in marriage is to project an image of self as worthy, under conditions where the one who can discredit the assumption may have good reason to do so.*

Conclusion

Voice is, in our way of thinking, intimately connected with who we are, and this is especially so of the singing voice. Revealing it, and revealing ourselves through it, can therefore understandably be enormously threatening. One's voice is intensely personal. It says far too much about us, and must say something different about us if we are to adopt the identity of 'performer'. I would argue that the greatest source of anxiety singers face is how to be convincing *as a performer*, how to not only convince the audience of the role or idea one is portraying, but how to convince them in one's identity *as a singer*. This will require not just a cognitive reconstrual but a physical one too, as we exhort our bodies to leave behind their sedimented attitudes and encourage them to adopt strange postures signalling psychological capacities and states that we may to some degree find unacceptable or incompatible with who we take ourselves to be. After nearly 20 years of singing in my adult life, after 10 years of singing lessons, and after now numerous solo performances, I think I may finally be becoming a singer.

References

Burr, V. (1995). PCP and the body. Paper delivered to the 11th International Congress on PCP, Barcelona, July.

Burr, V. (2001). The Art of writing: embodiment and pre-verbal construing. Paper presented at International Congress on PCP, University of Wollongong, July.

Burr, V., Butt, T.W. (1989). A personal construct view of hypnosis. *Brit. J. Exp. Clin. Hyp.* Vol. 6, no. 2, 85-90.

Butt, T. W. (1998). Sedimentation and elaborative choice. *J. of Constructivist Psychology*, 11, 265-281.

Goffman, E. (1967). *Interaction ritual*. Penguin.

Kelly, G. (1955). *The psychology of personal constructs*. New York: Norton.

Mair, J. M. M. (1976). Metaphors for living. In A. Landfield (ed) *Nebraska Symposium on Motivation* Lincoln, Nebraska: University of Nebraska Press. 243-290.

Mair, J. M. M. (1977). The community of self. In D. Bannister (Ed.), *New perspectives in personal construct theory*. London: Academic Press. 125-149.

Reé, J. (1999). *I See A Voice: A philosophical history of language, deafness and the senses*. London: Harper Collins

Salmon, P. (1985a). *Living in Time*. London: Dent

Salmon, P. (1985b). Relations with the physical: An alternative reading of Kelly. In D. Bannister (Ed.). *Issues and approaches in personal construct theory*. London: Academic Press. 173-182

Stand at the back and pretend – the experience of learning to sing

Mary Frances

I was probably 7 or 8 when the teacher told me to stop singing, called me tone deaf. I remember the shame. I got pulled out of the group and told to just stand at the back and pretend. What's interesting is that it led to a lifetime of standing at the back and pretending. I spent a lot of my life making sure no-one could see or hear the real me. That had been the real me you see – that singing boy. (Alan)

Alan has been learning to sing with a community choir, overturning his former construction of himself as a non-singer. He is one of several people I have met during my own journey of learning to sing who give vivid life to the assertion of George Kelly (1955) that we need not be victims of our autobiography. Joining a choir or taking lessons has revealed a hidden singing self, and has sometimes been part of a major process of personal reconstrual.

For my part, although I had little confidence or practice, I always knew and believed that I could sing – I was just nervous about doing so when anyone else was listening. But at the first meeting of the group I joined, I was surprised by the number of people who described themselves as completely unable to sing, or as 'tone deaf'. I was impressed by the level of fear and threat they must have overcome to be there. It seemed that they were facing the potential of a repeat invalidation ('it's true, I really can't sing'), or the uneasy surprise of a new validation ('I can sing after all') with its life-story changing implications ('perhaps I always could sing').

This chapter draws on the stories of seven singers I have met in the past few years, and is the result of elaborative interviews and conversations. The emergent themes from these interviews are considered through the lens of Kelly's Personal Construct Psychology. The findings reveal a close connection between singing experiences in childhood and our developing sense of self, and they also highlight aspects of teaching and learning which resonate with Kelly's necessary conditions for psychological change and personal reconstruction.

Singing at school

From Africa comes a saying: 'If you can walk you can dance, if you can talk you can sing'. Natural voice teachers such as Frankie Armstrong (1985) have noted that it seems to be a unique aspect of our present-day western culture that so many people are told as children that they can't sing. As she says, the label sticks: "Anyone so labelled is bound to get tense and anxious around singing, and this tension makes it difficult to listen and to really hear sounds and pitches: all you hear when you listen with this kind of tension is your own panic".

As Director of Music at the Institute of Education in London, Graham Welch (2003) has spoken of the "lifelong perception of musical disability" resulting from being labelled as unmusical at an early age, and has expressed concern about a "self-perpetuating expectation of musical incompetence" which endures through adult life. He believes it a misconception that some children are not musical and believes that most 'out of tune' singing stems from a mismatch between the child's level of singing competency and the tasks set by their teachers, and from the combination of text and music in many school singing experiences. Research would indicate that singing expertise develops in a sequential way, with musical aspects such as melodic fragments being mastered before complete songs, the text of which can trigger 'speech mode' and lead to a perception of being out of tune. "Everyone is musical... Much perceived musical disability is a product of enculturation, including inadequate education and/or inappropriate experience."

The change from uninhibited singing child to withdrawn non-singer is described by Alan and others as happening rapidly in the wake of a shaming experience at school. From a Personal Construct Psychology perspective, Phil Salmon (1970) has talked about children's 'watershed points' – events which may have been trivial to others but which had a tremendous impact and lasting influence on the child's construing of self. The shaming which has accompanied many people's experience of being told they can't sing seems to have been just such a watershed.

> *I was told from a very early age that I couldn't sing. Tone deaf, tin ear, flat. Up to age 10 or so it didn't really matter, I just sung anyway, but then the message got through. Public humiliation was the thing – being told to stop singing in front of everyone. Being the only one told to be quiet.* (Tess)

> *Being told to 'stop droning' when practising carols for my first Christmas concert. Our teacher said to me 'Well, you can't possibly be a carol singer'. I felt humiliated, disappointed not to be allowed to sing, sad to have confirmation that I really couldn't sing.* (Lynda)

Mildred McCoy (1977) has defined shame in PCP terms as 'the awareness of dislodgement of the self from another's construing of one's role'. We experience shame as our personal failure in living up to another's expectation of us, within a significant role relationship. The dislodgement is from our core role structure, which is both our frame of reference for social interaction and the basis of our identity. A significant invalidation of self might be likely to occur in incidents such as those described, given the formative vulnerability of children being named by their early teachers.

Similar ideas have been expressed by psychoanalyst Helen Lewis (1989) who described shame as being "directly about the whole self. It is the vicarious experience of the other's scorn of self, so that it is experienced in one's own and others' eyes. The self in the moment of shame is felt to be 'in the eye of a storm' of disapproval". She adds that it is difficult to find a way of releasing this "humiliated fury", and predicts the likelihood that such experiences will be succeeded by more shame.

Construing self as a non-singer

In the wake of these early experiences, the construct of 'being able to sing v not being able to sing' appears to have had a wide ranging influence on identity and life choices:

> *I was silenced basically. I became very very quiet, and rather afraid of what might come out of my mouth. I hid effectively for years.* (Tess)

> *I learned it was better to keep quiet. I withdrew and detached myself from the experience so it did not touch me* (Lynda)

> *I've never felt like I could have a view about music – what was any good, what wasn't, because of being tone deaf. I couldn't know could I? I couldn't have an opinion. I think I projected my creativity onto other people, going out with arty types and being a bit in awe of them, admiring them like they had this great gift that was completely out of my reach.* (Beth)

> *Not being a singer or performer I identified myself as more serious, more academic in contrast to them. I was very serious and studious growing up.* (Eva)

> *In all areas of life I have been at pains to hide my deficiencies. 'Standing at the back and pretending' has been part of that. I think it influenced my professional life a lot. Becoming a teacher, you take on a role, a persona. The boys have no interest in who you really are, you are just 'sir'. You stand at the front and pretend. The real you is not the issue. Or that's how it seemed for many years.* (Alan)

PCP would suggest that in construing themselves as non-singers, this group would be likely to have developed an elaborated opposite pole about singers – the 'not me' dimension. The change towards becoming a singer would mean not only leaving behind familiar aspects of self, but potentially taking on a new set of self-constructs with similarly core implications. So what was implied by being a singer?

Good singers for me are people in their power, strong people. And they are creative people. From my background that's not who we were. And being powerful can be scary. (Debbie)

Being a singer would be about being confident, very confident, having a big personality. Creative, expressive, a bit arty. None of that was anything like me. (Beth)

Singers? Strong, confident, powerful, visible, noisy, there! And a bit bohemian, flowing scarves... (Tess)

Being a singer would mean being a performer, front of stage, being outgoing and flamboyant, confident, expressive, not afraid to let your hair down. And powerful, in control, commanding. A bit frightening really! (Eva)

Singing for me would imply extraversion, power, knowing who you are and demanding your place in the world, 'here I am!'. (Polly)

Several clusters of constructs appear here:
- strength, power, and confidence, (also connected with being rather scary or frightening);
- creativity, expressiveness and being artistic;
- and having 'big' personalities, being extraverted and 'being there' (in contrast perhaps to 'standing at the back and pretending').

As people told their stories it was clear how little they identified themselves with these qualities before learning to sing. This was reflected in a multitude of comments about being quiet, silenced, hidden, afraid, more academic, studious and so on.

While the self-descriptions of the former 'non-singers' seemed in tune with the label they had been confronted with in those early shaming experiences, it seems that an echo of the small singing child still survived. Paul Kotmann (2000) has suggested that the pain we experience when we are negatively labelled is not total invalidation of the self, but includes the feeling that "who one is is *not* being addressed and indeed has no place in the name-calling scene at all". As Alan told us earlier, *"that was the real me, you see, that singing boy"*. Kotmann, introducing the work of Adriana Cavarero (1997), draws on her ideas that our 'linguistic vulnerability' can be re-cast as a constitutive feature of our uniqueness, that "opening to be hurt or affected by what we are called might even be that which gives us the sense, through the pain or shock we feel, that *what* we are called does not correspond to *who* we feel ourselves to be".

McCoy emphasised that the partial invalidation of core structure resulting from a shaming experience "does not involve the abandonment of the constructs involved". The child who was happily joining in the carols or nursery rhymes before labels such as 'tone-deaf' forced their way in to colonise their construct systems was evident perhaps in the continuing desire to sing.

From about 15 I got into the folk scene and there were excellent singers. I remember once starting to join in, really wanting to sing, But then someone looked right at me and said 'Someone's singing out of tune'. I never joined in again. (Debbie)

The desire to sing was strong. Two girls in the 6th form set our A level poetry to music and I desperately wished to be them; at a student party a young woman spontaneously sang Summertime and I so wanted to be her; friends in the states sang together and I was too scared to join in for fear of 'droning' and ruining the sound. (Lynda)

I've always loved music, lived for music in many ways - my CD collection is phenomenal - and I dreamed, really dreamed of being able to perform those pieces I loved so much. But it was crazy dreaming, like being a millionaire. (Alan)

I think I did have this yearning to sing, every time I heard the singing side of the family together – it was frustrating sometimes not to feel able to join in but I wouldn't have dared. *(Eva)*

The decision to sing again

Kelly's emphasis on enactment and behavioural experimentation continually reminds us that personal reconstruction is not located in an internal linguistic change, but in a relational and performative process. This resonates with the ideas of Fred Newman and Lois Holzman (1997) who describe learning and development in terms of 'revolutionary activity' which is not "expressed in our actions as thinkers, perceivers, conceivers, constructors, or interpreters (even if relational and situated), but completed in our creative performance as collective developers of our lives". Singing is most particularly an embodied construct, an action to be performed.

The decision to embark on the great experimental activity of learning to sing in adult life seemed to be triggered by another watershed point. This may have been a consequence of finding oneself in a new set of relationships or an unfamiliar geographical area, stimulating a need to consider who we might be in that changed context. Alternatively the decision had sometimes grown out of a personal crisis which had shaken and disrupted the paths along which life was lived to the point where re-construal became possible, and a revised construction of self became essential.

It was after my divorce I went to the singing class. I had promised myself life would be different, I would start doing more, trying new things. (Beth)

My husband had died after a long illness. There had been a long period of stress and tension, and 18 months on part of me was ready to begin something new. And I thought singing would be refreshing, get me out of my head, stop me wallowing. (Polly)

Post-divorce, new town, not knowing anyone, wondering if this could be a way of getting to know them. Beneath that, being 50, realising I had nothing left to lose, wanting to be different, realising I was so sick of who I was. Some part of me thought singing, finding my real voice, might be a key to that. (Alan)

Being too much alone, and too often silent after my husband died. I needed to be with people and be doing something. And not talking, not bloody therapy, nothing to do with P's death. (Tess)

PCP contrasts the deterministic idea that we remain the same through life with an elaborated belief in development and choice. These adult watershed moments perhaps highlighted a contradiction between our sense of ourselves as beings in motion with potential to reinvent ourselves, and the old negatively phrased labels and self-categorisations such as 'non-singer'. Additionally, it may be a reflection of the close connection between core self and singing self that singing was the alternative therapeutic choice at these times of transition.

The scale of these reconstructive experiments is very well articulated in stories of the first lesson. Making the phone call or filling in a booking form was quite a leap, but the day of the class brought an extraordinary level of anxiety and threat.

Kelly suggested that we are likely to be threatened "by hauntingly familiar things" about which we have developed fairly comprehensive constructs. He describes us as feeling at risk of regression when our "perceptual field is flooded with material which is familiar to childhood's eyes". And even when our experiment is successful, we may be equally alarmed by the mounting proportions of an alternative interpretation of our self. Having moved far enough to feel able to approach singing again, some people still carried the fear that they wouldn't be able to do it and that their teachers were right all along. They also acknowledged a potentially greater fear that a new previously unknown self, with well-elaborated 'scary' aspects, might be about to emerge.

You are at the edge of danger (Polly)

It could be worse than you fear, it could be as bad as you remember, it could, just perhaps, be better than you imagine. A major step? Oh yes. (Beth)

Who would I be? (Tess)

Anticipation of the experiment caused anxiety and threat, the risk of further invalidation at core level:

Very apprehensive, for the first time in ages really not knowing what would happen to me. (Polly)

I didn't want my voice to be heard, it was the real me. All these new people and my voice would be heard and I would be judged (Debbie)

Terrified and convinced I would be the only one who really, really couldn't sing and would feel worse afterwards. (Lynda)

It may have been awareness of that mismatch between the labelled non-singer self, and the self we feel ourselves to be, that finally prompted the experimental leap:

Another part of me, a tiny rebellious bit, that said after all these years, 'Fuck that teacher, you <u>can</u> sing'. (Alan)

The moment of arrival in the group was remembered with great vividness:

When I joined the singing group it was terrifying – like exposing a shameful secret I'd had for years – who I was. Sick with nerves, really throwing up sick, didn't think I'd be able to make a sound. (Alan)

I have no idea how I got there. I mean I saw the poster, applied, turned up, but at another level I have no sense of how I made the connection between that and me. It was like being someone else. And it wasn't till I was there and realised I'd have to sing in front of these 30 people. I don't know how to describe to you the terror, absolute blinding terror. (Tess)

The morning of going there I felt really ill, I nearly backed off. I walked up and down the street outside, I thought about going home. In the group, everyone looked young and confident. I was so scared I kept telling myself 'we're all in the same boat, starting from scratch'. then we were asked to get in a circle, and the man next to me turned to the woman on the other side and said 'I recognise you, aren't you in the Bach choir?'. I had a kind of panic attack, I could hear my heart beating. I thought I am so in the wrong place. (Beth)

Teaching and learning – with a difference

One of the most important features of these groups seems to have been instant and unconditional validation from the teachers, unexpectedly including validation as singers. This assumption seemed to surprise people into a provisional re-construing of self which allowed change to happen.

The first thing [the teacher] said was 'Everyone can sing'. I remember I felt like crying because suddenly after all those years, I believed her. The whole day was very emotional, the whole experience was. (Alan)

The teacher said two really important things. She asked if anyone had ever been told they couldn't sing. Loads of people put their hands up and one woman was crying. I felt really OK then about myself, about being there. And she said, 'Just sing what I sing, and if you find you are singing something else, that's called a 'harmony''. Everyone laughed, but it felt great. it felt like there wasn't a right way to sing. You could all just sing. And the sound we made was great, we sounded like a choir. it was unbelievable. (Tess)

All the teachers mentioned used a varied repertoire of songs from all over the world. There is sometimes criticism of the appropriation of music from other cultures, but in these situations it seems that the choice of world music was a great leveller. Firstly, the repertoire reduced threat levels by being unfamiliar to childhood's memory, avoiding a flooding in of past experience. Equally importantly, those more experienced singers in the group who may have been confident working through the usual choral repertoire were as nonplussed as the novices by the pronunciation of a Gaelic chorus or the open-throated sound of a Bulgarian folk-song. In some cases it would seem that the unfamiliar rhythms and unlikely harmonies posed bigger challenges for those with musical experience, as they had better elaborated constructs of what sounded right or wrong which they would have to unlearn.

> *It helped that we started with just noises really, and breathing. It was more like yoga. I calmed down a bit. And the things we sang were kind of talky. Not really singing melodies but calling stuff. It helped a lot that we didn't have to 'sing'. We built up to that quite slowly and by the time we were singing you hadn't noticed it happening, you were just singing.* (Beth)

> *The technique was to build up from making sounds based on shouting, to 'call' as if to a friend on the street....It was an atmosphere of support and encouragement, small steps to build confidence and experiment without judgement and any sound is interesting, not right or wrong.* (Lynda)

Kelly described three conditions favourable to re-construal:
- the provision of 'fresh' sets of elements from which new constructs might emerge;
- an atmosphere of experimentation, where we can 'try things on for size';
- and the availability of validating data.

Both by chosen style and technique, and by intuitive gift, the singing group leaders met these conditions by:
- the provision of unfamiliar song and rhythm styles, of which few people had any previous experience;
- emphasising process over performance, and offering a wide variety of songs and exercises in each session. They described themselves as experimenting, regularly trying things which they weren't sure would 'work';
- and by finding individual contributions and unexpected outcomes interesting, delightful or amusing, but never problematic. *'I sang one line really wrong twice and the teacher said 'I like that, we'll all learn that'* (Tess)

Similarly, Kelly highlighted conditions unfavourable to change:
- the presence of threat;

- a preoccupation with old material, as our existing habits inhibit our finding new ways to deal with events;
- and the lack of a suitable social 'laboratory' for our experiments.

To avoid these conditions, the group leaders were:
- keeping threat levels to a minimum, not least by recognising these feelings as normal from the start, and by offering validation without evaluation;
- avoiding preoccupation with old material by using world unfamiliar repertoire and the oral teaching style. Even those with experience in music weren't given the music to read but required to learn by ear in the group;
- and a rich social laboratory was provided by working primarily with quite large groups, typically 20-40 people, thereby offering a diverse range of validational evidence.

The choice of music from other cultures provided an additional stimulus to change, by enabling a reconstruction of the purpose of singing in life. Singing is a universal human activity and, in most cultures, is a natural component of many everyday activities and communications as well as being central to celebrations and rituals. It is the exception rather than the norm to reject most singing that doesn't conform to a narrow interpretation of what is beautiful and technically correct.

This social-cultural connection between singing and critically evaluated 'correct' performance was evident in the comments which drove many of the voices featured here into silence. Singing in our culture seems to have been largely removed from the everyday, and given special status. Installed on a stage in a concert hall, or perfected in a professional recording, we have a special category of people who sing, and to have singers, there must necessarily be non-singers.

Half the family, my mother's side, were singers and performers, and the other side were definitely not singers, they couldn't hold a note. I identified with the non-singing side very early because I couldn't sing like my mum, couldn't perform, and I can remember being told to 'stop that noise' by the ones who could sing. (Eva)

The requirement to stand at the back and pretend, rather than add whatever your voice brings to the group, privileges severely constricted understandings of what is a good sound over an activity which has its original purpose in everyday human connection. As Gergen and Gergen (1986) have noted, we are limited to a vocabulary of action that has currency in our own culture, and we cannot compose an autobiography of cultural nonsense. Being a non-singer seems to be well-established cultural construct. For this reason, the content and meaning of the songs learned in the singing groups was of prime importance in beginning to reconstrue oneself as a singer.

> *I managed to inhabit the spirit of the songs very quickly – they were important songs with good things to say, and I wanted to be part of saying them..'.* (Tess)

> *I have had the experience of being so completely in the meaning and expression of the song that the sound has taken care of itself and (I'm told) been note perfect and sounded 'musical'.* (Lynda)

Where we have become used to performances by paid professionals in a concert setting, the idea of performing in public would provoke anxiety and threat in many of us, but where the song is to heal a sick child or protest an injustice, we are likely to want to add our voice. Few people are inhibited about joining the chants in the football stadium to spur on a winning team, or praising the 'jolly good fellow' when they truly appreciate a job well done. The repertoire of the singing groups has usefully extended the range of convenience of singing, embracing situations where some heartfelt (as opposed to expert) singing might be both possible and appropriate.

> *It totally changed my framework of what music was, what it could be, and what it was for.* (Eva)

What became apparent was that for the sick child or the oppressed neighbour it was your familiar and loved voice that would be wanted, and a professional singer however skilful would be no substitute. The performance measures would be true comfort and real solidarity, not technical brilliance, and this was a major re-construal after years of not being 'good enough' to perform.

> *I was able to sing at a friend's wife's funeral and it felt so important, such a good thing to do. Enriching. You had to take a risk, but it was beautiful. The risk was acknowledged there, people knew you were doing a big thing. the risk was acknowledged by accepting the gift.* (Debbie)

The most critical difference in the teaching and learning experienced here is the absence of shame or the risk of shaming. The school teachers described had pre-formed standards of competence against which children were judged. They seem to have construed their role as developing the best and weeding out those who couldn't reach the standard – a process typical of many people's educational experience. Graham Welch suggests that many children have been "misunderstood and compared (wrongly) to adult notions of what it is to be musical". The singing group teachers described here started from an entirely different assumption – that everyone could sing. There was no weeding out to be done. Newman and Holzman have described truly creative and reconstructive activity as "created through (and simultaneous with) practicing method rather than being an appraisal generated from hypotheses prior to, or interpretations after, practice".

When my own singing teacher formed a small choir, she invited those people who had had individual lessons with her and who were regular attenders at the larger group. I remember how impressed and surprised I felt that she had selected those with a commitment to developing their voices rather than those with the most 'talent' or 'best voices'. I was still using the old school-based constructs; she construed her role quite differently – here were people who really wanted to sing and would put time and energy into it. Her role would be to work with us to have us sound our best and create a new musical experience together.

A new singing self

During the process of these interviews, the stories of not being able to sing and of early singing experiences, were told as anecdotes familiar to the teller. My questions about the impact of becoming a singer on self identity, life, and the imagined future were rather different as several people declared themselves surprised by their own answers – these were newer stories, many being told for the first time.

Interestingly, the worries about needing to be extraverted and a flamboyant personality seemed unfounded and these aspects of being a singer had been reconstrued by some:

> *We share something incredibly deep, and that's an important thing to do with other people, and yet we don't really know each other at the everyday level – I couldn't tell you what people do as jobs, or how they live.* (Alan)

> *There's a privacy and anonymity about it. I can just be me sharing something rich with others, but we don't need to small talk or get to know each other. We really don't know one another except at the level of singing.* (Polly)

Alternatively, some people had embraced a new rather more performative self:

> *Singing and performing gives me a chance to have a show-off side – the part that you would be slapped down for as a child.* (Debbie)

We do perform now and I really enjoy the stage and spotlight. We laugh about it in the group, say that we've released our inner Liza Minnelli! (Beth)

The emphasis on the community of the singing group, on working well together and helping each other, seems to have been emphasised continually by the teachers and to have *"kept in check the potential to become a scary prima donna"'* (Beth). It seemed that singing was not really about that after all.

So what has resulted form these bold experiments in singing and change? The level of personal reconstrual was evident in many comments. We might simply listen as these voices, no longer standing at the back and pretending, speak for themselves:

The personal confidence has been wonderful. I relate quite differently to people now, more relaxed, more myself. And I go to concerts now and I'm quite opinionated - I can have an opinion now, I'm a singer! (Beth)

I'm much less self-judgemental. I think 'blow it, I'll have a go!'. It's helped me let go and have a social, fun side. (Eva)

Singing has given me confidence to find my voice in other arenas. Speaking to people, raising things with people, speaking up on issues, saying what I think and feel. Less afraid of my own power and strength. (Debbie)

It got to that part of me to do with emotions, feelings beyond words, but you don't need to find words to express it all. It's access to a new self, enriching, life-enhancing, a new beginning. (Polly)

To be honest I think I was quite lost for years. Singing has been the key for me. I found myself. I heard myself. And to my amazement I liked myself. (Tess)

I have always thought of myself as a rather boring person, a bit dull, but that's changed a good deal. Learning to sing at my age makes me wonder what else I can do. I might try stuff I've shied away from. Finding I'm not tone deaf has led me to question other aspects of myself. I wasn't tone deaf after all. I'm a singer, with the gift of music. My life story has changed. (Alan)

My warmest thanks to all the singers who shared their stories with me, to Lynda Jessopp who developed my ideas about the cultural aspects of the construction of singing, and to Jenny Goodman who helped me find my own singing voice.

References

Armstrong, F. (1985). Finding our voices. In: N. Jackowska (Ed). *Voices from arts for labour.* Pluto Press/Arts for Labour.

Gergen K. J. & Gergen, M. M. (1986). Narrative form and the construction of psychological science: In T. Sarbin (Ed). *Narrative Psychology: The storied nature of human conduct.* NY: Praeger

Kelly, G. (1955/1991). *The psychology of personal constructs*, vols 1 &2, 2nd printing: London: Routledge

Kotmann, P. A. (2000). Introduction to *Cavarero, A. (1997). Relating narratives.* London: Routledge.

Lewis, H. B. (1989). Some thoughts on the moral emotions of shame and guilt. In: L. Cirillo, B. Kaplan, & S. Wapner (Eds). *Emotions in ideal human development,* Lawrence Erlbaum.

McCoy M. M. (1977). A reconstruction of emotion. In Bannister, D., (ed), *New perspectives in personal construct theory.* London: Academic Press.

Newman, F., Holzman, L. (1997). *The end of knowing, a new developmental way of learning.* London: Routledge.

Salmon, P. (1970). A psychology of personal growth. In: D. Bannister (Ed.). *Perspectives in personal construct theory.* London: Academic Press. pp. 197-221.

Welch, G.F., Adams, P. (2003). *How is music learning celebrated and developed?* British Educational Research Association.

DANCING

Construing through body: The dancing experience

Sabrina Cipolletta

It may be useful for psychologists, therapists, teachers or anybody else working with learning and change – knowledge in general – to investigate how art experiences, like dance, can be used in their working fields. People often say that they practice dance or other body experiences as a therapy, but usually they cannot explain the reason why. Some people say that dance is simply therapeutic in itself: if you dance you feel fine. Some other people claim that dance therapy produces a bodily change, and this in turn determines a mental change. The first case may be seen as an example of common sense explanation, which is not able to explain the difference between dance and dance therapy. The second answer is the expression of a dualistic point of view: mind and body are two different substances and each one can interact with the other. The category-mistake pointed out by Ryle (1949) can be detected in this point of view: if mind and body are two different logical categories, it is not possible to say that one determines the other, in the same way as it is not possible to say that "He came back home in tears and stretcher", as an English joke goes.

I shall here analyze dance through the framework of constructivist psychology, in an attempt to surpass the questions I mentioned above.

Construing through the body

Constructivism dissolves the historical dichotomy between subject and object, mind and body, realism and idealism, putting meaning and experience as superordinate notions to the old ontological mind-body issue (Varela, Thompson, Rosch, 1991). Mind and body simply become distinctions made by an observer of a unique reality (monism). The emphasis is therefore placed on the observer as an active construer of meanings.

When we consider the construing process, we do not refer to experiences about which we may speak or think privately. The construing process can be usefully applied to processes traditionally regarded as physiological. The 'butterflies in the stomach' one feels when one meets the person he or she fancies is a good example of a construct described in physical terms, but it represents neither a physical event nor a mental one–or we could better say that it represents them both. This feeling is actually an anticipation, a form of knowledge. Knowledge is action, as Maturana and Varela (1980) claim. Anticipations, on which our construct systems flow, are neither physical nor mental but can be construed in both ways, because each change in one of the knowledge domains, co-emerges (although not in relation) with a change in the other (Maturana, Varela, 1980, 1985).

Emotions are a good example of this notion. Kelly's definition of transition as the awareness of movement within one's own system of constructs goes beyond the traditional debate concerning whether emotions originate in the body to be then transposed in the mind, or the cognition comes before the resulting physiological changes. Kelly's framework reads emotion as a process which involves the entire person. As some linguistic expressions seem to point out (e.g. 'pale with fear', 'red in the face' or 'green with envy'), we live much more unitarily than how we think, and even than how we talk (Binswanger, 1955).

Therefore bodyhood, interaction and conversations can be considered as complementary: just as what one recognizes as emotions in everyday life are dispositions of the body to the action (Maturana, 1988), in the same way language is construed through conversations made up by gestures and actions. This fact is inseparable from the corporeal being: changes in the body involve changes in the conversation and vice versa (Kenny, Gardner, 1988). One's way of appearing, of dressing, for example, varies in relation to the other people and their response. Namely, one will act in a different way in front of a 'big and strong man' than how he or she would in front of a 'frail and humble woman' (Burr, 1995). The same can be said about the opposite situation: a change in one's way of feeling will imply a change in one's way of appearing. How many such personal and professional examples can we think of? Let us think about the changes we observe in our patients, or in our everyday life. One such example may be pregnancy. What is the best way to define it? Should one define it in terms of hormonal changes, or should one describe the growing of the womb? But how much more complex is the chain of transformation which takes place in the woman's body?

For this reason Kelly (1955) speaks about 'anticipation' in terms of 'postures': it is not a meditation on something, but a way of placing oneself in relation to it, a 'form of movement' in a situation. The action/construction is then indissolubly connected to the 'scene' in which it takes place, as Goffmann (1959) too proposes in his dramaturgic approach.

Instead of speaking about 'body' and 'mind', we may then focus on the 'self in relation' and we can examine the meaning of our physical experiences or ask ourselves what kind of development in anticipation or meaning can be brought by an experience we usually label as physical. In other words, body experiences become part of our professional reflection and action, perhaps breaking through in the therapeutic setting and in the world of consultancy and training, and changing them. We can start thinking how to use them in such contexts.

Why dance?

In trying to find an answer to this question, I take into account the question Bateson (1972) imagines his daughter asks him in the conversations of the 'Metalogues' which open his book 'Toward an ecology of mind':

D: *Dad?*
F: *Yes?*
D: *Would it be a good thing if people gave up on words and began to use gestures only once again?*
F: *Umm... I don't know. Of course in that way, it would be impossible to have a conversation. We could only bark and miaow, and laugh and groan and cry. But it might be fun... life would be like a kind of dance ... where the dancers make their own music.*

In the answer given by the father, that aspect of dance which is of interest to us is underlined. Dance is usually identified with technique and we imagine that without technique, there would be no dance. Here, rather, dance is considered as a human action that has movement at its centre, movement free from impersonal a priori codes. This distinguishes it from ballet, for example.

I refer to that form of dance which, since the beginning of last century, has developed as a reaction to the 'muscularism' and the abstractness of the late 19th century dance, as a return to 'natural' movements, thanks particularly to Isadora Duncan and without any doubt under the influence of Delsarte's teaching, who referred to life directly to find the meaning of each gesture (Casini Ropa, 1990).

Other fundamental references are Jacques-Dalcroze who, with his research on rhythmical movement, has established a practice whose aim is to reach balance (eurhythmy) and go beyond the arrhythmia (imbalance/disharmony) which characterizes many of our habitual gestures, and Rudolf Laban, who concentrated on the body in his meticulous study of movement. Progressively, dance has loosened the knot which tied it to music, as Cunningham's works show, and has come to configure itself more and more as "the poetry of bodily actions in space" (Laban, 1960, p. 21). I consider it here then as "the art that stems from life itself, for it is but the action of the whole of the human body; in other words it is an action transposed in a world, in a sort of *space-time* which is not the same as that of practical life." (Valéry, 1957, p. 68)

This last aspect, which outlines dance as metaphor, configures dance as a form of play as that suggested by Bateson (1972): play may occur only if the participant organisms are able in some way to meta-communicate, namely to exchange signals which carry the message: 'This is a play'.

In the metalogue 'Of Games and Seriousness'[19] it is pointed out how in the 'mess' which can occur in a play setting there is actually a great seriousness, generated by the choice done by each participant to comply with the fundamental rule of play: one has to play 'as if' it were a serious thing. The moment one discloses that it is a play, he or she would end the play itself. A condition for the play to continue is therefore its being taken seriously by the participants, though the 'things' occurring during the play are not serious. Bateson (1972) deals in this way with the conversations he imagines to have with his daughter. We may deal in the same way with our considerations so far, for, as Rovatti (2000) underlines, that is life: in some way it is not possible to go out of the 'fiction' of our construction of possible worlds.

Actually, as Gadamer (1960) points out, it is not possible to leave the play just as it is not possible to leave the 'hermeneutic circle' of our reciprocal understanding: for play to be, one has to plunge completely in it. "The players are not the subject of the play, but it is the play that is produced through the players" (p. 133). We may therefore say that "each player is a played subject" (Gadamer, 1960, p. 137), in the sense that, as with dance, there are no external aims or purposes for the movement which constitutes the play itself. Moreover, from the metaphoric use of the term, which Gadamer (1960) finds in some expressions, as for example 'the play of lights', comes the "idea of a movement of coming and going which is not bound to a precise purpose in which it may find its end. This is connected also to the original meaning of play as dance" (p. 134). Again: "It is exactly during the play that the movement is not only without intention and purpose, but also free from every effort. It goes as if by itself" (p. 136).

This image of play is consistent with what has been said about knowledge as action, and it may suggest that dance too can be used as a means to reactivate movement, therefore fostering change and creativity. I will try to explain how this can occur.

Dimensions of dancing

As a starting point, I will use my experience with two groups, a dance-therapy group and a dance training class. I shall examine these dancing experiences in terms of the dimensions of movement individuated by Laban (1960) and the main scholars of psychomotor studies (Aucouturier, Derrault and Empinet, 1984; Frostig and Maslow, 1978, Lapierrre and Aucouturier,

---

[19] Here is a significant passage:
Daughter. Dad, are these conversations serious?
Father. Of corse they are
D. Are they not a sort of game you play with me?
F. Heavens forbid... they are however a sort of game we play together.
D. Then they are not serious!

1974, Russo, 1986). Then I shall try to translate these dimensions into the terms of Kelly's personal construct psychology. The two theoretical systems refer to different fields, but share the assumption of the bipolar nature of constructs (it is not by chance that Lapierre and Aucouturier speak of 'contrasts') and of an existence not subject to the distinction between mental and physical. Integrating these approaches allows me to describe and read in professional terms some personal experiences within a group.

Space

The spatial experience may be considered starting from the distinction between *inside* and *outside*, which represents one of the fundamental contrasts on which we base the important distinction me or not-me. In this we also find the recognition of the limits which denote internal and external space. The first is derived from an experience of our body as a container and on this we build our corporeal scheme, understood as the three-dimensional image which everyone has of him/herself (Schilder, 1950).

From this point of view we can observe the extension of movement and of the body on the basis of the contrast *large-small*, the postures into which one is organised, movement to one side (left-right), the level (high-low), the use of single parts or of the whole body and that aspect of co-ordination regarding spatial organisation of movement. We may therefore try to read these dimensions in terms of self in relation.

The dimension *inside-outside* can be read in terms of *permeability* of the group: the more this construct is permeable, the easier it will be for the person to include new elements, such as a video-camera, a leader, him/herself; the more the system is impermeable, the easier it will be for these elements to remain outside.

All that has been said with reference to an individual can be applied to the group.

The space of the group is defined by the initial 'ritual' of removing shoes and sitting in a circle, as indicated by the facilitator in the first meeting. The two groups to which I refer already show a difference: whereas the first accept the invitation, in the second, positions are less defined. Only three of the nine people present at the first meeting take off their shoes and two remain seated on the chairs outside the circle. We can read this difference in terms of the different definitions of context, which characterise the two groups. Whereas the first is characterised by free participation in the activity proposed by the association, the second is inserted in a course attended by people who are not necessarily being informed of the proposed activities. Those in the second group who choose to remain outside, continue simultaneously to maintain a position inside because they continue to be present in the construction shared by the participants of the group. In fact these people define their position 'leaving early' rather than simply 'not being present'. Vacillating between in and out, the group identity is maintained, dividing the group dimension into two levels: on the one hand, participation in the activity, where some people are 'outside'; and on the other hand, belonging to the group, where everyone is 'inside'.

Another way to define position in the group could be found in bodyforms, described in terms of *open-closed, large-small* which we have often found together. To illustrate both poles of each, I will present the examples of Lilli and of Claudio, two participants in the second group. Lilli is a smiling young woman with a diagnosis of spina bifida and hydrocephalus who can only walk with support and still has an unstable walk. Claudio is a robust boy who participates in Lilli's group because of 'problems in relating'. Closed and introverted, if Claudio can avoid speaking he will; and if he does speak, he hesitates.

When requested to introduce oneself with a movement, Lilli responds with a rotation of her head and her bust stretching forward and looking out, whereas Claudio responds with a small contraction of the shoulder. In general, Lilli's movements are large and open like a circle with stretched arms. Claudio's movements are small and contracted, as when he responds to the request to lie down in a comfortable position by keeping his head raised and closing his shoulders with his arms stuck close to the sides of his body.

We can read in Lilli's movements an openness in relation which we can translate in terms of an enlargement of the perceptive field (*dilation*), with the aim of reorganising it on an upper level which includes also many elements external to herself and belonging to the group. This becomes an availability to others, which puts her in a position of protectiveness towards those she perceives as being needier, and in a position of readiness to meet the requests of others, which can sometimes mean almost unbearable efforts. This availability, at times, we might read as a hostile attempt to establish a role as helper, which has been invalidated by a series of experiences that have shown her that she cannot be of help to others as she would like. If, on the other hand, she renounced this role she would meet a sense of guilt hard to sustain because of her lack of an alternative role.

Claudio's closeness, on the other hand, seems like an expression of *constriction,* which works to eliminate the incompatibility he perceives in the elements which are present in his perceptive field; given thathis role constructs appear impermeable, they do not admit new elements. Indeed this is how the group map outlined by him appears to an observer: isolated shapes without any particular relationship between them (Fig. 1).

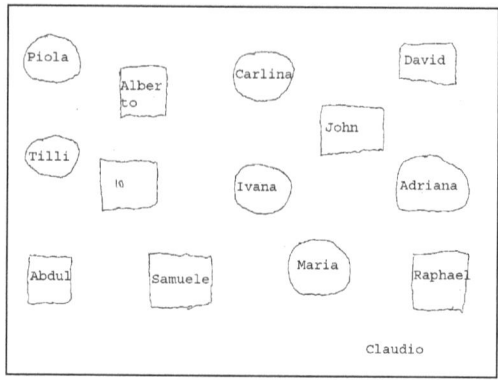

Fig. 1: Claudio's group map

But what is Claudio protecting himself from in this way? What does he think might happen if he considered the new data which experience offers him in relationships? Let's hypothesise that he might discover that he is more adequate than he always believed. This may be too large a revolution and probably unsustainable in his significant relationships!

We can see another contrast on this dimension, *near-far*, as an attempt to shorten distance in order to keep the relationship when it exists in terms of dependency. The same attempt can be observed on another dimension: time.

Time

In time, indeed, it is possible to find the characteristic urgency typical of dependency constructs, which express the attempt to reduce succession to simultaneity, to shorten the duration, to eliminate the delaying between desire and its satisfaction according to the characteristics of a 'concrete thought' (Piaget, 1937).

I observed in the group the attempt to be uniform, to seek *commonality* rather than *sociality*, in Kelly's terms. For example, this is noticeable when to the proposal of walking together towards the centre of the circle and returning, as long as the speed is constant or steps are counted in ascending or descending order from one to four, agreement is maintained because everyone does the same thing. When each one of them has to lead, the agreement is broken: the rule neither precedes nor defines the action but it must be negotiated *in action*. This requires welcoming into one's own temporal horizon that of another, to understand his/her request in order to respond. Some remain perplexed, stopping and looking about; others 'flee forward', accelerating the pace and leaving the others behind.

It seems that we can see in the two solutions two different ways of moving through the action cycle: on the one hand stopping at length in the phase of circumspection without making any decision or passing into control; on the other hand a drastic shortening of the first phase to pass into action. This is what Kelly calls *impulsiveness*.

The best example of this may be represented by the case of a participant in the second group: Alberto. We can read Alberto's fast movements in this way; his rapid switching from one action to another does not leave space for reflection. He verbalises this himself in the fourth meeting when, speaking about decision-making, he says that he is fast in this: 'I leap before I look,' he says.

Flow

Every process of artistic creation is built, on the one hand, on moments of improvisation and, on the other hand, on the carrying out and repeating of sequences. The first favours the extension of a construct system and allows the emergence of submerged constructs. The second favours the definition of existing constructs through their validation. We can therefore relate these two practices to the process of *loosening-tightening* which form the cycle of creativity. Whereas the flow of free movement fosters loosening (it is not by chance that this is recognised as a relaxed, mobile, dreamy aspect), controlled movement fosters tightening and brings about a vigilant, controlled and stable aspect.

In fixating on only one of these modalities, we can recognise what we regard as disorder, an interruption of the movement. So it is particularly important to observe how the passage from a phase of loosening to a phase of tightening in the movement of a person is made in order to understand his/her construct system.

Perhaps the dimension in which this is most evident is flow.

The person in the second group who distinguished herself for flexibility was Ivana (Fig.2). Hers can be read as an attempt not to choose a clear direction in relation (*loosening*). This locates her 'out of reach'. In her case, this could be a way of avoiding 'contact'. Closeness evokes repeated experience of mistreatment, which she cannot define in a precise way to avoid close relationships with the most significant people for her. In fact, were she to tighten her definition of her parents, she would probably construe them as 'bad'. And that for her is intolerable. She prefers to live in an imprecise relational world, which is nebulous, but which allows her to avoid the consequences of validation.

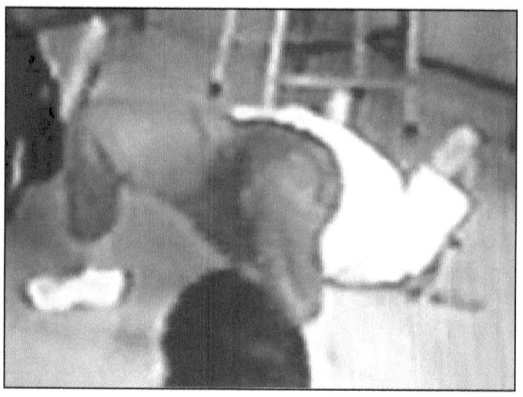

Fig. 2: Ivana's fluid movement

On the other hand let us look once more at the example of Claudio: his rigid, contracted geometrical movements (Fig.3) can be read as the process of *tightening* leading him to an anticipation so precise as to constrain him to immobility. The links between his constructs are so tight and defined that the result is one big, simple and rigid monolith, moving through the world, is the result. On the other hand it may be the only possible solution to maintain stability and not to fall apart.

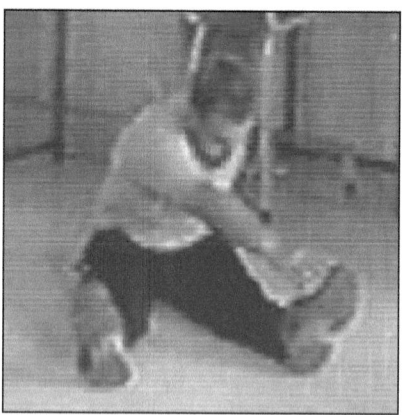

Fig. 3: Claudio's contracted movement

Speaking of stability, let's enter another dimension - weight.

Weight

Movement does not happen in a void: it always begins from something, and above all it moves toward something. We can read it in terms of push and pull. So to jump or to stand on our toes, we must call on an 'effort" from inside or a force which pulls us from outside. Otherwise we could consider it part of a larger system which organises itself. Therefore, much less effort is needed if we simply push on the ground, leaving our weight on it. It will be the same ground to push against us and allow us to go up.

Think of the importance which this could have for the maintenance of equilibrium. Often we try to reach it in the opposite way, calling on our willpower and forcing ourselves.

It is possible to distinguish between different combinations of giving and receiving weight. From strong to weak, from tense to relaxed; passing through the different phases of simple contact, in which weight is still entirely on itself, in the complete abandon in which you give to or receive from the other completely.

Let us look at the case of Ines (participant in the first group), a sweet and pretty girl who seems to be walking on eggshells. She evokes the sensation of fragility and precariousness, just as her figure is fragile and her equilibrium is precarious. She uses grace to conquer you in a way that is sometimes seductive, and then entrusts herself entirely to you in order to stand and to exclude all others from the privileged relationship which she tries to establish: you are only her support, nothing else. How can she be helped to get out of this construct which, while guaranteeing her survival, condemns her to permanent childhood?

Maybe one way would be to allow her to experience different forms of support: I can give my weight to another in different ways, just as the other can be viewed in different ways (a solid rock, moving sands or a running torrent), I can discover that I can use other things as support, for example the ground. The ground is our main support if we do not place ourselves in relation to it on causal terms, as Ines does. She forces herself to stand, placing herself against the ground as if it were a battle. But if we listen we can receive the stability which comes to us from being in accord with it. In this way, perhaps, it will be possible to stand in relation to others on different terms considering them as people and reconstruing their point of view, thus entering a role relation. In therapy, you can help a person to have this experience through small experiments which allow alternatives to be created and validated.

...Toward an end

We can summarise the analysis of movement conducted so far referring to Laban's synthesis (1960) of the motion factors with reference to the four

fundamental questions which defines an action (where, when, how and what). These four questions refer to four main human faculties:
- *attention*, which aims at finding one's way and a relation with an object in either a direct and instinctive or a cautious and flexible way, and can therefore refer to a spatial factor;
- *decision*, which can either be taken "unexpectedly and suddenly, letting one thing go and replacing it with another in a precise moment," or gradually "keeping some of the previous conditions for a certain time" (Laban, 1960, p. 114); it is therefore associated with a temporal dimension;
- *precision*: by which one can control and constrain the progression of the action or let it flow freely, and which refers to the flow of the action;
- *intuition*: the desire to do a determinate thing, holding firmly and with determination, or lightly and gently, which refers to weight.

From the combination of the two contrasting poles that can be identified in each of these dimensions, the following table may be drawn:

FACTOR	CONCERNED WITH	FACULTY	CONTRAST
SPACE	where	attention	*flexible linear*
TIME	when	decision	*extension abbreviation*
FLOW	how	precision	*release restraint*
WEIGHT	what	intention	*relaxed energetic*

I tried to interpret these dimensions according to personal construct psychology, as synthesized in the following table. It does not take into account the other professional dimensions which I introduced to read each action (corresponding to the previous faculties) as it is a complex action.

DIMENSION OF MOVEMENT	PROFESSIONAL CONSTRUCT
space	*dilation-constriction*
time	*circumspection-impulsiveness*
flow	*loosening-tightening*
weight	*dispersed - undispersed dependency*

I am aware that such a schematisation is reductive, for it leaves out of its perceptive field a set of elements which are necessarily part of the understanding of a complex phenomenon. Nonetheless, I will illustrate its inner coherence–with reference to Kelly's personal construct theory, from which the professional constructs I used derive–and outer coherence, which refers to Laban's movement scheme of the constitutive elements.

Space refers to a construct dimension in which the narrowing or the widening of the perceptual field aims at including or excluding new elements. Time is applied to the CPC cycle, circumspection-preemption-control, which controls the decision: at one end there is the extension of the circumspection phase, which leads to consider different possibilities and to procrastinate the decision; on the other end there is the shortening of this phase and the immediate leap to action, defined with the term 'impulsiveness'. Flow refers to one aspect which characterises the precision of a construct: from one end of extreme vagueness, typical of relaxation, in which the construct is applicable to all the elements, one comes to the much more binding end of tightness. Finally I translated the last dimension, weight, in terms of dependence: I realized that in all the cases of insufficiently distributed dependence, one can find a particular energy and tension if the dependence is focused on oneself, and relaxation and abandon if the dependence is focused on someone else. Balance and coordination with the others and with the ground–elements which define the body's harmony with space – are attainable through a more highly distributed dependence.

This is an attempt to give voice to questions regarding the meaning of body experiences without giving up theoretical rigour or awareness of the assumptions from which I work. It therefore regards people as immersed in a social process which implies, in terms of anticipation, the maintenance of their identity, observing how these experiences may easily bring about change in both phenomenological domains: mental and physical.

Furthermore, as Gadamer says (1960), 'play' means 'to be played': in these experiences my clients and I were playing the same game/play, that is the dance we joined in. I believe that these embodied experiences enriched me as much as them. We were all plunged into one creative cycle, and I believe that this allowed all of us to explore new directions of movement and to develop alternative personal and professional paths.

References

Aucouturier, B., Derrault, I., Empinet, Y.L. (1984). *La pratique psychomotrice. Rééducation et therapie*. Paris: Doin.
Bateson, G. (1972). *Steps to an ecology of mind*. New York: Ballantine.
Binswanger, L. (1955). *Ausgewählte Vorträge und Aufsätze*. Bern: A. Francke AG Verlag.
Button, E. (1988). Music and personal contructs. In: F. Fransella & L. Thomas (eds.). *Experiencing with personal constructs psychology*. London: Routledge & Kagan.
Casini Ropa, E. (ed.) (1990). *Alle origini della danza moderna*. Bologna: Il Mulino.

Frostig, M., Maslow P., (1978). *Educazione motoria: teoria e pratica.* Torino: Editrice Omega.
Gadamer, H. G. (1960). *Wahrheit und Methode.* Tübingen: J.C.B. Mohr.
Goffmann, E. (1959). *Presentation of self in everyday life.* New York: Doubleday.
Kelly, G. A. (1955). *The psychology of personal constructs.* vol. 1-2. New York: Norton.
Kenny, V., Gardner, G. (1988). Constructions of self-organising systems. *The Irish Journal of Psychology*, 9, pp.1-24.
Laban, R. (1960). *The mastery of movement.* London: McDonald & Evans.
Lapierre, A., Aucouturier, B. (1974). *Les contrastes et la decouverte des notions fondamentales.* Paris: Doin Editeurs.
Lapierre, A., Aucouturier, B. (1975). *La symbolique du mouvement.* Paris: EPI.
Maturana, H. (1988). Reality: the search for objectivity or the quest for a compelling argument. *The Irish Journal of Psychology*, 9, pp. 25-82.
Maturana, H., Varala, F. (1980). *Autopoiesis and cognition: the realization of the living.* Boston: New Science Library.
Maturana, H., Varala, F. (1985). *The tree of knowledge.* Boston: New Science Library.
Piaget J. (1937). *La costruction du réel chez l'enfant.* Neuchatel: Delachaux et Niestlé.
Ryle, G. (1949). *The concept of mind.* London: Hutchinson.
Valery, P. (1957) Philosophie de la danse. Paris : Editions Gallimard.
Varela, F., Thompson, E., Rosch, E. (1991). *The embodied mind: cognitive science and human experience.* Cambridge: The MIT Press.

Music and mirrors: Dance as a construction of self

Sara K. Bridges

When Jörn and Kenneth approached me to write a chapter on dance and personal construct theory, I was very interested. Kenneth and I had been talking about our shared love for theatre for many years and we always said that we should "do something" with the combination of art and PCT. I was very pleased that he and Jörn had had similar conversations and had put together a truly impressive list of contributors who had interests and expertise in both PCT and the arts. Kenneth suggested that I write about dance and constructivism, not necessarily from a theoretical or dance therapy perspective, but instead write from my personal experience of being both a constructivist theorist and a dancer. This seemed to make a lot of sense to me and I eagerly looked forward to putting a presentation together for the International Congress on Personal Construct Psychology conference and to writing this chapter. Yet, quickly this initial eagerness turned to hesitation, then to anxiety and trepidation, and finally to dread and denial. Writing or presenting about my theoretical orientation or my approach to therapy is relatively simple – the difficulty came instead from the process of 'coming out' as a dancer to my PCT friends and colleagues (or to anyone else). In the multiplicity of selves or roles inhabited within my life, dance has existed as a way of meaning making and a way of internally defining myself. To move this internal definition to a public domain required exposing my self imposed title ('a dancer') to the scrutiny of others and to the possible invalidation of a core construct. Yet, the question that arose for me was: "Who truly gets to decide how we internally define ourselves?" The following chapter describes my experience of preparing the presentation for the conference and of writing this chapter. I will cover my history of dance, the threat experienced when openly calling myself a dancer, the aggressive approach I adopted in coping with the threat (from a Kellian sense) and how, in the end, dance and constructivism are both aspects of the multiplicity of selves or roles co-habitating within my personal construct system. Furthermore, throughout this chapter I will examine the many different roles we inhabit on a daily basis and how these roles influence our internal sense of self.

Personal story

I started dancing when I was 7 years old and I thought I would dance forever. I took lessons in an old mansion that had been converted into a school of dance – the ballroom was the largest studio, with the smaller rooms upstairs and down (including a beautiful solarium) turned into the studios for the more beginning students. All of the rooms had wooden floors, ballet barres on the walls and at least two walls filled floor to ceiling with mirrors. All the floors and stairs squeaked and the lighting was bright in the studios and dim everywhere else. Some of the rooms had record players or reel to reel tape players that could be adjusted for the speed of the class, however the ballroom dance studio (Studio 1) had an actual piano and a small grey haired woman who would play for the classes. I loved the structure and movement of the classes, the sound of the music filling the old house as I sat on the floor doing my homework between classes, and the thrill of a muttered "good" from my teachers. Dancing helped me to focus; the count of the music, the exact position of my arms, hands, legs, feet and head, and the complex dance combinations removed all other thoughts from my head, at least for the two hour class.

As I improved, the teachers moved me up to harder classes and to larger studios. Dancing in Studio 1 meant that you were good – good enough to have captured the attention of the teachers and perhaps even good enough to "do something" professionally in dance. I was dancing in Studio 1 the first time my knee gave out. I was 16 years old. I kept dancing but I knew something was wrong. I started wrapping my knee, using ice and taking lots of ibuprophen. I went to physical therapy, used electrodes to help strengthen my muscles and eventually had two knee operations. To this day, I wonder if the classes were getting too hard and I used my knee injuries as an excuse to stop dancing. However, I recently checked with my parents and they reminded me of what the doctors had said before my first operation, "You need to stop dancing now if you want to be able to walk when you are 30." So, I stopped dancing. I wondered aimlessly for awhile performing in musicals occasionally and studying theatre. Occasionally I would dance a small bit in a performance and the choreographer, not knowing my background would say something like, "You should really look into dance… you could be pretty good." I know they were trying to be encouraging, however their comments often reminded me of how other people viewed me. To them I "could be a dancer," but in my way of understanding me, I still was.

Who is a dancer?

Recently I started dancing again. I decided to take an 'adult ballet exercise' class after a more than 20 years hiatus (I had taken a class or two in college, but nothing very seriously). At the end of the first class, the instructor suggested that I join the advanced adult classes and I found myself in a 'real' ballet studio again. Of course I am not as involved as I once was, however I enjoy the total focus of the class and the companionship of being with other dancers. By coincidence, Kenneth approached me about a presentation and this chapter when I had been dancing again for about 6 months. As I stated earlier, I was initially quite enthusiastic about the project, yet as I began to formulate my ideas I felt stuck. Was I really a dancer? Did I still have the right to call myself a dancer after being away from a studio for so long? And perhaps the more difficult question, whom or what defines the label of being 'a dancer' or for that matter 'a' anything?

These questions prompted me to start talking with other women in my dance classes. None of us were making a living by being dancers, we all had other occupations and interests, and we all were "past our prime" in dance years. Yet these women were beautiful, skilled dancers who took the classes quite seriously. "So, do you consider yourself to be a dancer?" I asked. Their responses startled me and reinforced my trepidation in revealing my internal construct of 'dancer' to anyone. Some of the responses that stood out the most were:
- "Oh no, it's just something I enjoy doing."
- "No, I have never danced in a company."
- "I'm not good enough to call myself a dancer"
- "I used to be... now I just teach."

Yet the most surprising and troubling response came from an absolutely talented and stunningly beautiful dancer who was a fairly recent Russian immigrant. She told me that only the dancers who were invited to dance in the Bolshoi school when they were small (3 or 4 years old after proving they had natural physical talent), and who actually went to the school to dance 6 hours a day, leaving their families and regular school behind were allowed to call themselves dancers. She had received an invitation, however because her family wanted her to get a quality academic education, growing up she only danced 5 or 6 times a week as a 'hobby.' If she could not or would not call herself a dancer, how on earth could I? In the past I had questioned my ability or skill as a dancer, but never my identity. Now, I questioned both my skill and my identity. I then began to beleaguer my friends, family and students with my questions... What are you and who or what gives you permission to call yourself by that label?

Multiple roles

Every day, in every moment, we inhabit different roles that come replete with their own labels and associated meanings. There are roles we occupy with very clear social and personal definitions of label ownership defined by our genetics (i.e., I am a mother, father, son, daughter, etc.), our relationships (i.e., I am a partner, wife, husband, friend, etc), our occupations (i.e., I am a teacher, carpenter, psychologist, forester, student. etc), and/or our beliefs (i.e., I am a Muslim, Catholic, Christian, Jewish person, etc.). However there are other roles undertaken with less clear messages about label ownership such as our hobbies, avocations, and interest areas (i.e., 'recreational' sports, writing, art, music, etc.). Because our hobbies and avocations are, by definition, peripheral to our activities of daily living, they are rarely included in the external ways we are defined. For example, a man who is an electrician, a father, a devote Catholic, and a weekend piano player would tend to be defined by his occupation, relationships and beliefs rather than by his hobby; playing jazz piano for friends and family. Thus, this man would most likely not be defined as 'a musician' by others, yet this may in fact be one of the ways he internally defines himself.

In talking with others about this chapter, I asked them how they defined themselves ("How do you define yourself? Apart from the obvious [meaning the clearly defined roles] what are you 'a' something."). The responses I received were fascinating to me: A woman who played soccer for over 10 years including being a starting player on her college team for 4 years told me that she used to be a soccer player, but now she was just someone who plays soccer, not a soccer player; a woman who writes creatively and journals regularly said she wasn't "really a writer" but she always wanted to be; and a man who sings in choirs and has sung for friends at weddings said he sings, but wasn't a singer. In each conversation there seemed to be an element of awe or admiration that accompanied the labels they were disavowing; a soccer player, a writer, a singer. Further inquiry revealed that they rejected the coveted labels because they believed these labels would not 'hold up' to the scrutiny of others (e.g., "I am not really a soccer player because I have never been paid to play," "I have never published any of my work, so I am not really a writer" or "I am not a professional singer"). It seemed that it was the act of externally defining themselves as 'a' something that was troubling because they lacked proof or validation for the label.

Obviously, there are many occupations and roles that have clear educational and training requirements that preclude people from simply adopting the title or label (i.e., lawyer, psychologist, doctor, contractor, etc.), yet there are also avocations that cross professional/non-professional delineations (e.g., sports, arts, music, dance, etc.). When the boundaries are blurred, how does one go about deciding whether a label or role fits for them internally and whether or not this translates to an external definition recognized by others? It may be that the threat of invalidation produces a discrepancy between how people define themselves internally and how they define themselves externally. Internally I may define myself as a dancer; however, writing this chapter called into question my right to use the label 'a dancer' as I represented myself to others; a very threatening experience.

Threat and aggression

Threat is the awareness of an imminent comprehensive change in one's core structures" and *"Aggressiveness is the active elaboration of one's perceptual field"* (Kelly, 1955/1991, Vol. 2, p. 7/1991).

In Personal Construct Psychology threat represents the feeling of being on the verge of encountering deep changes within one's core constructs or ways of understanding and making meaning in the world. Aggression, is a response to threat by actively attempting to expand one's reality and the willingness to "risk[s] being wrong in order to set something right" (Kelly, 1969, p. 286). The process of exposing my internal core construct of being 'a dancer' to the danger of invalidation was very threatening. Moreover, my hesitation to reveal my internal construct of being a dancer after learning that so many people I consider to be dancers did not use that label or feel they truly embodied the role of being a dancer, indicated an impending shift in my core constructs.

At first it seemed that I would have to surrender the label of 'dancer' to the opinions and viewpoints of others (i.e., if they do not consider themselves to be dancers, than neither should I). If I have never danced professionally, took a 20+ year hiatus, and probably would deny being a dancer should Mikhail Baryshnikov ask, I saw myself coming to the sad conclusion that I was not truly a dancer. All in all, this would not have necessarily been a horrible event, nor would have inextricably impacted my daily living. Yet, somehow inside there was a small defiant voice that said, "I am a dancer, no matter what you say." This was not a hostile voice refusing to consider that my core construct as a dancer was no longer valid. Instead, this voice represented the part of me that recognized that although I may not meet the external criteria for being a dancer, the feeling of being a dancer simply did not disappear.

With time and reflection, I gradually adopted a position of adaptive aggression. By facing the fact that I might not be a dancer, room was created for alternate definitions of being a dancer and ways to understand the role of dance in my life. Rather than relinquishing the label of being a dancer, I was able to pursue elaboration of dance as a construction and define the personal, internal ways in which dance influences my life and helped me to make sense of my world.

Dance as a construction

An alternative to saying that I am a dancer is to simply say that "I dance." Yet for me, simply saying I dance does not fully capture the role dance plays in my internal processing and how I make sense of my surroundings. Through the combination of art, science and movement dance creates an avenue for understanding self in space, time, and relation. Additionally, dance is clearly a way of focusing and creating room for introspection. Even when I was not dancing in a studio or taking classes, dance was a form of identity for me and a way of orienting to the world. For example, I rarely listen to music without choreographing in my head and it is for this reason that I can not write with classical music playing in the background – I need music with lyrics and it helps if the time structure is somewhat sporadic (currently I am listening to Joni Mitchell's *Blue* for just that reason). Yet, having music helps me to focus when writing, very much like it does in a dance class. Further, where some may feel intimidated or anxious when entering a room with floor to ceiling mirrors, entering a studio with mirrored walls and a wooden floor reduces my anxiety. I know exactly what is expected of me in this space; concentrate, listen, watch, work hard, and focus.

Although at this point I fear misrepresenting myself, being a dancer is one of my first and seemingly most resilient constructs. Dance is one of the predominant lenses I use for understanding how I interact within my environment and it is where I turn in times of joy, frustration, anxiety, sadness or when I simply am feeling unsettled in the world. For me, dance is a hidden superordinate construct; a silent construct whose existence has been so ingrained that its overarching impact had been obscured prior to writing this chapter. In my opinion, many of the people I spoke with also have hidden superordinate constructs; soccer player, writer, singer. Those activities are ways of being that are core to their existence, but may not stand up to the critique of others. By negating those parts of the self that internally feel true but externally seem presumptuous, the opinions of others are favored over ones own personal constructions.

Recently I have heard people define themselves as 'a recreational' something (drummer, singer, writer, golfer, etc) or as 'an amateur' something (musician, actor, bird watcher, collector) and I suppose that is one way of representing their fondness for the activity without feeling as though they are misrepresenting themselves or their abilities. Additionally using the term recreational or amateur may help to appropriately situate the role of the activity in the multiple roles inhabited on a regular basis. Yet, although there are some that champion having one main role that supersedes all the others, it is my belief that multiple roles can coexist simultaneously. Perhaps it is my need to 'multitask' as a psychologist, mother, partner, mentor, or friend on a daily basis that helps me to feel comfortable occupying all of these roles without having to prioritize one role over another. Even as I wrote the last sentence I did not feel a need to place the roles in a hierarchical fashion – to me there is no 'right' order of roles and if the need to prioritize one role over the other presents itself, the decision is based on the available information about need and urgency rather than on a preconceived notion of a hierarchical ordering of roles. As a college student with several divergent interests and activities, my father would often ask me, "What are you?" This question was his way of indicating that I should prioritize my education over my friends, work, volunteering, etc. I always knew the correct answer was 'a student' (without rolling my eyes), yet I still felt the pull of the other roles in my life. To this day I feel pulled by the many roles I play; however, there does seem to be more room for engaging in multiple roles throughout many moments of the day. The role of being a dancer is one of these multiple roles – it may be a background voice or construct, but it is a constant and foundational component of my meaning making.

Conclusion

For many, there are obvious roles inhabited on a regular, if not constant, basis. Often these roles come with clear external validation based on genetics, relationship, education and training, or explicit beliefs. Yet, after writing this chapter and communicating with others, I have come to believe that there are equally important roles that are concealed because of the absence of external validation. These roles are equally important for meaning making processes, but remain hidden because their disclosure invites the threatening possibility of invalidation. Additionally, there are some who have received education and training that permits them to officially use a label or occupy a role, but are hesitant to reveal it because they are either not working or work in a different field (e.g., an attorney who is working as a teacher, a psychologist who is working in administration, etc.). Once again, it is the risk of invalidation from others or perhaps the fear of misrepresentation that inhibits disclosure. Yet the covert nature of the role does little to remove the personal importance of the construct for an individual's meaning making processes.

Clearly I am not saying that it is necessary to reveal hidden superordinate constructs to the scrutiny of others in order to make them more tangible – quite the contrary. Writing this chapter and giving the presentation in Columbus helped me to recognize the importance and existence of being 'a dancer' as a superordinate personal construct for me. Further, after much deliberation I concluded that I do not need external validation for this construct to exist in my meaning making processes. Thus, it would seem that for many, having constructs that are protected from the opinions of others does not mean that they are any less true or integral in their daily lives. Claiming the role of soccer play, writer, singer or dancer as constructs or ways of making meaning can be an internal process, independent of the validation so readily available for other roles. By writing this chapter, I have elaborated the role of being a dancer and have come to the conclusion that this role is more than what I do, and even without obvious external validation, dance truly is a construction of my self.

References

Kelly, G. A. (1991). *The psychology of personal constructs: Vol. 2 . Clinical diagnosis and psychotherapy*. London: Routledge. (Original work published 1955)

Kelly, G. A. (1969). The threat of aggression. In B. Maher (Ed.). *Clinical psychology and personality: The selected papers of George Kelly* (pp. 281-288). New York: John Wiley.

ACTING

Construing characters and casts: Personal constructs on the stage and in the dressing room

Kenneth W. Sewell

Over the past decade, I have combined my professional work in the field of psychology (as a clinician and researcher operating from a constructivist perspective) with a personal passion for the stage (as a patron, frequent actor, and occasional director). Throughout these coincidental aspects of my life, I have found constructivist psychology and theatrical experience to be mutually informing. On the theatrical side, this reciprocal utility has been most apparent in how constructivist psychological knowledge enhances the tasks involved in character development and on-stage interactional listening. From the perspective of my work as a psychologist, role-portrayal and on-stage focusing skills offer immense carry-over into the role of psychotherapist—both the committed enactment of that role with diverse clientele, as well as the focus required to stay present in the stage-space of the therapy room. Only rarely (e.g., Sewell, 1998) have I attempted to formalize the combination of these parallel paths via scholarly writing on the subject. This chapter will venture into such scholarly analysis by offering a conceptualization of experiential and relational aspects of stage acting from the perspective of Personal Construct Psychology (PCP; Kelly, 1955).

Terminology

Although many readers may be familiar with basic concepts and terminology used within PCP, readers not already familiar with PCP might benefit from explication of such terms. The following is an overview of important concepts that will be referenced throughout the subsequent PCP analysis of stage acting. In explaining these concepts, I will generally avoid using theatrical examples simply because the remainder of the chapter is devoted to placing these concepts into the theatrical world.

Commonality and individuality. When two individuals use similar dimensions of understanding and anticipation to construe an experience (be it an experience in the past, present, or future), we can consider these persons to be psychologically similar. Having a common psychological perspective (herein called *commonality*), even if in a circumscribed range of experience, provides a basic building block for communication, affection, and social interaction (considered below). By the same token, when two persons use different dimensions to understand an experience, they are psychologically different (*individuality*)—a state that has implications for how they might then interact.

Sociality. Human social interplay requires more than coordinated activity or even commonality. To be involved in social interaction, a person must begin to construe (however imprecisely) the psychological realities of another person. Only when this mind-reading is attempted can people engage in the fearsome process of having human relationships.

Experience Cycle. Human beings (at least the ones who are alive) rarely wait for environmental cues to begin exercising their psychological muscles. Instead, anticipation is critical to how people experience any phenomenon. Thus, all of human psychological experience can be seen as proceeding through successive and interlacing cycles of anticipation (What is coming next?), investment (How much do I care?), encounter (What is happening?), validation/invalidation (Did I get what I expected?), and change (Now that I see what happened, should I hold on to the theory that led to that anticipation or should I revise it?). This *experience cycle* can be identified in moment-to-moment experiences, such as your anticipations of what words will ensue during the course of reading this sentence. Experience cycles also span great durations; for example, a person might spend several decades building a theory (coordinated set of anticipations) about what life will be like as a retired person, and another few decades encountering retirement and evaluating the anticipations.

Fragmentation and suspension. Humans are not computers. Computers have a hard time making 2 plus 1 equal 3 in some situations, while making 2 plus 1 equal a *ménage a trois* in other contexts. But humans have no trouble with *fragmentation*—or having psychological subsystems that are not necessarily compatible with each other. Likewise, aspects of our psychological realities can be laid aside (*suspended*) when not in use, almost as if they were not a part of our psychological make-up. Consider the committed socialist who happily and seemingly ruthlessly celebrates his victory in a poker game. The enjoyment of taking the resources (chips) of the weaker (unluckier or less-skilled) participants and putting them to use for his own desires is experienced in the virtual absence of his sociopolitical beliefs that all should share equally in the fruits of existence.

Domains of construing. I have argued elsewhere (e.g., Sewell, 2005) that humans simultaneously are construing two related but importantly-different domains: the field of events (happenings in the world) and the field of the social (relationships). I have found this distinction critical in my work with traumatized persons, given the differential implications of severe breaches in these two domains of construing. This distinction offers a parallel application in the realm of stage acting. The event domain is the story to be told via the play in which I am cast. The social domain involves the others in the story with me. For an actor, the social domain has two subdomains. First, relationships *within the play* are those that will be contrived, rehearsed, and ultimately enacted on the stage. Secondly, relationships *within the cast* are those that are developed, elaborated, and enacted in the para-theatrical space (backstage, at the local pub following a rehearsal, etc.).

Applying PCP to stage acting

The Magic of Threes

As a heuristic organizational structure for the remainder of this chapter, I have adopted the oft-chosen triad. Stories have a beginning, a middle, and an end. Events are often explained in terms of before, during, and after. Involvement in a stage play likewise consists of a triad: engagement, rehearsal, and performance.

The Beginning: Engagement

For the present analysis, I have chosen an arbitrary starting point: reading the script with the knowledge of the character to be portrayed. Some earlier point could have been chosen, such as deciding which audition to attend, or the audition process itself. I have intentionally avoided including the audition process here, simply because it contains complexities that would merit a full chapter of its own. Thus, we begin with engagement as a cast member.

The lamplight read-through. Reading a script takes the actor into the world of the play's story (event domain) and into the character's world of relationships (social domain). As a part of anticipating and investing in the actions and characters (cf., the experience cycle), the cast member begins to evaluate the events and characters. What do I (the actor reading the play) like and dislike? Who do I (the actor) like and dislike? The actor begins developing sociality for the character to be portrayed. What is he thinking and feeling? What does *he* like and dislike? Who does *he* like and dislike? What is driving him? The actor continues in the experience cycle by beginning several kinds of anticipations. How I will portray this character? How will other characters be portrayed in relation to my character?

The full-cast read-through. When a cast comes together for a read-through, there already exists a certain degree of commonality based upon the shared commitment to the play. Likewise, there is considerable individuality based upon the differing roles being portrayed and on the differing interpretations the actors have applied to the script during their respective lamplight read-throughs. The full-cast read-through is the first opportunity for these building blocks (commonality and individuality) to begin influencing the various levels of sociality that lie ahead.

In the full-cast read-through, a dynamic hierarchy begins to be established between the stature/status of the actors (in their pre-existing relationships or conceptions of each other) and the 'importance' of the roles being portrayed (e.g., lead, supporting, chorus, cameo, etc.). Consider the following quip which is meant to be a jargonized variant of an oft-quoted saying: "There are no small parts...only small vantage points from which to construe a play and my role in it." As human beings, we are always invested. In a scene from 'Shakespeare in Love', the cast preparing for the original production of 'Romeo and Juliet' were recreating in a pub/brothel following a rehearsal. As was the custom during Shakespeare's time, the cast was all male. The actor who was to portray Juliet's nursemaid, a particularly large and burly man, was seated with an interested young woman on his lap. "So you're in a play..." she remarked, "What's it about?" The large man replied, "You see, there's this nursemaid..."

In addition to initiating the hierarchies amongst cast members, the full-cast read-through also provides the laboratory for experiments (cycles of experience) to begin that are based upon listening. *Listening* in the theatrical sense can be defined as "genuine/real sociality experienced by characters in the artificial life-world of a play." What does it feel like to be spoken to that way? Does the portrayal I had begun to anticipate based upon my previous reading ring true in light of these feelings and relationships? Who do I (the character) like and dislike? Are my (the character's) feelings getting adequate air...and how can I best air them? The evolving results of these experiments inform my anticipation of my character and his roles in relation to these other characters. Ultimately, they inform the range of choices I see as available to me in portraying my character (cf. Kelly's choice corollary).

Other experiments begin that are based upon actor-level sociality. With whom will I have the opportunity to try new things (a kiss, a slap, a cry, or the notorious 'head-up-the-dress' which I did several times with my friend Polly in Christopher Durang's 'Marriage of Bette and Boo')? Who will be fun to go out for drinks with? How can I tolerate that I've had problems with before?

The middle: rehearsal

The sheer intensity and density of the time investment typical of rehearsal processes for a stage play has effects across all constructional domains.

Event domain (story). Living with the story-line with such deep and frequent involvement gives it significance by default. The choice of involvement being now foregone, it is as though I *conclude* that anything on which I spend this much time and effort *must be* important. That conclusion generalizes from my participation in the play per se, to the story itself. I come to care deeply about the story (even if there is an awareness that it is campy, melodramatic, or otherwise divergent from events that would normally evoke such an investment). Along this same line, the overarching anticipations associated with the performances of the play (how successful they will be, how 'good' I will be, how moved the audience will be, etc.) become imbued with great investment (a la the experience cycle). It is during this period of time that the 'fourth wall' is constructed. The fourth wall is the imaginary wall that encloses the space of the play—the 'wall' through which the audience is viewing the play. From the perspective of the actor, constructing the fourth wall (i.e., suspending extra-play construing during the concentrated focus on the story) lends genuineness to action in the stage-space.

Social domain (within the play, between the characters). To live out the interactions as prescribed by the script, the actors must experiment with how characters will relate with each other in meaningful ways. The novelist and screenwriter Larry McMurtry has mentioned in a radio interview how the writing process is so much easier for him in a play than in a novel because so much room is left between the lines...room that must be inhabited and elaborated by the actors. In order to fill that space, the actor must experience the character in a variety of tentative and experimental ways. The enactment is tentative in that it is not crystallized or 'final', but that is not to imply a lack of investment. Thus, in order to do this kind of experimentation, the actor has to risk insanity (i.e., a portrayal that goes beyond what can be experienced by others as disconnected, inappropriate, or just plain *wrong*) in order to adequately explore the extremes of potentialities for the character. This experimentation always takes place as interaction; thus, the tentative portrayals invent and test out a variety of (often extreme) frameworks for experiencing each other (the characters in relation). This kind of risking creates 'drama', which can be seen as a particular kind of extremity of circumstance and interaction.

The role of the body becomes important in this context of dramatic experimentation. The body is the vehicle of emotional communication. We tend to think about verbal communication as somehow divorced from the body, in that we talk to each other in ordinary circumstances with little conscious reflection on the implications of the body in the interaction. However, in order to explore the extreme potentials of a character, even the manner of speech must be 'on the chopping block' and open to revision and replacement. When I do that, I become keenly aware that I use my body to speak...to use it differently (in order to speak differently) I become more aware of my bodily presence. The result is something profoundly intimate and vulnerable. When that is received by the other, the interaction takes on a kind of physical validation that, although often present in ordinary verbal interactions, rarely registers at an overt level. Perhaps the most intense example of this body intimacy in my own experience came during rehearsal of the crucifixion scene in 'Godspell'. In portraying Jesus, this was the first rehearsal during which we 'ran' the scene (as live action, rather than going through the blokking with the director's involvement). Thus, it was my first time to experiment with the expressions of pain and agony that my character was to experience. As my character writhed in pain and wept/sang the words "I'm dying," I (the actor) became aware of one of the other actors in the scene. As a sympathetic witness to the crucifixion, her character was to be expressing grief and horror. Her wails were of an intensity I had not anticipated. Having never been in a show with her before, I recall briefly thinking, "Wow, I didn't know she was that good." When the scene ended and the director broke the action, I quickly became aware that the actor was still weeping. She rushed to me and asked me for a hug. The emotional communication that took place between our characters (and, ultimately, between us as actors) led to an intimacy that persists to this day when we encounter each other.

Social Domain (within the cast, between the actors). The same practicalities that make the fictive story of the play loom large for the actor makes the social context of the cast a predominant feature of the actor's world, however temporary the particular cast might appear to be. In a sense, the cast becomes, of necessity, a majority block in reference to the actor's social sphere during the course of a rehearsal process. In the development of friendship relationships, we intentionally do things to increase commonality; we attend movies together, we elaborate on shared past experiences, we plan common experiences for the future. These common experiences/anticipations yield a sense of identification. As a member of a cast, you and your cast-mates are doing much the same thing (i.e., engaging common experiences) as a matter of course. This way of developing commonality is also seen in other team-oriented endeavors, ranging from the pleasant (playing on the same sports team) to the horrific (fighting in the same combat unit). Regardless of whether chosen or by happenstance, the commonality developed in extreme coordinated activity provides a strong basis for interpersonal identification. Being in a cast together is a prime example.

Fragmentation between various levels of functioning for an actor is almost always present (and is likely necessary). Fragmentation of the 'regular me' versus 'show me' expresses itself in many ways. For example, fragmenting the actor from the character takes on great importance when the character has aspects/actions that are morally objectionable. In order to portray a racist, wife-abusing bigot in 'The Little Foxes', it was imperative for me both to give Oscar's bigotry heart-felt sincerity, and to treat my wife and the black members of the cast with the dignity that I (the actor) know they deserve. Another example involves fragmenting the role of 'star' in a show from the other contexts in life that respond better to an egalitarian stance. Having what is known as a 'diva moment" because the sound technician is not responding to my need to have a better body microphone (a tantrum which might be tolerated or even reinforced as the lead actor) will lead to a very different outcome than the same level of self-important demands with my boss or with my fellow actor in the dressing room. The reverse also demonstrates the point. Having accepted the role of an extra, certain self-deprecatory behaviors are seen as natural in the context of the cast; but carrying them into the workplace or the home would be seen as senselessly masochistic.

Although fragmentation is natural and even healthy between these levels, suspension of one subsystem in favor of another (e.g., suspending the sociality developed in the within-play subsystem once the actors are backstage) is rarely complete. Thus, there can be osmotic carry-over from one subsystem to the other. Bigoted actions on stage can result in subtly hurt feelings between cast members, even though everyone knows that it was scripted and demanded. Love-relationships on stage not-surprisingly evoke love affairs between actors. Certainly, an actor playing a leading role might inadvertently carry the expectations for validation and appreciation that are forthcoming from the cast into a primary relationship that lacks those qualities (which could result in relationship enhancement or even dissolution). Interpersonal dynamics among cast members (pairings, alliances, attributions regarding mistakes, etc.) often mimic the dynamics of the characters portrayed by those actors.

Even emotional reactions of actors can mimic those of the character. In a recent production of '42nd Street', the talented young lady portraying Peggy Sawyer broke down during an intensive dance rehearsal, sobbing and saying, "I just can't do it." Despite the sincerity of the reaction, the actor's tears were mixed with ironic laughter as she became aware that she was doing exactly what Peggy Sawyer does in the middle of Act II.

The End: Performance

It may seem obvious that the putative intent of rehearsal is to place the desired interactions of a play into such a refined habitual enactment that the performances should be exact replications. A statistics professor once gave my class a definition of the scientific term *replication*: the repetition of an experiment exactly as it was done before...*except for at least one crucial difference*. His point was that no one ever does an experiment exactly as it was done before, even when it is called a replication. Instead, researchers inevitably try to correct things perceived as flawed in the previous experiment, and/or make new mistakes in the current one. Actors do the same thing. Thus, performances represent unique points along the path of a stage play, points that evoke discernable experiences across the domains of construction.

Event Domain (within the actions of the play). The audience itself and audience members' reactions become events of the play. Validation and invalidation are communicated in a variety of ways: laughter, applause, quiet, tears, and so on. As validation/invalidation, these items of feedback become part of the actors' and characters' experience cycle, and thus influence what happens on stage.

Social Domain (within the play, between the characters). What seemed so real in the doing (rehearsals) now seems like just so much speculative daydreaming. *Having* the argument (during the actual performance) can evoke new and different construals, feelings, and counter-behaviors that were never expected. This is because the energy of the audience, which provides the dreaded consequences for 'faking it', makes the suspension of the extra-play construction system more pronounced.

Social Domain (within the cast, between the actors). Performances bring a continuation of the isomorphic processes seen during rehearsals, wherein intra- and inter-personal dynamics of the characters come to life in the experiences of the actors. Now that the show is in the performance phase, these processes have the added complexities of the new subjects of sociality: the audience. Now that the audience is *out there*, the actors become aware that they are *back here*; this creates a palpable sacredness to the backstage space. An insider-outsider dichotomy develops wherein validation takes different forms and is given differing weights. A pre-performance 'Good-show!' admonition from a fellow cast member can take on grand importance, as can the withholding of backstage encouragement following a mistake. This dichotomy is often most clearly revealed when it becomes problematic. For example, occasionally, a minor character can 'steal the show' according to the response of the audience. When this occurs, it is as if the audience is reaching into the backstage space and meddling in the *business* of the cast (who had already worked out its interpersonal dynamics on the basis of the basis of the anticipated stars).

The performance process also has a quality of ice on a hot stove—a ride that is being transported by the very vehicle of its own demise. There is a ticking clock in performances (no matter how long the run) such that valued relationships launch into a variety of defensive maneuvers. Romances are established or social lives are otherwise interconnected in ways that are overtly meant to endure beyond the run of the show. Anticipatory grieving and senseless arguments, serve the function of creating distance before it is externally imposed. Likewise, actors commonly exchange token gifts as a way to create transitional objects beyond the duration of the show. The post-production cast party often serves as a ritualized concentration of these processes (laughs, tears, gifts, spats, and all).

The Narrative Arc of Three

In attempting to conceptualize stage acting from a Personal Construct Psychology perspective, I have made many choices that have both guided this chapter and simultaneously closed off potential alternative avenues of consideration. Even the choice to punctuate the experience between engagement, rehearsal, and performance could have been aborted in favor of alternative frameworks. I make no claim to the *correctness* of my choices. However, I do assert that this process of choosing (and thereby both opening and closing off consequential choice possibilities) illustrates the stage actor's task. At every point in the process, choices are made and their implications reverberate. Speak softly, or scream. Say "I love you" sweetly, or add a bit of sarcasm. Stride proudly, or limp. To the extent to that the choices are salient (extreme) and coordinated in honest communication of a story and a set of relationships, effective drama has been achieved. To the extent that the choices I have made in this chapter are salient and coordinated in honest communication of the experience of stage acting, the effort has been worthwhile.

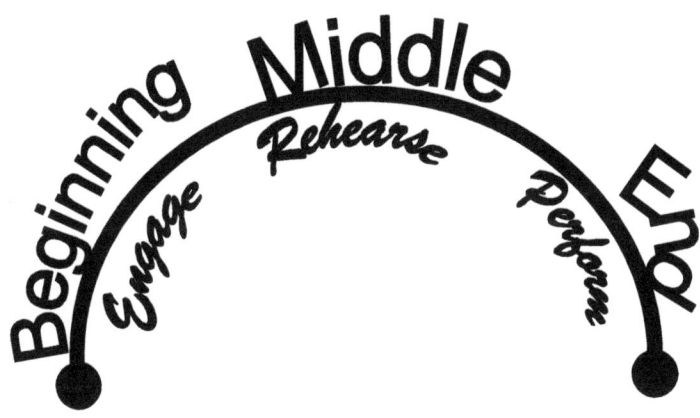

References

Kelly, G. A. (1955). *The psychology of personal constructs* (2 vols.). New York: Norton.

Sewell, K.W. (1998). Embodiment, sexuality, and self-understanding: Constructivist elaborations of theatrical acting. *Constructivism in the Human Sciences, 3*, 56-69.

Sewell, K. W. (2005). Psychotherapy with traumatized clients: A constructivist framework for healing. In D. Winter & L. Viney (Eds.). *Advances in personal construct psychotherapy*. London: Wiley.

Sociality and the sitcom

Jonathan D. Raskin

Because constructive alternativism encourages us to challenge traditional distinctions to see where new ones might lead, I have chosen to examine an art form of questionable artistic merit: the television sitcom. I have chosen sitcoms not just because I happen to enjoy many of them, but also because of their marginal acceptance as an art form:

> There is a strong sense in which television and everything connected to it is seen as unworthy: unworthy certainly as a serious intellectual pursuit, unworthy as a source of ideas or of stimulation, unworthy of critical evaluation, unworthy even as a pastime. The entertainment it provides has long been considered inferior to the entertainment provided by books or films or plays; its information more ephemeral and less substantial than that provided by newspapers, books, magazines, or journals. In short, in the classic dichotomy between high art and low art, television definitely occupies the region of low art. (Attallah, 2003, p. 93)

I have chosen to examine TV sitcoms in part because I appreciate the opportunity to challenge constructions of high versus low art. Of course, television is not just commonly construed as low art. It is also construed as downright harmful. People routinely denounce TV as a mind-numbing waste of time that serves only to alienate people from the world around them. However, new cultural technologies are often attacked for disrupting people's 'natural' ways of life. For example, in the 1830s Ralph Waldo Emerson warned Americans "against an intellectual dependency on books that could make them into 'bibliomaniacs' " (Marc, 1997, p. 130). Yesterday's bibliomaniac is today's couch potato!

Though taking up this topic helps challenge constructions of TV as low art unworthy of attention, more broadly I worry about personal construct psychologists such as myself who decide to provide insight to the arts community by filtering artistic experience through the prism of Kelly's grand theory. There is nothing per se wrong with such an endeavor. After all, applying Personal Construct Psychology (PCP) to the arts promises to be fun— generative, even! It challenges the 'art versus science' construct that sometimes impedes our imaginations. Yet we should keep in mind that a flourishing body of humanities based scholarship (much of it already steeped in the constructivist and postmodern themes we value) predates our arrival on the arts scene. Take the following quote: "We experience the world through systems of representation that, at the very least, condition our knowledge of the world and, some would argue, construct that world" (Allen, 1987, p. 5). This quote would fit nicely into just about any journal article or book chapter on Personal Construct Psychology. However, it comes from a far different source. The quote is drawn from the introduction to a 1987 book called *Channels of Discourse*, a volume that uses "semiotics, narrative theory, genre theory, and reader-response criticism" in analyzing television (Allen, 1987, pp. 1-2). Such media studies approaches resonate quite nicely within a PCP worldview. Just as PCP therapists contend that personal constructs are not windows on truth but rather uniquely meaningful ways to understand our selves and our relationships, media studies critics such as Allen (1987) hold that the question is not "does television gives us the 'truth' about the world" but instead "how does television represent the world?" (p. 5). Thus, we personal construct psychologists should not only be mindful of our own deficiencies when it comes to familiarity with arts scholarship, but we should also be careful not to reinvent the wheel for media studies and related arts scholars who already seem to have an excellent handle on their subject matter.

As an additional caveat, we should remain cognizant of Burr's (2003) warning that if we work too hard to resolve the ambiguities associated with experiencing art, we risk turning that experience into an overly analytical activity in which we forget that the very ambiguity and multiplicity of meaning in artistic forms is what makes them so affecting in the first place. This does not mean we should refrain from applying PCP to art for Burr (2003) also observed that PCP, while created within the clinical realm, potentially proves quite powerful in thinking about other areas of lived experience. Art is one such area. As long as we remain aware of the dangers of resolving artistic ambiguity in a once and for all way, PCP analysis of the arts can be quite enriching.

These observations duly noted, let's examine the sitcom. After discussing the 'art versus commerce' construct dimension that often leads people to discount sitcoms as worthy of analysis, I briefly review the history of the sitcom and provide some background on its commonly delineated characteristics. I argue that the sitcom, like all narrative forms, constitutes a socially constructed narrative genre and that the power of any narrative genre is its ability to be appropriated for different purposes by relying on shared constructions of its own stylistic conventions. The cultural 'embeddedness' of sitcom conventions is crucial to how sitcoms are meaningfully understood on the personal level. I suggest that sitcoms which stand the test of time and make an artistic contribution are able to do so because their creators—whether they know it or not—are able to exploit sitcom conventions in a variety of implicit and explicit ways that continue to "evoke a riot of meanings" (Burr, 2003, p. 61) in audiences.

Sitcoms: worthless junk masquerading as art?

Sitcoms are routinely criticized for being formulaic and cliché driven, their status as an art form remaining relatively precarious (Attallah, 2003). For example, critic James Bowman sees sitcoms as "worthless junk" masquerading as art—slickly packaged fluff without a lick of artistic integrity or vision, cynically foisted on the unassuming masses to fill the space between commercials (Bowman, 1999). In this estimation, those who watch sitcoms are complicit in the very dreadfulness that characterizes them:

> *Are we to believe that the people who watch them [sitcoms] don't realize that they are clichés? Much more likely, I think, is that clichés are exactly what they want. Like most sitcoms, these depend on well-established types, rather than character development. It is important that each character be recognizable, which in practice means that his actions have to be all but completely predictable. In fact, it is more and more the case that the characters are only platforms for the launching of one-liners and double-entendres. All television these days aspires to the condition of stand-up comedy, which is the ultimate in passive, no-fault entertainment. Never have the 'coms' been as 'sit' as they are now. Not only are the characters within each series stock types, but they are more or less interchangeable between series.* (Bowman, 1996)

This is quite a condemnation. While I agree with many of the specifics (particularly the parts about stock characters and one-liners), I also find myself wondering about a central premise of the argument, one Bowman (1996) spells out more precisely elsewhere: "We seem unable to refrain from responding to it [the sitcom] as if it were not packaging but art, as if it had some genuine content." This is fascinating, as it suggests a construct dimension of 'art versus commerce,' in which the genuinely artistic never concerns itself with sales or profit. True art, in this conception, remains unaffected by the corrosive impact of market influences. Sitcoms, conceived and created under the very auspices of such influences, are necessarily devoid of artistic status.

In responding to Bowman's indictment of the sitcom, let me paraphrase one of my favorite television characters (Dr. McCoy of *Star Trek* fame): "Damn it, Jim. I'm a psychologist, not an art critic." Consequently, perhaps my naiveté is showing here, but art and commerce strike me as having a long intertwined history. There have been many artists who died penniless or refused to compromise their vision in the face of enormous social and economic pressure. But there's also an impressive list of artists who succeeded economically, sometimes even anticipating market forces while creating their masterpieces. Didn't Shakespeare write plays with mass appeal in order to keep his theatre company running? Wasn't Picasso a pretty savvy entrepreneur? Andy Warhol? Woody Allen? The Beatles? None of these artists were free of economic forces that impacted their work and they all seemed to do pretty well monetarily, too. Thus, I reject the idea that because sitcoms are mass-marketed and commercial, they are necessarily lacking in artistry.

This is not to say I enjoy most sitcoms. Bowman's criticism hits the mark in many respects. Most would agree that all too often, sitcoms are pretty bad. Again, though my training in psychology does little to enhance my credibility as a critic, I might go so far as to suggest that *most* artistic endeavors are unsuccessful over the long haul. Only art that continues to speak to people across many years gains the status of 'timeless classic.' Shakespeare survived, but the work of many of his contemporaries did not. An enormous number of novels are written; few become part of the 'literary canon.' Just like personal constructs that no longer help us anticipate events, art that no longer speaks to people eventually is discarded. The overwhelming majority of sitcoms suffer from the problems Bowman identified. However, the sitcom itself as a *dramatic form* with identifiable (albeit socially constructed) conventions is not inherently better or worse, intrinsically more or less subject to the pernicious influence of economic necessity, than other dramatic forms. Yes, few sitcoms stand the test of time and emerge as great art, but this applies to work across all artistic mediums—most of it is pretty mundane and ultimately forgettable. Outstanding sitcoms use the conventions of the sitcom form to great effect. Accordingly, what I wish to offer herein is a constructivist psychological approach to sitcom, one that sees market-driven considerations and timeworn dramatic conventions as part and parcel of sitcom artistry.

A little bit about sitcoms

History and definitions

Sitcoms are commonly described as owing a great deal to radio comedy that preceded them, much of which was based on vaudeville and music hall shows popular in the early part of the 20th century (Baker, 2003; Hartley, 2001; Mills, 2004). Sitcoms are typically 24-30 minutes in length and have self-contained narratives that are resolved by the end of the show (Baker, 2003; Feuer, 2001; Mills, 2004). They have regular characters in recurrent locations (usually work, home, or some combination of both) (Baker, 2003; Mills, 2004). Families are a common focus and when they are not (as in workplace sitcoms), the characters usually function much like families anyhow (Hartley, 2001). Sitcom plots tend to be circular in that the end of each episode returns the situation and characters back to the state they began, allowing episodes to easily be viewed in any order. Visually, this narrative structure is represented as 'Episode = Familiar status quo → Ritual error made → Ritual lesson learned → Familiar status quo' (Marc, 1997, p. 190). Sitcoms commonly, but not always, employ a live audience or laugh track (Baker, 2003; Mills, 2004). Consistent with this, sitcoms often look like filmed stage plays, with the TV audience occupying the spot where the 'fourth wall' would otherwise be (Baker, 2003; Mills, 2004). However, some sitcoms diverge from this visual style, instead appearing more like traditional films in which camera angles vary and the audience's vantage point is not limited to the 'fourth wall' perspective (e.g., $M*A*S*H$ and *The Wonder Years*) (Mills, 2004). Finally, it is common in sitcoms for the main characters to use recurrent comic catchphrases[20] and for minor character portrayals to frequently rely on stereotypes (Baker, 2003; Mills, 2004).

Sitcom as genre

Because TV sitcoms fall outside my psychology training's range of convenience, I explored what media studies scholars say about television genres. Genre is French for 'type' or 'kind' (Feuer, 1987; Neale, 2001). Generic taxonomies allow art forms to be "grouped into categories," with each genre "marked by a particular set of conventions, features, and norms" (Neale, 2001, p. 1). As such, television "does not simply reflect the world in some direct, automatic way. Rather it constructs representations of the world on the basis of complex sets of conventions—conventions whose operations are hidden by their transparency" (Allen, 1987, p. 2). Though some insist that genre categorization should remain the exclusive purview of genre critics, many media studies scholars stress that genre delineations are contestable constructions (Mittell, 2004; Neale, 2001). Thus to Neale (2001) the term genre has multiple meanings:

> *Genre can mean 'category' or 'class, generic can mean 'constructed or marked for commercial consumption'; genre can mean a 'corpus' or 'grouping', generic can mean 'conventionally comprehensible'; genre can mean 'formulaic', generic can mean 'those aspects of communication that entail expectation'; and so on.* (p. 3)

Personal construct psychologists are likely to endorse the claim that genre definitions are contestable (Mittell, 2004; Neale, 2001; Turner, 2001b) because they probably view 'sitcom' as a constructed category. A recent book by Mittell (2004) seems especially in keeping with both PCP and social constructionist accounts of 'sitcom' as constructed generic classification. Mittell (2004) argued that television genres are most usefully understood as cultural

---

[20] Examples of catchphrases abound. Among the more notorious: "Watchu talkin' 'bout Willis?" (*Diff'rent Strokes*); "To the moon, Alice" (*The Honeymooners*); and "Dy-no-mite!" (*Good Times*).

categories. For Mittell (2004), TV shows are not defined as westerns, cop shows, soap operas, or sitcoms because these are preexisting natural categories that describe the timeless 'essences' of these shows. Shows have no generic essences because "there is nothing internal to texts mandating how they are to be generically categorized—in some instances, the same text becomes 'regenrified' as cultural contexts shift" (Mittell, 2004, p. 8).

This strikes me as quite consistent with PCP and social constructionism. As Mittell (2004) observed, those who make, air, and watch television shows continually relate shows to one another. They say things to themselves like "Gee, *Two and a Half Men* is a lot like *The Odd Couple* for the twenty-first century," or "*Smallville* is *Beverly Hills 90210* meets *Superman*." These linkages are not dictated by the shows themselves, but instead "come together only through cultural practices such as production and reception" (Mittell, 2004, p. 8). The meaning of texts—in this case sitcoms—is not something found solely in the texts themselves but something humanly mediated and invented. Yes, the sitcom genre is in part located in texts and narrative conventions, but it is also a product of how television producers, networks, advertisers, media critics, and audiences come to categorize television forms for practical, as well as artistic and entertainment, purposes. As such, genre construction is *intertextual*, requiring people to socially engage with each other in an ongoing process of categorization and meaning making (Mittell, 2004).

This sounds a lot like PCP's *sociality* (Kelly, 1955/1991a, 1955/1991b) and social constructionism's *joint action* (Burr, 1995; Shotter, 1993). In the former, people are able to comprehend others by construing their construction processes. In the latter, people collaboratively create and sustain shared understandings as they relationally engage and respond to one another. Instead of conceptualizing television genres as entities unto themselves, both sociality and joint action suggest that genres are human creations developed by contextually grounded persons engaging in ongoing interpersonal relationships with one another. A genre's 'essence' holds only in the ongoing coordination of human meaning making practices. As social and cultural relationships evolve, the constructed genre categories people have developed together change, too.

Therefore, the sitcom—like all entertainment genres—becomes a perpetually evolving socially constructed form. Even though "the form shows no signs of being exhausted or of not being adaptable to all kinds of socially and comically complex circumstances" (Feuer, 2001, p. 69), it continues to be used in new ways that expand or revise socially shared understandings of what it is. Television audiences, producers, and critics share this historically and culturally shifting understanding of sitcom's conventions and style (Mittell, 2004). They remain literate in the visual, linguistic, and storytelling devices that the socially consensual 'sitcom' category typically employs. When watching a new TV show for the first time, people often quickly agree on whether or not it is a sitcom because they already know the constructed conventions of the form—even when these conventions are not explicitly acknowledged or discussed (Mills, 2004). That is, "the seemingly self-evident manner by which we are able to make sense of television" is "a result of our having learned those conventions of television reading—even though we are usually not conscious of their operation, nor can we remember having been taught them" (Allen, 1987, p. 2). As reception theory has suggested (Fish, 1980), how audiences classify what they are watching influences how they make sense of it: "meaning does not reside 'out there' in words on a page or dots on a television screen, but comes about as a result of a confrontation between viewer and image, reader and text" (Allen, 1987, p. 2). Perhaps most importantly for my purposes herein, once a genre is socially constituted and internalized by people as an identifiable narrative form, it becomes possible to utilize that form in unlimited ways for a variety of purposes.

Three approaches to sitcom genre

I submit three ways in which the sitcom has been effectively used as a socially constructed narrative form. What I put forward is offered in the spirit of the invitational mood (Kelly, 1964/1969a). It is merely one way of constructing a meaningful analysis of the sitcom genre, one that makes transparent the perspective I apply when evaluating the artistic merit of different sitcoms.

The modernist approach

Most sitcoms practice 'modernism.' A favorite pastime of constructivists is pointing out how modernist orientations to science and knowledge frequently accept the conventions of research and inquiry without spending much time paying explicit attention to them (Ashmore, 1989; Gergen, 1994; Neimeyer, 1995). Likewise, when sitcoms take a *modernist approach* they unreflectively abide by genre conventions because their primary concern is not to comment on the genre but rather to appropriate its conventions in examining particular dramatic themes or issues: "In fact, one could say that it has been the *ideological flexibility* of the sitcom that has accounted for its longevity. The sitcom has been the perfect format for illustrating current ideological conflicts while entertaining an audience" (Feuer, 2001, p. 70). Just as modernist science has been (and continues to be) extremely fruitful, a modernist approach to sitcom production can generate highly enjoyable and artistic results. For example, *All in the Family* (CBS, 1971-1979) and *Everybody Loves Raymond* (CBS, 1996-2005) are modernist sitcoms to the extent that they do not alter or draw special attention to the genre's conventions.

Of course the 'realism' of sitcoms is always precarious because the 'fourth wall' filming style and audience laughter clearly diverge from people's everyday experiences and make it obvious that one is watching a constructed form (Mills, 2004). However, in modernist sitcoms the audience is encouraged to suspend disbelief by overlooking aspects of the situation that seem quite unlike daily life. There is no self-conscious reflection—by the audience, by the performers, or in the script—on the ways in which sitcom reality differs from lived experience. When Archie Bunker insults his 'meathead' son-in-law and the audience roars with laughter, the characters do not pause and wonder where precisely this laughter is coming from. Were they to do this, the 'realism' of the dramatic situation would be compromised and draw attention to the artifice of the entire enterprise.

The best modernist sitcoms are effective because they master, but do not challenge, the basic rules and structure of sitcom. They seek to use the genre as a way to convey a more general point of view. They abide by the genre's rules in order to grapple with particular themes, issues, and character relationships. For example, *All in the Family* used the sitcom genre as a means to explore prejudice and class structure in American society. The show made no effort to negate the conventions of sitcom form because it was via those very conventions that it was able to explore race and class issues effectively. And certainly all the conventions were there. There were catchphrases ("Get away from me, Meathead"), circular narratives (Archie's declining political and economic status was regularly confirmed by the end of episodes), and the seminal 'fourth wall' visual style. Within the confines of sitcom rules, the show explored the relationships between the four principle characters (family members, in keeping with sitcom genre conventions) and in so doing examined topical issues. Each week, conservative Archie and his liberal son-in-law Mike (a.k.a., 'The Meathead') would wrestle over the day's sociopolitical issues, with the comedy coming out of their somewhat stereotypically hostile in-law relationship. While *All in the Family* stretched the sitcom form by having characters delve into controversial topics as no TV show had before,[21] the basic sitcom structure remained uncontested. This worked to the show's advantage by keeping the audience's attention on the characters, stories, and issues. *All in the Family* used the very familiarity that audiences had with the sitcom genre to engage (often hilariously) the political concerns

---

[21] For an interesting discussion of *All in the Family* see Marc (1997), Chp. 5 ('The Sitcom as Literate Peak: Post-Vietnam Refinements of Mass Consciousness'). Marc labeled 1970s sitcoms *All in the Family*, *M*A*S*H*, and *The Mary Tyler Moore Show* as 'litcoms' because of what he perceived as their sophisticated social analysis and literate qualities, but lamented that the "waning of the literate sitcom was sudden" (p. 165)—as exemplified by "Garry Marshall's self-conscious return-to-normalcy trilogy—*Happy Days*, *Laverne and Shirley*, and *Mork and Mandy*" (p. 166).

of the day. By accepting the conventions of sitcom and mastering them most effectively, the show was able to tackle the prejudices that occur in all families and cultures.

Everybody Loves Raymond is a more recent sitcom that falls within the modernist approach. Whereas *All in the Family* examined prejudice in 1970s America, *Raymond* tackled the complexities of family dynamics as they manifest themselves in the all-too-ordinary events of everyday life. As with *All in the Family*, *Raymond* exploited the sitcom's conventions to great effect but never questioned or negated them—the 'fourth wall,' audience laughter, a family-centered focus, and circular narratives were all hallmarks of the show. The relationships between the characters generally remained the same throughout the series (i.e., the situation was almost always returned to the status quo by the end of each episode) and the comedy grew out of the audience's familiarity with these relationships. The problems the characters dealt with were the 'small' things that epitomize much of everyday life: annoying and intrusive mother-in-laws, petty squabbles between husband and wife over house chores, sibling rivalry, and embarrassment over the presumed insanity of one's closest relatives. Within the recognizable boundaries of the sitcom genre, *Raymond* conveyed the centrality of how mundane daily events often are quite significant within one's personally meaningful and idiosyncratic family system.

From a dramatic point-of-view, modernist sitcoms like *All in the Family* and *Everybody Loves Raymond* are able to explore their respective themes so effectively because they rely on the relationships between their recurring characters. From a PCP perspective, these shows depend heavily on sociality (Kelly, 1955/1991a/, 1955/1991b). Their dramatic effectiveness is contingent upon how well they convey the illusion that their characters are real people able to construe one another's construction processes and form role relationships. Of course, audiences also need to engage in sociality for these shows to be effective. Audiences must construe the characters' constructions—and this process only works if the characters' constructions seem complex enough for them to appear as reasonably fleshed out human beings to a wide swath of those watching. In the many less-than-entertaining sitcoms that populate the TV landscape, the characters are so poorly written that audiences only see them as stock types (Bowman, 1996); there is little for viewers to sink their teeth into when it comes to construing the characters' construction processes and forming what seem like genuine role relationships with them. However, in the best modernist sitcoms, not only do the characters appear to have role relationships with each other, but the audience also has to work to form role relationships with the characters. The sexual conflicts between Raymond and his wife Debra (he wants more sex, while she wants more help around the house!) are much funnier when audiences understand these characters' respective constructions of themselves and one another, as well as are able to relate to them by empathizing with their respective (but quite divergent!) personal realities.

The postmodernist approach

In its many guises postmodernism self-consciously focuses on the rules and assumptions implicit in taken for granted social practices. Accordingly, postmodernist researchers are as interested in *how* scientists 'do' science as they are in actually doing science themselves. For example, the sociology of scientific knowledge literature is 'postmodern' to the extent that it takes as its subject matter the processes by which scientists construct rules about how to study the world, what kinds of questions are legitimate to study, what counts as legitimate data and analysis, where to draw the line between one scientific discipline and another, and so forth (Ashmore, 1989). In the same vein, sitcoms that adopt a *postmodern approach* purposely draw attention to sitcom's traditional stylistic conventions. Such shows seem as interested in exploring the conventions of sitcom as they are in using those conventions for dramatic effect. Hence, they have a more self-conscious 'postmodern' feel. Examples have appeared throughout television history, including (but certainly not limited to) *The George Burns and Gracie Allen Show* (CBS, 1950-1958), *It's Garry Shandling's Show* (Showtime and FOX, 1986-1990), *The Simpsons* (FOX, 1989-present), and *That's My Bush* (Comedy Central, 2001). These shows strike me as postmodern because rather than diverting audience attention away from sitcom conventions and emphasizing the dramatic narrative, these shows instead purposely draw the audience's attention to the generic conventions employed in order to celebrate them, critique them, or just make you aware of their invented status.

Sitcoms employing a postmodern approach aim to make audiences aware of sitcom conventions. That is, their purpose is very different from sitcoms using a modernist approach. Modernist sitcoms rely on, but downplay, genre conventions in order to focus audience attention on the *content* and *drama* they pour into the form itself. They use the form to concentrate on characters, issues, and themes. For postmodernist sitcoms, the sitcom form itself *is* the issue! Characters, plots, and broader themes (when present at all) are secondary—they exist only to serve the larger postmodern goal of drawing attention to the socially constructed rules and regulations governing the entire sitcom enterprise.

The George Burns and Gracie Allen Show is an early example of postmodern themes within sitcom genre. The show relied on several devices that drew the audience's attention to the fact that they were watching a TV show. For example, George Burns regularly talked directly to the audience, commenting on the plot going on around him. Further, George often went upstairs to his study and tuned his TV to the very show he was participating in downstairs just moments before! Unlike the characters in *All in the Family* and *Everybody Loves Raymond*, George was aware of his status as a character in a sitcom. As a result, he was usually coolly detached from the proceedings (after all, he knew they were pretend!). By contrast, the characters around George were not in on the secret. They lacked George's awareness that they were in a TV show and therefore a lot more was at stake for them. However, the audience identified with George, who constantly reminded them the whole situation was a fictionalized manipulation. The meta-communication was "this is all make-believe so please don't take it too seriously." The comedy came from George being able to manipulate the other characters via his awareness of being in a show.

George Burns and Gracie Allen played 'themselves.' In postmodern sitcoms actors often play themselves, which helps further advance audience awareness of the show's artifice. When actors play themselves, audiences are left wondering about whether the 'selves' played are 'real' or not—after all, even though the actors are 'themselves,' their words are scripted and their performances staged. The George Burns who went up to his study to watch his own show on TV was not the 'real' George Burns. His going upstairs and eavesdropping on his own show, which ostensibly seemed more 'real' then the fake goings-on downstairs, was also scripted and pretend! The resulting reflexivity likely left audiences guessing about how much of George and Gracie's performances mirrored their off-screen identities. Ironically, these kinds of questions are more readily dispensed with when watching sitcoms where the actors clearly are playing fictionalized characters. In such instances audiences 'play along' with the charade and accept that what they are watching is 'made up.' There is no doubt that the 'selves' the actors are playing are fictionalized rather than real. Thus, audiences are free to stop wondering about the 'real' and instead lose themselves within the dramatic world of make believe at hand. By having actors play 'themselves,' postmodern sitcoms blur the line between 'real' and 'pretend.' This makes it harder to suspend disbelief and become engrossed in the narrative. When audiences cannot clearly discern what is 'real,' their attention is diverted from the dramatic action before them to questions about the constructed status of the entire enterprise, often producing a more emotionally detached experience. The audience is distanced from the dramatic action when made to attend to its constructed nature.

It's Garry Shandlings's Show is a more recent example of the 'postmodern' approach to sitcoms—one that pushed the envelope further than *Burns and Allen* by making sitcom conventions themselves the entire focus of the show. The main character Garry (playing 'himself,' of course!) often 'stepped out' of the action and made comments to the audience. Garry's comments were aimed specifically at addressing (and making fun of) sitcom conventions. Every episode seemed to be a vehicle for sending up the sitcom form. The show's theme song exemplified this by making clear the show's premise. Sitcom theme songs often inform audiences of the show's comic intentions (Mills, 2004). Rather than explaining the premise of the show (as many sitcom themes do), *Shandling's Show* used the funny theme song genre device to make us aware of said device with lyrics such as:

> *This is the theme to Garry's Show,*
> *The opening theme to Garry's show.*
> *This is the music that you hear as you watch the credits.*
> *We're almost to the part of where I start to whistle.*
> *Then we'll watch 'It's Garry Shandling's Show'*
> (Blackcatter's World of TV Theme Song Lyrics)

In a review, *The New York Times* said that Shandling's show "is a loose affair, allowing the comedian to slip in and out of his sitcom character," with the result being that "he can talk directly to the camera, commenting on the supposed action, and he can even walk into the studio audience, gathering reactions and shaking hands" (O'Connor, 1987, p. C18). Comparing Shandling's show to the 1950s *George Burns and Gracie Allen Show*, the *Times* considered the former "far more sophisticated, almost post-modern, if you're partial to buzz-words" (O'Connor, 1987, p. C18). However, from my perspective both shows are postmodern because one of their primary effects (intentional, I suspect) was to find comedy in making audiences aware of the genre conventions they utilized.

A different, even more recent, sitcom that I consider postmodern in its approach is *That's My Bush*—a controversial and short-lived show. The show presented a fictionalized version of George and Laura Bush in the White House, utilizing and exaggerating every possible sitcom convention imaginable. Because its subject matter and style were so discordant, the effect was to draw audience awareness to the absurdities of the sitcom genre. Only in a sitcom can George Bush attack another country and have the consequences quickly reversed during the show's final minutes! And yet in a strange way it made sense because, as we all know, sitcoms situations are always 'homeostatically' reset to their familiar status quo. *That's My Bush* parodied other tired sitcom elements, as well: audience cheering upon each recurring character's initial entrance; the sassy, wisecracking maid; the intrusive neighbor; and the annoying (often misogynistic) catchphrase ("One of these days Laura, I'm going to punch you right in the face!"). The impact was that audiences came to experience the gulf between the sugarcoated and straightforward world of sitcom conventions (the George and Laura in *That's My Bush*) and the messy complexities of everyday life (the George and Laura currently occupying the White House). In juxtaposing these two worlds, the sitcom structure was both made transparent and implicitly criticized for its often-simplistic assumptions and structure. An additional impact was that audiences realized how fully they have internalized the socially constructed conventions of sitcom genre.

The Simpsons is another sitcom (one still in production) with many postmodern elements. Because it is animated rather than 'live-action,' it can readily mock the circular narrative element of sitcom genre. Animated characters never age and their relationships and situations therefore need not ever change. Bart Simpson remains nine years old even though *The Simpsons* has been on the air for fifteen years! Periodically, the show draws attention to this strange state of affairs and in so doing makes audiences aware of the artificiality of sitcom reality. Another way in which *The Simpsons* draws attention to the circular nature of sitcom plot is the relationship between Homer Simpson and his boss, Mr. Burns. In episode after episode, Mr. Burns is introduced to Homer as if they are just meeting for the first time. This seems reasonable once or twice. After watching multiple episodes, however, audience members become aware of this dramatic device. Based on how *The Simpsons* stretches use of this device to a ridiculous point, audiences may even begin to think about how other sitcoms also use this device—sometimes in an only slightly subtler manner! As such, *The Simpsons* qualifies as 'postmodern' because it constantly draws the attention of viewers to well-worn sitcom conventions. Interestingly, *The Simpsons*, despite all its postmodern elements, also fits nicely into my third and final way of approaching sitcoms.

The constructive alternativist approach

Whereas the modernist approach to sitcoms aims to make genre conventions transparent and the postmodernist approach endeavors to highlight those very same conventions, the *constructive alternativist approach* works to develop alternatives to generic regulations. 'Hybridized' shows are those that are difficult to categorize neatly within socially accepted genre distinctions (Turner, 2001a). From a PCP perspective, hybridized shows are constructive alternatives in which new possibilities for what a show can be are attempted. When successful, constructive alternativist shows alter or expand existing genres—and potentially lead to the development of entirely new genre categories.

The Office (BBC-2, 2001-2002) is a nice example of a sitcom that expanded the genre by realizing it in new ways. Mills (2004) noted "in many ways *The Office* conforms to the expected characteristics of sitcom, with the single setting, the recurring characters with conflicting personalities and the single narrative problem in each episode" (p. 69). However, the program diverges in numerous ways from typical genre conventions. First, "the programme—as $M*A*S*H$ before it—does not look like a sitcom." (p. 69). For example, the show's "opening titles do not signal to an audience its comic intent" (p. 69). The song is downbeat and dreary, "in contrast to the standard upbeat music and brightly lit opening titles associated with many other sitcoms" (p. 69). Again, recall the aforementioned theme to *It's Garry Shandling's Show*, which (despite the show's postmodern elements) retained the 'upbeat' theme concept.

In addition to breaking with the theme song conventions of sitcom, *The Office* also employs the visual style of the 'docusoap' (Baker, 2003; Mills, 2004). The docusoap is defined as

> *a form in which traditional documentary shooting techniques are aligned with editing practices more associated with popular drama or soap opera. Beyond these formal qualities, docusoaps also differ from traditional documentaries in their choice of more obviously entertaining subjects.* (Mills, 2004, p. 70)

Docusoaps are more commonly referred to as 'reality TV.' *The Office*, unlike more conventional sitcoms, is shot in a reality TV style, even though it is a scripted show. That is, it "uses the aesthetics and conventions of docusoap, but for comedic ends" (Mills, 2004, p. 71). The show's docusoap visual style breaks with the traditions of sitcom: there is no 'fourth wall' filming technique; the show is not filmed before a live audience and no laugh track is added. Further, the docusoap style allows much of the humor to stem from the fact that the characters do not always know they are being filmed (Mills, 2004). When aware of being on camera, they often behave differently by trying to manage the impressions they make. Brent, the lead character and boss at the office where the show takes place, creates much of the comedy through his blithe ignorance of how badly he comes across on camera. He makes off-color jokes, appears incompetent, and generally is held in low esteem by his underlings—who often look appalled by what he says and does (Mills, 2004). By blurring the lines between sitcom, documentary, and reality TV, *The Office* creates a 'constructive alternative' to customary television show categories and their corresponding conventions. In Mills' (2004) words, "by using the conventions of documentary for humour, *The Office* undermines the distinctions between sitcom and documentary, between seriousness and humor, demonstrating that the outcomes of one can be achieved through the conventions of the other" (p. 74).

Mills (2004) alluded to the *M*A*S*H* (CBS, 1972-1983) in discussing *The Office*. *M*A*S*H* is another nice example of the constructivist alternative approach to sitcoms, though the show did not go nearly as far as more recent shows in 'breaking away' from conventional constructions of sitcom genre. Some of this may have been due to network pressure to cram the show into a more traditional sitcom format. Larry Gelbart, who wrote many of the early episodes observed that battles with the network generally "stemmed from the fact that we wanted to veer so far from what was considered half-hour comedy" (Kalter, 1984, p. 29). The show's setting, an American mobile army hospital during the Korean War, did not immediately seem notable for its comedic possibilities. Though classifiable as a 'workplace' sitcom, the workplace presented was a bit different than what sitcom audiences of the early 1970s had come to expect. The main characters were surgeons operating on wounded soldiers, healing them so they could go back to the front to fight some more. Themes surrounding the horrors of war were not typical sitcom fodder.

Stylistically, the show seemed to slot-rattle a bit (Kelly, 1969b, 1955/1991b), alternating between the visual styles of sitcom and cinematic film. This is not surprising, given that the TV version of *M*A*S*H* was based on the 1970 movie of the same name. So whereas *The Office* combined aspects of sitcom with docusoap, *M*A*S*H* combined aspects of sitcom and cinematic film. Like *The Office*, *M*A*S*H* had a somber theme song and credits. The credits showed helicopters flying into the M*A*S*H unit and unloading wounded soldiers as Johnny Mandel's 'Suicide in Painless' played. This song was the same one used in the 1970 movie. However, a 'musak' version of 'Sucide in Painless' was used in the show, leaving out the original lyrics heard in the film. This may have been done so the song broke less fully with sitcom theme song conventions. By leaving out the song's depressing lyrics, much of the song's sting was removed. Even without its words, the theme song's downbeat tempo and mood, along with the dreary images in the accompanying credits, gave no indication that one was watching a comedy. *M*A*S*H*'s credits clearly contradicted the genre convention of using cheerful songs as sitcom themes.

M*A*S*H presented a generically hybridized style, using both sitcom and filmic elements. The scenes shot on indoor sets seemed more traditionally 'sitcom-like.' They relied on an only slightly more expansive use of the common 'fourth wall' sitcom filming technique. For example, audiences always were shown the operating room, the character's tents, and the camp's administrative offices from the same point-of-view, with the fourth wall removed. This is classic sitcom style. However, sequences shot outside 'opened up' the show and were much more three-dimensional and cinematic. Whenever the main characters left the hospital and ventured out into the war zone, the show suddenly dropped the fourth wall style and instead allowed the camera to rove more freely as in a traditional film. In these segments, the show took on a visual grittiness and realism lacking all together in most sitcoms. Perhaps because large parts of the show did not look like a typical sitcom, the show's American network (CBS) required that a laugh track be added (Kalter, 1984). Interestingly, the laugh track was excluded when the show aired in Great Britain (Mills, 2004). Given the less obviously 'sitcom-like' visual style and subject matter, CBS may have worried that audiences would not be able to clearly identify *M*A*S*H* as a sitcom without a classic genre convention such as the laugh track.

In both *The Office* and *M*A*S*H*, constructive alternatives to typical sitcom conventions were employed. Genre conventions were combined in new and clever ways. Many shows can be viewed as 'constructive alternatives' to classic sitcom genre conventions. For example, *The Simpsons*, referred to earlier for its postmodern elements, also can be seen as adopting a constructive alternativist approach by combining aspects of sitcom and cartoon genres. Examples of constructive alternativist shows that are difficult to classify cleanly because they combine different genre elements in unique ways are *The Wonder Years* (ABS, 1988-1993), *Northern Exposure* (CBS, 1990-1995), *Scrubs* (NBC, 2001-present), and *Desperate Housewives* (ABC, 2004-present). *The Wonder Years*, like *M*A*S*H*, used a more cinematic, on-location style of filming. Its elimination of the laugh track and use of a narrator clearly offered a stylistic alternative to classic sitcom genre conventions. *Northern Exposure* challenged genre conventions somewhat differently, by merging elements of hour-long drama (location filming, multiple plotlines, and a large ensemble cast) with the comedic kinds of characters and situations more readily associated with half-hour sitcom. More recently, *Scrubs* commingled elements of sitcom and medical drama genres in unique and new ways; the doctors and situations on *Scrubs* are handled in a light way that hews more closely to sitcom conventions than the ultra-seriousness usually found in doctor shows. As a final example, *Desperate Housewives* is a current show that has combined soap opera and sitcom by emphasizing ongoing plots and cliffhangers that typically are left unresolved at the end of each episode. At the same time, the storylines are treated in a much more comedic manner than usually found in soap operas. All these shows are nice examples of the constructive alternativist approach to genre. They are difficult to classify purely as sitcoms because they diverge from socially accepted constructions of what 'rules' a sitcom should follow. At the same time, by hybridizing or altering commonly understood genre conventions, they potentially challenge or modify socially shared constructions of what counts as a particular genre.

Conclusion

In examining the scholarly literature on sitcoms and trying to relate it to PCP, I have been struck by the extent to which constructivist themes resonate within the media studies literature. The more I scrutinized the literature, the more daunting writing this chapter became. I became increasingly aware that my engagement with the relevant literature was facile at best. And yet I think PCP and related constructivist psychological approaches have a great deal to offer in thinking about TV sitcoms specifically and the arts more broadly.

Distinguishing modernist, postmodernist, and constructive alternativist approaches to sitcoms helps me think about the artistic merit of various programs. I use different criteria for evaluating shows that I feel employ sitcom conventions in traditionally modernist ways versus those that adopt a postmodern point of view versus those that offer a constructive alternativist hybridizing of styles. That is, I evaluate different shows based on my constructions of what they are trying to accomplish and how well they do so. Obviously, my interpretations of what particular programs aim to accomplish are not *the* interpretations. There is no final answer about what makes great art. My interpretations are merely personal constructions I created to make sense of my own idiosyncratic experience of sitcoms. Of course, when my personally devised constructions about sitcoms fit with those others have privately constructed for themselves, commonality in constructions occurs and we have agreement about what constitutes 'good' art. However, even when commonality does not occur, the potential for role relationships formed around artistic evaluation becomes enhanced any time people try to construe one another's art-related constructions. And therein lies the fun.

References

Allen, R. C. (1987). Introduction: Talking about television. In R. C. Allen (Ed.), *Channels of discourse* (pp. 1-16). Chapel Hill: University of North Carolina Press.

Ashmore, M. (1989). *The reflexive thesis: Wrighting sociology of scientific knowledge*. Chicago: University of Chicago Press.

Attallah, P. (2003). The unworthy discourse: Situation comedy in television. In J. Morreale (Ed.), *Critiquing the sitcom: A reader* (pp. 91-115). Syracuse, NY: Syracuse University Press.

Baker, J. (2003). *Teaching TV sitcom*. London: British Film Institute.

Blackcatter's World of TV Theme Song Lyrics. *It's Garry Shandling's Show*. Retrieved June 24, 2005 from http://www.cfhf.net/lyrics/its-garry.htm.

Bowman, J. (1996). Groupthink TV. *The New Criterion, 14*(5), Retrieved May 17, 2005, from http://www.newcriterion.com/archive/2014/jan2096/bowman.htm.

Bowman, J. (1999). Childish wish-fulfillment. *The New Criterion, 18*(3), Retrieved May 17, 2005 from Academic Search Elite Database.

Burr, V. (1995). *An introduction to social constructionism*. London: Routledge.

Burr, V. (2003). Making sense and the ambiguity of the lived world. In G. Chiari & M. L. Nuzzo (Eds.), *Psychological constructivism and the social world* (pp. 59-66). Milan, Italy: FrancoAngeli.

Feuer, J. (1987). Genre study and television. In R. C. Allen (Ed.), *Channels of discourse* (pp. 113-133). Chapel Hill: University of North Carolina Press.

Feuer, J. (2001). Situation comedy, part 2. In G. Creeber (Ed.), *The television genre book* (pp. 67-70). London: British Film Instititue.

Fish, S. (1980). *Is there a text in this class? The authority of interpretive communities*. Cambridge, MA: Harvard University Press.

Gergen, K. J. (1994). *Realities and relationships*. Cambridge, MA: Harvard University Press.

Hartley, J. (2001). Situation comedy, part 1. In G. Creeber (Ed.), *The television genre book* (pp. 65-67). London: British Film Institute.
Kalter, S. (1984). *The complete book of M*A*S*H*. New York: Harry N. Abrams.
Kelly, G. A. (1969a). The language of hypothesis: Man's psychological instrument. In B. Maher (Ed.). *Clinical psychology and personality: The selected papers of George Kelly* (pp. 147-162). New York: John Wiley. (Original work published 1964)
Kelly, G. A. (1969b). Personal construct theory and the psychotherapeutic interview. In B. Maher (Ed.), *Clinical psychology and personality: The selected papers of George Kelly* (pp. 224-264). New York: John Wiley.
Kelly, G. A. (1991a). *The psychology of personal constructs: Vol. 1. A theory of personality*. London: Routledge. (Original work published 1955)
Kelly, G. A. (1991b). *The psychology of personal constructs: Vol. 2. Clinical diagnosis and psychotherapy*. London: Routledge. (Original work published 1955)
Marc, D. (1997). *Comic visions* (2nd ed.). Malden, MA: Blackwell.
Mills, B. (2004). Comedy verite: Contemporary sitcom. *Screen, 45*(1), 63-78.
Mittell, J. (2004). *Genre and television: From cop shows to cartoons in American culture*. New York: Routledge.
Neale, S. (2001). Studying genre. In G. Creeber (Ed.). *The television genre book* (pp. 1-3). London: British Film Institute.
Neimeyer, R. A. (1995). Limits and lessons of constructivism: Some critical reflections. *Journal of Constructivist Psychology, 8*, 339-361.
O'Connor, J. J. (1987, April 14). Following his whimsy, Shandling finds success. *The New York Times*, p. C18.
Shotter, J. (1993). *Cultural politics of everyday life: Social constructionism, rhetoric and knowing of the third kind*. Toronto: University of Toronto Press.
Turner, G. (2001a). Genre, hybridity, and mutation. In G. Creeber (Ed.). *The television genre book* (pp. 6). London: British Film Institute.
Turner, G. (2001b). The uses and limitations of genre. In G. Creeber (Ed.). *The television genre book* (pp. 4-5). London: British Film Institute.

COMING TO TERMS

Art proustifies Kelly's PCP: Personal searchings and revisitings

C. T. Patrick Diamond

> *All manner of actions, ... , so many different methods of scientific [and artistic] investigation, each one having a definite intellectual value and being legitimately employable in the search for truth.* (Proust, cited by Nabokov, 1980, pp. 239-240)

> *Methods remain the personal concern, approach, and attack of an individual, and no catalogue can ever exhaust their diversity of form and tint.* (Dewey, 1916/ 1950, p. 173)

Introduction

After 40 years I have come to believe that arts-based versions of personal inquiries can create understandings that are 'truer than true,' contributing to a process of never-ending self-invention. Given that George Kelly in his theory of personal construct psychology (PCP), through largely suppressed references and making few appeals to authority, sought to encourage readers to make what they will of things, I am searching here for ongoing changes in my understandings, including those that were first incited by others. I cite Kelly and Don Bannister citing Kelly—and me citing myself. I feel qualified to give this self-recital because I experienced the events and "I can at least write about what I now recall" (Kelly, 1969, p. 46).

One of my self-authored turning points was a paper published in 1993a as 'Gridding a grid.' In an act of what I now realize was one of written self-palmistry I then claimed that:

> *Kelly's meta-theory of perspective provides an artistic-temporal metaphor for how artists [and all of us] come to know and for how they know that they know. Since what they see is governed by the place from which it is seen, any present insight is only partial and relative and might be changed by movement to another vantage point* (pp. 174-175).

That paper helped mark the beginning of my gradual movement from a literary perspective through a grid-based phase to finally one that was fully arts-based. Kelly's PCP has continued to provide me with a series of vantage points from which to view my work and its development—and myself. Any careful, reflexive, and sustained study of an experience undertaken to advance understanding can count as an inquiry.

Coming to Kelly

The search that led me to Kelly's 'man-the-inquirer' began after I completed my BA in 1963 at the University of Queensland in Australia. My personal concern had mainly been with the convergence of experimental fiction and humanistic psychology as in the psychological novel. Pioneered by Henry James, Virginia Woolf, James Joyce, and of course Marcel Proust, this form of narrative evoked the ebb and flow of characters' thoughts and impressions in the midst of all their discontinuities and transitions. Inner monologues and streams-of-consciousness. During my year of teacher preparation in 1964, I was reintroduced to the teacher as sergeant major or feared disciplinarian. I was also disappointed to learn that learning theory was itself narrowly thought of in terms of animal behavior; that of sluggish earthworms, pecking chickens, cats struggling with portions of their brains abated, mice lost in mazes, and deprived rats banging on bars in cages. Confined to memory drums and nonsense syllables, there was no mention of how Proust memorialized experience or of how he periodically contrived to have a pair of starving rats in separate cages set together on his bed, end-to-end, and then the doors slid open. The famished rats attacked each other with piercing screams. Artist as 'turned on' rat-man.

I taught high school English and History until 1969 when I was appointed as a lecturer in English language and Literature at a Teachers' College. At the very last moment I had had second thoughts about accepting the headship of the English department at the Brisbane Grammar School. I had completed a BEd during which I had been introduced to Kelly's work in an Ed. Psych. course. Presented as a cognitive theory of personality complete with its own purpose-built Repertory grid technique. I was intrigued to learn that, by construing learning not just a special class of psychological processes but rather as what people do every day to define who they are, Kelly had kicked learning theory 'upstairs.' PCP then seemed more readily accepted in England, especially at the London Institute of Education by a group of 'psycho-rhetoricians' or language and learning scholars led by Jimmy Britton and Nancy Martin. They were also conducting what was known as 'the writing project.' It would later inspire the model of 'teachers teaching teachers.'

In 1973, I was appointed to the Faculty of Education at my old university as a lecturer in English Method (Curriculum and Instruction) after having just completed a MEd dissertation on academic achievement motivation and library usage. I had been introduced to Jimmy Britton in person earlier in 1973 when he was the keynote speaker at a UNESCO conference at the University of Sydney. Britton who would be one of my external doctoral examiners in 1979 reminded us that Kelly (1969) had described "an afternoon with the obvious" during which he proposed that the activities of dissertation students could provide a model for all inquirers. Dreaming and planning, loosening and tightening. Because "the events of this world do not march up to us single file, [and] differentiate themselves by announcing their names our task is to pull [our] innermost experience apart and then to put it together again" (Kelly, 1969, p. 196) as best we can. Deconstruction followed by naming and reconstruction.

Although I had published English textbooks, teaching materials, and chapters, I doubted if I would ever manage to get more academic work published. However, in 1980 'A note on measuring teachers' constructs' appeared in *Research in the Teaching of English* and it was followed in 1982a and b by 'Understanding others: Kellyian theory, methodology and application' in the *International Journal of Intercultural Relations* and by 'Teachers can change: A Kellyian interpretation' in the *Journal of Education for Teaching*. While the first two papers revisited my 1979 dissertation, the third provided a real point of departure.

Finding Kelly

In 1974 I had begun my five-year, doctoral research into how high school English teachers understood their teaching of writing (English essays or composition). I had supplied my 93 participating teachers with a Vygotskian sorting task for classifying cards with statements on them (the elements) about the teaching of writing. I was interested in the names that the practitioners gave to the clusters of statements that they formed. Their superordinate constructs. My supervisor, a psychometrician lately returned from the Ontario Institute for Studies in Education (OISE) (later to be amalgamated with the University of Toronto, UT), suggested that I use a Latent Partition analysis to tease out the underlying cognitive structures. To do research in education then meant I had to do 'Ed.Psych.' As a researcher, I had to move from words to numbers.

My Kellyian recollections are those of an occasional visitor and casual observer from Down Under. While on sabbatical at the London Institute in 1980, I met Fay Fransella and Don Bannister who from their hospital settings had just published the breakthrough PCP Penguin, *Inquiring man*. When I met Don in person, he remarked that Kelly had often acknowledged, though seldom attributed, his debt to Lev Vygotsky and John Dewey. Kelly's clinical practice and theory confirmed Vygotsky's claim that the structure of the language and constructs that people habitually use always influences the ways in which they perceive the surrounding world, including their place in it. As Kelly (1969) wrote in the autobiography of his theory:

> *Not only ... [do] the words man (sic) uses give and hold the structure of his thought, but, more particularly, the names by which he calls himself give and hold the structure of his personality. Each of us invests [him or her] self with a particular meaning* (p. 56).

Over lunch eaten with plastic cutlery in the hospital cafeteria, Don seemed mainly interested in how I responded to his first triad of psychological novels[22]: *Sam Chard, Long day at Shiloh,* and *Burning leaves.* For him novel writing provided an exercise in the controlled elaboration of an author's personal construct system[23]. Autobiographical experimentation. We continued to correspond and Don invited me to contribute an essay to his 1985 book, *Issues and Approaches in Personal Construct Theory.* I called it 'Becoming a teacher: An altering eye.' I next contributed a chapter called 'Turning on teachers' constructs: A process approach to exploration and elaboration' to Fay Fransella and Laurie Thomas's 1988 book, *Experimenting with Personal Construct Psychology.* The use of 'turning on' did not then alert me to the dangers of appropriating the meanings of others while ignoring my own. Psychologists are always slow to realize that they are people too.

Mourned for his early death in 1986 Bannister had confessed that, when he was visiting Kelly in 1965, Kelly had warned Don jokingly that he was in danger of becoming PCP's first dogmatic proponent. But no one did more to extend its range of convenience (Scheer, 2003). Responding to Don's literary turn, I began to wonder if the range of convenience of 'man-the-personal-scientist' might not also include 'man-the-novelist' or 'man-the-artist'? And even the teacher as educational artist. I was beginning to find my way back from numbers to words. I remembered that Kelly had written about the cycles that Hamlet had found himself in and that Vygotsky's 1925 doctoral dissertation on *The Psychology of Art* (not published until 1968) contained a long essay about Hamlet. In this existential case study of his own inner world, Vygotsky tried to grasp the workings of the mind in its most revealing aspects, creating and responding to a literary text. Hamlet, the mourning self-conscious son, is himself often construed as the intellectual's intellectual. Vygotsky cleared his text of all references and scholarly comments, relegating them to final notes. A year later he produced an introductory Ed. Psych. textbook for beginning teachers.

---

[22] see Farrar, M. (2006). People, poetry and politics – the novels of Don Bannister (in this volume, pp. 17-28) (Eds.)

[23] see Bannister, D. (2006). A PCT view of novel writing and reading (in this volume, pp. 12-16) (Eds.)

Coming to arts-based inquiry

Just when I had been in danger of being preemptively construed as another 'gridder,' I published (through the good graces I am sure of Maureen Pope, one of the most innovative of PCP's educational inquirers) another paper in 1993b called 'Writing to reclaim self: The use of narrative in teacher education.' This marked the beginnings of my searching in more arts-based directions. According to Don, Kelly regretted ever having designed the 'Rep. grid' which, after a flurry of over 1,000 published studies, had become what he had described as one of the best ways yet invented to avoid all contact with PCP theory. Just another form of the semantic differential or the acceptably hard face of an essentially soft psychology.

In 1989 I took a wrong (but thankfully brief) turn to become Director of Australia's largest post-secondary College of Art. My plan had been to develop a graduate program for the College and to take it downtown, joining Brisbane's burgeoning cultural cluster at the South Bank. By the time that I resigned six months later all I had succeeded in replacing was the caravan that had served as the faculty and students' eccentric on-site cafeteria. I had, however, been working with some of the graphic design artists at the College to explore self-directed professional development. I had used Sebastian's self-described 'grid paintings' as the elements in a Rep. grid that I elicited from him. Our joint reflections on its FOCUS-ed solution (see below) led to learning conversations about painting and postmodernism. Realizing it was time to rake and burn the leaves, I left for Toronto where I was appointed in 1991 as a professor in the Center of Teacher Development (CTD) at OISE/UT. Britton again acted as one of my referees; Dave Hunt, a former Master's student of Kelly's and then a professor at OISE, was the other.

The CTD was internationally renowned for the work of Michael Connelly and Jean Clandinin (a former dissertation supervisee) in narrative inquiry and personal practical knowledge. I ended my 1991 book, *Teacher Education as Transformation: A Psychological Perspective*, by gesturing towards more aesthetic approaches in which the teacher might be construed as reaching out to the world from the vantage point of a postmodern novelist-dramatist. References to postmodernism had also appeared in the paper that I had begun writing at the College of Art about an artist's reviewing his own art-making. It was finally published in *Empirical Studies of the Arts* in 1993a as 'Gridding a grid.' In that paper, however, I was still writing about myself in the third person and making dismissive references to 'non-empirical' approaches. Indeed the avowed purpose of empirical paths is to avoid the so-called distorting influence of personal perspectives and the complications of subjective properties. But, as it occurred to me, if all the researcher does is follow the positivist trail, it can all become a pointless, forced march. Whenever we forget that more than one ending is possible, the range of action that is allowed becomes restricted rather than facilitated. Even 'empirical' I realized originally referred to that which is based on experience and not just on measurement. And so I have spent my last 14 years at OISE/UT working through the implications of this position and helping to conceptualize and experiment with those 'non-empirical' techniques that have come to be known as arts-based (AB) inquiry. Building on my PCP beginnings I have become a collaborative AB-educational researcher.

In 1999 I published a book with Carol Mullen, my first Canadian doctoral supervisee, called *The postmodern educator: Arts-based inquiries and teacher development*. Carol and I provided a rationale for art-based approaches to inquiry and professional development. We highlighted the work of 17 teachers from four countries as they acted out the metaphor of the 'person-as postmodern-educational-artist.' In the first chapter, 'Art is a part of us,' we argued that art is not the reserve of a select few operating at what Vygotsky might call the 'acme' level of human activity. The ability of artful engagement to engage and transform individuals is not the exclusive province of genius. Striving to make meaning through metaphor making and artistic shaping is a fundamental human need. We all take experience out of the ordinary and make it 'special.'

In arguing that narrative research, educational inquiry, and teacher development are forms of 'art,' Carol and I returned the term 'art' to its older usage as the skillful fashioning of useful artifacts. However, since the 19th century, art had become associated with upper class leisure and over-cultivated sensibility. Proust could be easily caricatured as the archetype of just such an indulged recluse, writing by night and sleeping by day in his cork-lined bedroom. Yet this novelists' novelist has provided the most compelling account yet of how experience becomes fully significant only in re-collection as it is arranged in a meaningful if provisional pattern. Using art to transform life, Proust evoked the flickering nightlife of the mind even as he filled the cultural storehouse of his mind with exquisite epiphanies. Far removed from the passageways and historical detritus that later fascinated Walter Benjamin.

Arts-based inquirers do not presume to produce works of 'capital A-Art' or to satisfy the demands of some ascetic canon. Instead, they shape experience by using a variety of aesthetic forms. From this democratic viewpoint, we are all artists—art just is part of us. By using a catalogue of artful forms, including short stories, poems, plays, and collages, as well as postmodern, fragmentary multi-form forms such as split text, duologue, and palimpsest, teacher (educator) inquirers like Kelly's personal scientists can evoke and invoke greater meaning from their experience. Arts-based inquiries allow us all to tap into imagination and to break with what is supposedly fixed, objectively and independently real for all time. We can learn to see beyond what is taken for granted as normal and so reconstrue past experience. We can even carve out "new conceptual routes" (Kelly, 1955, p. 128) through previously uncharted territory.

So many different methods

By imagining fresh possibilities an inquirer can "release facts, long taken as self-evident, from their rigid conceptual moorings. Once so freed, they may be seen in new aspects hitherto unsuspected" (Kelly, 1955, p. 1033). In chapter 3, Carol and I suggested ways for teachers and teacher-educators to imagine and represent ever-changing combinations of their present, past, and possible selves, including the teacher 'I am,' 'fear to be,' and 'hope to become.' In order to mark my self-reflexive turn and to take my 1993a paper to heart, in chapter 7, 'Reciting and Reviewing the Educator Self: An Exhibition of Five Self-Works,' I used self-narrative to inquire into and generate knowledge about my own teacher educator or writing self. After having previously explored the different ways in which others might access their respective reflexive self-consciousness (Diamond, 1991, 1993b), I summoned up my own experiencing self and cited it in a narrative site so as more fully to research its different aspects.

Using five arts-based fragmentary pieces of writing, I explored my engagement with my own writing and inquiries. Because the third person, expository voice is usually preferred in academe to that of the first person, expressive voice, I used arts-based narrative to reclaim this marginalized aspect. And then, more collaboratively, I wrote in a chorus of voices to contribute to shifts in my overall developmental pattern. Even as one of my semi-autobiographical works now in progress (see below) consists of a dual memoir written in the form of a factualized novel with all sorts of introduced changes.

In chapter 7 of the 1999 book, I peered out through a curtain of narrow leaves and trailing tendrils to share a short story fragment about the cutting down of a boyhood tree house. Until 1993b I had been using the FOCUS computer program (Shaw, 1990) to provide a two-way cluster analysis to reorder the construct rows and the element columns (like Sebastian's paintings or aspects of teacher selves) to produce FOCUS-ed Rep. grid solutions. The construct and the element relationships were visualized as dendrograms that showed the least similarities in the clusters which were then named and reflected upon by the artist or teacher. Dendrograms display relationships among clusters, showing the multidimensional distances between objects in a tree-like structure. Elements or constructs which are closest to each other in the multidimensional data space are connected by a vertical or horizontal line, forming a cluster which can be regarded as a 'new' focus for reflection. That cluster and the remaining original data are once again searched for the closest pair, and so on. The distance of the particular pair or degree of similarity of clusters is reflected in the height or length of the lines. Now I am using literal trees and arts-based self-narratives rather than multivariate statistical procedures to represent personal experience with more author-ity—as of whispering willows with ground-sweeping branches and soft, rustling leaves. But even deep roots and an enclosing canopy may not be able to protect a child.

Inquiring into arts-based dissertations

In 1994 I published a chapter that I called 'From numbers to words' in an OISE Press book devoted to advising doctoral candidates about the dissertation. Developments in my writing were being paralleled by those in my graduate teaching and supervision. I named my courses 'Arts-based teacher development,' 'Doing an arts-based dissertation,' and 'Works in-progress: Preparing a dissertation proposal.' Like Proust my students and I seek to embark on real voyages of inquiry that consist not just in seeking new landscapes but also in having new eyes. Altering eyes.

The challenge for dissertation inquirers is to find a form that can accommodate all the possibilities. So I suggest that my students assemble their responses to the invitations that they select from the course text chapters and to their own inquiry journeys in the form of an artist's narrative reflective portfolio. It also includes their pastiches of and reflective responses to each of the following clusters: a novel or book of short stories; an anthology of poems; a film or play or dissertation; and a music concert or art gallery visit. I ask then to consider how their encounters with arts-based forms help inform their dissertation journeys.

Other entries include more autobiographical life writing, including chronicles or time-lines (rivers and snakes), self-and group-portraits (verbal and mixed media), journaling (duologue), together with arts-based accounts and re-storying of their on-going inquiries such as their dissertation or proposal. I encourage them to focus on the teaching dilemmas, critical incidents, or turning points that inciting them to reconstrue their personal histories of learning to teach or becoming dissertation candidates. They then select which of these portfolio materials to share and reflect on.

The portfolio itself, like a personal construct system, can take whatever overall form they choose to imagine. It has consisted in the past of an expanding file or ring binder, the compartments of a toolbox, a packed suitcase or picnic basket, a quilt or cloak with commodious pockets, a revisited family album, a school yearbook or diary, a clothesline, a playbook, or a favorite, appropriated book with additions and annotations all couched within it. Proust's novel about his search provides an extended self-study punctuated by a series of epiphanies or moments of heightened self-awareness. His preferred method of working involved keeping numerous *cahiers* or draft notebooks with the right-hand pages being written on initially with the left-hand ones being left blank for later notes and additions, forming a split text. In 1914, his novel consisted of a *bricolage* of fragments to which he added *paperoles*. These were loose sheets of paper of different format and length stuck together and interpolated throughout the manuscript—and even the corrected galley proofs. These reworked manuscript pages could reach two meters in length.

Like Proust's novel, a dissertation is a constantly evolving work in progress with everything being not quite finished until the very end. He experimented by removing whole sections from one part to another, constantly rereading, re-thinking and re-writing. From the point of view of composition, a dissertation like a novel is so complex that it cannot be clear until quite late when everything has begun to be combined. There is no rigid order through which chapters must proceed. Like Proust, candidates can use metaphor and visuals, memoir, scholarship, etymology, poetry, music, essay, art criticism, photographs, and translated paintings to enchant their work. Arts-based inquiry is neither formless nor subscribes to 'anything goes.' It provides experience, method, form, and developmental impact.

And so

As an associate editor for *Curriculum Inquiry* since 1995 I have written a series of arts-based editorial essays. Most recently with Christine van Halen, a distinguished doctoral supervisee, I am co-editing a special series on arts-based inquiry. For example, in 'Searching ways: Art Proustifies science' (2002) Christine and I considered the place of art in science. In 'Depths of (un)knowing: Arts-based spinning and weaving" (2002), we portrayed educational artists as restless inquirers whose introspective, multiple ways so catch them up in their imaginative webs that, like Proust, they may seem lost in forever searching for form as content. But there is no rigid distinction to be drawn between content and form, between what is done and how it is done. The inquiry or "[art]work itself *is* matter formed into aesthetic substance" (Dewey 1934/ 1980, p. 109). Particularly when the matter is an evolving personal construct system. The art is not just an ornament to be added onto or applied to gild the material. The art cannot be separated from the thought or impression that it renders.

But why Proust? The verb *proustifier* can denote an attitude that is overly self-conscious of form and perhaps overly full of extravagant expressions and deliberate digression. Overwrought. This may explain why Proust is more usually read about than actually read. However, *proustifier* also refers to a universal kind of yearning for connection and meaning that leads to and is released as the urgent, involuntary recollection of experience. Proust's way of re-searching experience makes him an exemplar of the arts-based re-searching inquirer. His work celebrates a fascination with a text that is forever just out of reach. A metaphor-laden story of inquiry whose end is not rushed.

By viewing art as a particular quality possessed by human experience, we can gain access to important insights from the wide array of imaginative activities in our own lives and not just from what are acknowledged as great works of high art. Using aesthetic forms, perceptions, and interpretations allows us to "recover the continuity of aesthetic experience within the normal processes of living" (Dewey 1934/ 1980, p. 10) and working—even within what many consider ordinary activities. Like Proust, we can try to find beauty or art where we have never imagined that it could exist, that is, in the most ordinary things, in the profundities of life stilled so that we can look out at time itself.

In 'Posted presences: Watching for sensuous intelligence and humanistic integrity.' (2004) and 'Catch us if you can': Arts-based interplay" (in press), Christine and I again inquired into arts-based approaches by citing Henry James, Virginia Woolf, James Joyce, and of course Proust. We are currently preparing a 'History of the arts in research: Passageways and byways' as a chapter for the forthcoming *Handbook of the arts in qualitative research: perspectives, methodologies, examples, and issues* (in press). Walter Benjamin and Proust will be our guides even as Kelly has long been mine.

Looking back for one last time at my 1993a paper, I had purported to be using a 'numerical phenomenological' way of studying what a person's aesthetic response to his or her artistic representations might mean to him or her. More fortunately for me I can also see that I ended the paper by citing Proust (1954):

> *What one has experienced is like those negatives which show us nothing but black until they have been held up to the lamp ... ; one does not know what it is until it has been help up before the intelligence. Only then, ... can one distinguish . . . the shapes of what one has felt.*
> (p. 895)

The imaginatively intuitive made intelligibly explicit. I had then gone on to recommend that the views of the outside expert need to be at least complemented by those of the artist him- or herself. Each vantage point offers an:

> *Essentially relative, human perspective which is constantly seeking to enlarge and review itself. Even the recommended practice of looking at where they are looking from is itself undertaken from a position and may need to be re-visioned. ... Postmodern art may be marked by the reassertion of the artists' mastery over their own work.* (p. 175)

Now, approaching retirement and searching for ways to continue writing but now as a novelist, I wonder if anyone will ever represent me as a literary agent or if my first psychological novel, drafted in 180,000 words, will somehow manage to get itself published. I am encouraged that Nabokov (1980) construed the writer as a teacher, storyteller, and an enchanter. Fiction writing may hopefully provide me with new ways in which I can re-enchant my truth-like fictional inquiries. Life writing as exemplified by Kelly.

Like Proust, Kelly has had his mix of translators, interpreters, revisionists, editors, and devotees. But his vision remains fundamentally his own. Kelly taught us that our lives are forms of motion and that the challenge for us as inquiring artists and practitioners is always to find ways that can take account, however temporarily, of the qualities and movement of experience and its cumulative significance in our lives. Finding such forms "invites us to look ... and wonder what vast and unforeseen alternatives might lie ahead" (Kelly 1969, p. 8). Each person's lifelong task is to continue to search for his or her own way and to form a self-constituted aesthetic. By sharing and even publishing my own 'make-believe,' I hope to find new ways in which to explore an even richer 'diversity of form and tint.'

References

Bannister, D., & Fransella, F. (1980). *Inquiring man*. Harmondsworth: Penguin
Dewey, J. (1934/1980). *Art as experience*. New York NY: Putnam's.
Dewey, J. (1916/1950). *Democracy and education*. New York: The MacMillan Company
Diamond, C. T. P. (1980). A note on measuring teachers' constructs. *Research in the Teaching of English*, 14(2), pp. 48-51.
Diamond, C. T. P. (1982a). Teachers can change: A Kellyian interpretation. *Journal of Education for Teaching*, 8(2), pp. 163-173.
Diamond, C. T. P. (1982b), Understanding others: Kellyian theory, methodology and application. *International Journal of Intercultural Relations*, 6(4), pp. 395-420.
Diamond, C. T. P. (1985). Becoming a teacher: an altering eye. In Bannister, D. (ed.), *Issues and Approaches in Personal Construct Theory* (pp. 15-35). London: Academic Press.
Diamond, C. T. P. (1988). Turning on teachers' constructs: A process approach to exploration and elaboration. In Fransella, F.& Thomas, L.F. (eds.). *Experimenting with Personal Construct Psychology* (pp. 173-182). London: Routledge & Kegan Paul.
Diamond, C. T. P. (1991). *Teacher education as transformation: A psychological perspective*. Milton Keynes: Open University Press.
Diamond, C. T. P. (1993a). Gridding a grid: An artist reviews and comprehends his own exhibition. *Empirical Studies of the Arts*, 11(2), pp. 167-175.
Diamond, C. T. P. (1993b). Writing to reclaim self: The use of narrative in teacher education. *Teaching and Teacher Education: An International Journal of Research and Studies*, 9(5/6), pp. 511-517.

Diamond, C. T. P., & Mullen, C.A. (1999). *The postmodern educator: Arts-based inquiries and teacher development.* New York: Peter Lang.

Diamond, C. T. P., & van Halen-Faber, C. (2002). Searching ways: Art Proustifies science. *Curriculum Inquiry,* 32(2), pp.121-130.

Diamond, C. T. P., & van Halen-Faber, C. (2004). Posted presences: Watching for "sensuous intelligence and humanistic integrity." *Curriculum Inquiry,* 34(4), pp. 383-393.

Kelly, G. A. (1969). *Clinical psychology and personality* (B. Maher, Ed.). New York: Wiley.

Kelly, G.A. (1955). *The psychology of personal constructs,* vols. 1 & 2. New York; Norton. .

Nabokov, V. (1980). *Lectures on literature* (F. Bowers, Ed.). London; Weidenfeld & Nicolson.

Proust, M. (1954). *Remembrance of things past,* Part II, C.K.S. Moncrieff & F.A. Blossom transls.). New York: Random House.

Scheer, J. W. (2003). Readers, writers and critics: A constructivist look at literature. Paper presented at 15th International Congress of PCP. University of Huddersfield, UK.

Shaw, M. L. G. (1990). *Repgrid.* Calgary: Center for Person-Computer Studies.

van Halen-Faber, C., & Diamond, C. T. P. (2002). Depths of (un)knowing: Arts-based spinning and weaving. *Curriculum Inquiry,* 32(3), pp. 251-266.

van Halen-Faber, C. & Diamond, C. T. P. "Catch us if you can": Arts-based interplay. *Perspectives Essays: Journal of Curriculum and Pedagogy, 1*(2), (in press).

van Halen-Faber, C. & Diamond, C. T. P. History of the arts in research: Passageways and byways. In J. Gary Knowles, & Ardra L. Cole (Eds.). *Handbook of the arts in qualitative research: perspectives, methodologies, examples, and issues.* London: Sage (in press).

APPENDICES

Appendix A

A short introduction to Personal Construct Psychology[24]

Jörn W. Scheer

Background

Readers not familiar with the Psychology of Personal Constructs might welcome a short introduction to the theoretical background of the papers compiled in this book. It can be short since there are several introductory books available in some of the major European languages. In English language, they are, among others, Butt & Burr (2004), Fransella (2005), and Jankowicz (2004).

Even in the United States, Personal Construct Psychology cannot be considered a part of mainstream psychology. One of the reasons is that Kelly developed his theory in sharp contrast to the reigning schools of psychological thought of his time: behavioural theory and psychoanalysis. And to transport his new ideas, he chose to use an idiosyncratic language, inventing or redefining terms not commonly used this way in academic psychology. Yet it is still a delightful experience to read especially the first three chapters of his main work (Kelly, 1955), in which he elaborates the properties of a good theory and shows how Personal Construct Theory could serve as a major superordinate theory for many psychological phenomena.

Another point concerns the content of the theory. From the point of view of a 'nomothetic', would-be experimental behavioural psychology, Kelly's approach is provocatively subjectivist. Psychodynamically oriented psychologists may (erroneously) consider his theory as being too cognitivist and lacking a thoroughly developmental perspective.

However, after the 'cognitive turn' of late in psychology, Kelly's theory seems to be more 'modern' than ever. On the other hand, with the relativistic ideas of constructivism, especially the 'radical' version having become more popular, Kelly's stance on empirical evidence (*validation* in his terms) has become increasingly attractive to researchers and practitioners who feel the need for empirical validation of their own concepts.

---

[24] An earlier version of this chapter appeared in Scheer & Catina (1996) (Eds.)

Personal Construct Theory

Anticipation

The limitation of space does not permit more than a very short overview of the basic concepts of the theory. Perhaps the most important idea is that of *anticipation*. Just as a scientist aims at better control of phenomena by predicting events, every individual tries to predict the course of events in his/her life and to control their outcome. Every one of us has his/her explicit or implicit theories about the world around us (including the persons important to us), develops hypotheses and checks them against 'reality', in an almost experimental (in any case empirical) way. Therefore '(hu)*man as scientist*' is the central metaphor of Kellyan theory. We anticipate events and experiences, we 'construe' our reality, and we find our constructions eventually validated or invalidated and subsequently keep to them or modify them.

The 'fundamental postulate' of Personal Construct Theory therefore is:

A person's processes are psychologically channelized by the ways in which he anticipates events.

In a number of 'corollaries', Kelly specifies these ideas, especially with respect to the properties of constructs and construct systems.

Constructs

- Constructs are not just theoretical concepts as opposed to observable variables, like in standard psychology. Superficially, a construct is a verbal label, but this label represents a conceptual distinction that an individual makes. We think and anticipate in terms of contrasts (the *dichotomy* corollary): the concept of 'big' does not exist without an idea of 'small'.
- It is important to note that constructs are not only names, or concepts, or attitudes, or opinions. Constructs have a function for the individual. In 'postmodern' talk they have been called 'self-guiding narratives'. They serve as tools to replicate events in our imagination, and to make up our view of the world by continuous confirmation or disconfirmation, thus 'to construe reality' (the *construction* corollary).
- Constructs are organised in systems, often hierarchical in structure. There are superordinate constructs, core constructs, peripheral constructs, according to their importance to the individual's life (the *organisation* corollary).
- We have different construct systems for different areas and realms which may even be partially incompatible or at least contradictory when involved at the same time (the *fragmentation* corollary).

- Constructs in principle can be changed through experience (the *experience* corollary).
- A person decides for him/herself which alternative of a construct pertains to him/her, assigns him/herself to a construct pole, 'chooses' the construct pole, if he/she can expect an extension or definition of his/her construct systems. Doing this, he/she 'construes him/herself' (the *choice* corollary).
- Constructs are significant characteristics of the individual (the *individuality* corollary). In other words, constructs are 'personal'.
- But the ways of construing of an individual are to some extent similar to those of another (the *commonality corollary*),
- and even if they are different – we have to be able to understand the other's constructions ('construe the other's constructions'; the *sociality* corollary) in order to be able to live in a society, and to maintain interpersonal relationships.
- Every construct has a limited applicability (its range of convenience) and also an area where it fits best (the focus of convenience; the *range* corollary).
- This also limits a construct's ability to change (the individual's capability of learning and re-orientation); the ability of a construct to include new events into its range of applicability may vary (the *modulation* corollary).

Core constructs are central to the individual's personality; they enable him/her to maintain his/her identity. They are *superordinate* to others, and have a wider *range of convenience*. If they are challenged and required to change, this is experienced as utterly stressful.

The focus of theoretical and practical interest of Personal Construct Psychology is the analysis of the construct systems that an individual uses to analyse, understand, structure, and change his/her environment. One might say that in a Piagetian sense, the use of constructs encompasses assimilation as well as accommodation processes. And, as Kelly points out, emotions and cognitions are inseparably linked in the construing process; it does not make much sense to separate them and even assign them different kingdoms in the world of psychology.

Repertory Grid Technique

Kelly's theory would probably be less known, and less influential, had he not invented an ingenious method of exploring constructs and construct systems: the *Repertory Grid Technique*. This is a kind of test that the 'subject' develops him/herself, guided by the psychologist. In a procedure described below the person first defines the area that the test is to be applied to (by choosing the 'elements'), then develops the items ('constructs'), then completes the grid that is made up by the two dimensions: elements and constructs. In

Kelly's original version (The Role Repertory Test), the famous 'significant others' constituted the elements. He had the subjects assign real persons to the 'role titles' supplied (such as father or favourite teacher). Then several selections of three elements each were compared *('please tell me, is there an important way in which two of these three* (you self, your father, and Auntie Nora) *are alike and thereby different from the third?'),* resulting in a list of bi-polar constructs. Finally the person had to decide which construct pole applied to every person (element) listed. A matrix (or grid) with 'ticks' and 'blanks' resulted that was considered a representation of the construct system pertaining to the set of elements involved. Nowadays, often a graded rating (e.g., on a 6-point scale) is used to assess the elements with respect to the constructs.

It can be seen that the information obtained in a repertory grid is highly individual, therefore the technique has been termed 'idiographic'. However, the procedure is more or less standardised, which gives it relevance in 'nomothetic' psychology. And, however personal the constructs are, certain properties of the construct *systems* can be distinguished and compared to those seen in other persons – irrespective of the *content* of the constructs.

Repertory Grid Variations

The procedure described above is still the standard procedure of taking a 'repgrid' today. However a huge variety of topics have been explored in the research on construct systems - after all, we have construct systems for most every field of life (and death). In fact, in repgrid research, elements as diverse as personal others, death situations, and British seaside resorts have been used. And the techniques of construct elicitation and of element assessments have been varied, too.

The main, almost revolutionary development has been the application of mathematical analyses (principal component analysis and cluster analysis) to repgrid data using personal computers.

It may be seen from this that Repertory Grid Technique as a data collection method lends itself to a vast variety of applications. And it can also be used by researchers and practitioners who do not share the theoretical positions of Personal Construct Theory. Many of them are more interested in the interrelationship of the elements used (e.g., self-parent relationship, expressed in quasi-Euclidian or Pythagorean distances, as representing 'object relations' in a psychoanalytical sense).

Other methods of exploring constructs

It has been argued that taking a repertory grid is comparable to a semi-standardised interview, with the procedure being standardised, not the content. So it does not come as a surprise that other methods of exploring constructs have been developed. Among these are the 'laddering' and 'pyramiding' procedures which require the subject to successively explore the personal implications of the constructs in question (and their poles). Thus hierarchical relationships can be analysed better this way than through a repertory grid. A related technique is the 'ABC model' which asks for the disadvantages and advantages of the opposite poles of a given construct for the person.

Outlook

Like other theories, Personal Construct Theory has a 'life', a kind of development in stages which has been described by R. Neimeyer (1985). The popularity of the Repertory Grid Technique has attracted persons with other theoretical observances. Some Personal Construct psychologists think that the time is right to reconsider theoretical orientations in view of the developments in other disciplines like cognitive psychology. The fact that the theory can be placed beside others with the idea of approximation, linkage, even amalgamating in mind, has been of concern to some of the leading theoreticians in Personal Construct Theory. On the other hand, 'orthodoxies in PCP' have already been identified and attacked. Kelly himself insisted on the limited 'range of convenience' of the theory and expected that at some time in the future it might become invalidated by the course of time. For the time being, however, PCP seems to be alive and well – as documented by the appearance of a new *International Handbook* (Fransella, 2003, 2005) and a variety of *Internet* sites, including an *Encyclopaedia* and an online *Journal*. Even the administration and analysis of repertory grids can now be performed online.

References

Butt, T., Burr, V. (2004). *Invitation to personal construct psychology*, 2nd ed. London: Whurr.
Fransella, F. (Ed.). (2003). *International handbook of personal construct psychology*. London: Routledge.
Fransella, F. (Ed.) (2005). *The essential practitioner's guide to personal construct psychology*. London: Routledge.
Jankowicz, D. (2004). *The easy guide to repertory grids*. London: Routledge.
Kelly, G.A. (1955). *The psychology of personal constructs*. Vols. 1 & 2. New York: Norton (2nd printing: 1991, London: Routledge).
Neimeyer, R. A. (1985). *The development of personal construct psychologY*. Lincoln, Nebraska: The University of Nebraska Press.
Scheer, J. W., Catina, A. (Eds) (1996). *Empirical constructivism in Europe – The personal construct approach*. Giessen: Psychosozial-Verlag.

Internet Resources

The Personal Construct Psychology Portal:
http://www.pcp-net.de

The Internet Encyclopaedia of Personal Construct Psychology:
http://www.pcp-net.org.encyclopaedia

Online Journal 'Personal Construct Theory & Practice':
http://www.pcp-net.org/journal

Repertory Grid Administration and Analysis - WebGrid III:
http://tiger.cpsc.ucalgary.ca/

Appendix B
Constructive Criticism

In 1991, a journal named *Constructive Criticism* was published that survived for one year only. In the four issues, the editor, *Cintra Whitehead*, published a theory of literary criticism from a Personal Construct Psychology (PCP) perspective, a number of analyses of classical plays and novels, and several short stories and poems. In an article on *Oedipus* – the legend and the original play by *Sophokles* – she contrasts a PCP approach to the psychoanalytical view, of course a pivotal point in psychoanalytical theorising (CC, 2, 1991). She follows Kelly in an analysis of *Hamlet*. Here is the last paragraph in her paper on Hamlet:

> *Hamlet and Fortinbras to a certain extent, and the audience to a greater extent, have come through the play with elaborated construct systems never permitted to the protagonist or the other characters in the play.* Hamlet *is thus the tragedy of knowing vs. not knowing, but of knowing with the emotions and the will as well as with the intellect. The personal construct theorist will suspect that the play's unrivaled position in English drama results from its dramatization of the human need for all of us, like Hamlet, to be man-the-scientist who must decide when to trust intuition and emotion (which is after all a way of construing through preverbal constructs) and when and how to state and test hypotheses about life and the universe in order to predict and control life events.* (p. 99)

In another paper *Hamlet* and *Macbeth* are seen as located on opposing ends of a number of constructs (CC, 2, 1991). *King Lear* is being analysed (CC, 2, 1991). *Thomas Hardy's* novel *Jude the Obscure* is interpreted as one novel illustrating most clearly the theory of personal constructs (CC, 2, 1991). On a more general level, *Tragedy and Comedy* are treated from a PCP point of view (CC, 2, 1991).

The introductory article of the journal authored by Whitehead, *A General Theory of Psychological Literary Criticism*, would have been an ideal entry in the present volume, either in an updated form or as a straightforward reprinting. However, our efforts to locate Whitehead and invite her involvement in the current project were not successful. The interested reader is encouraged to locate the short-lived *Constructive Criticism* as a companion volume to this book.
Eds.

2002 · 378 Seiten · Broschur
EUR (D) 29,90 · SFr 52,20
ISBN 3-89806-282-1

2004 · 198 Seiten · gebunden
EUR (D) 19,90 · SFr 34,90
ISBN 3-89806-372-0

Terrorism, Jihad, and Sacred Vengeance delves into the psychology of terrorism and religious violence. What comprise the ideas, impulses and fantasies of terrorists and suicide bombers? How do victimization and exposure to death affect the psyche? From fascistic and paranoid responses following September 11th, 2001, to dreams of entering Paradise and blissfully joining God through acts of self-destruction, to the symbolism of evil and sacrifice, Terrorism, Jihad, and Sacred Vengeance explores the madness and despair persisting in the wake of recent events.

Critics have called the book Narcissism and Power (2002), written by Hans-Jürgen Wirth, a »masterpiece of political psychology«. In 9/11 as a Collective Trauma he presents a collection of his most interesting essays about psyche and politics. He reflects on the psychic structure of suicide bombers and analyzes the psycho-political causes and the consequences of the Iraq War. The other essays focus on xenophobia and violence, the story of Jewish psychoanalysts who emigrated to the United States from Nazi Germany, and the idea of man in psychoanalysis.

Goethestr. 29 · 35390 Gießen · Tel. 0641/9716903 · Fax 77742
bestellung@psychosozial-verlag.de
www.psychosozial-verlag.de

2005 · 206 Seiten · gebunden EUR (D) 29,90 · SFr 52,–
ISBN 3-89806-495-6

2004 · 212 Seiten · gebunden
EUR (D) 49,90 · SFr 85,50
ISBN 3-89806-241-4

This exquisite collection of photographs is the first to assemble rare and personal pictures of psychoanalytic pioneers: Anna Freud, Melanie Klein, Marie Bonaparte, Paul Federn, Michael Balint, Sándor Ferenczi, Otto Fenichel and many others – taken between 1932 and 1938 by Edward Bibring, a close colleague of Sigmund Freud. Edward Bibring (1894–1959) belonged to the small group of Viennese analysts who worked closely together with Freud after World War I. He was also editor of the »Internationale Zeitschrift für Psychoanalyse«, which Freud had founded and continued to support. Being a passionate photographer, Bibring managed to take very personal photographs of his fellow psychoanalysts mostly during psychoanalytic congresses. To escape the Nazis, Bibring and his wife Grete emigrated to London and later to Boston, where he retained his interest in photography and recorded this psychoanalytic era in pictures.

Den Ausgangspunkt dieses Buches bilden 16-Millimeter-Amateurfilme, die der Psychoanalytiker Philip Lehrman in den 20er Jahren des letzten Jahrhunderts während seiner Analyse bei Freud drehte und aus denen ein von ihm kommentierter Dokumentarfilm entstand. Fast 50 Jahre nach Lehrmans Tod veröffentlicht seine Tochter Lynne Lehrman Weiner die Transkription des Filmes sowie eine Auswahl zentraler Standfotos in Form eines Text- und Bildbandes. So entsteht ein sehr persönlicher Einblick in Persönlichkeiten der klassischen Psychoanalyse und »ihr« Europa der 20er Jahre. Ergänzend geben Kurzbiografien sowie Essays internationaler Psychoanalytiker einen Überblick über die Geschichte der Psychoanalyse in Berlin, Wien, Frankreich, London, Budapest sowie New York.

Psychosozial-Verlag

Goethestr. 29 · 35390 Gießen · Tel. 0641/9716903 · Fax 77742
bestellung@psychosozial-verlag.de
www.psychosozial-verlag.de

www.ingramcontent.com/pod-product-compliance
Ingram Content Group UK Ltd.
Pitfield, Milton Keynes, MK11 3LW, UK
UKHW041947230426
12048UKWH00008B/185